Demonstration Elections

Demonstration Elections

U.S.-Staged Elections in the
Dominican Republic,
Vietnam, and El Salvador

Edward S. Herman
and
Frank Brodhead

SOUTH END PRESS   BOSTON

Library of Congress Card Number 83-051284
ISBN 0-89608-214-8 paper
ISBN 0-89608-215-6 cloth
Cover design by Bonnie Acker
South End Press
302 Columbus Avenue
Boston, MA 02116

Table of Contents

"They use thought only to justify their abuses, and employ words only to conceal their thoughts."

(Voltaire, *The Capon and the Pullet*.)

"Our objective became simple: if we could not expect more GVN [Saigon government] efficiency, we could at least get a more stable and legitimate GVN. This required a constitution and free elections. Moreover, if we could not have the reality, we could start with appearances."

(*Pentagon Papers*, Vol. 2, p. 284 [Gravel edition].)

Preface

This book focuses on the use of "free elections" as a tool of public relations. From our vantage point it is therefore highly appropriate that the next El Salvador election, and perhaps one in Grenada, will be held in the year 1984, which George Orwell's novel *1984* has made into a symbol of word manipulation in the service of "people control." It is also fit that these elections will be organized under the general supervision of Ronald Reagan, Jeane Kirkpatrick, and company, who are bold in their use of evocative words in circumstances where the facts cry out for the use of their opposites. An "armed minority" using "violence" in Reaganspeak is not the junta we are supporting in El Salvador, it is rebels who are less well armed, have greater popular support, and do not systematically kill and mutilate unarmed civilians.

Or consider Kirkpatrick's assertion that we should not "finance the consolidation of totalitarian regimes."[1] In saying this, she does not mean that we should cut off aid to the military regime in El Salvador, which has murdered thousands of community and organization leaders in a process that conforms well to models of the totalitarian state.[2] She is not referring to the culture of fear which has engulfed El Salvador, where the population lives in a state of "fearful passivity," in the words of Leonel Gomez, a former land reform official in that country.[3] Juan Corradi describes this spiritual environment in even more evocative language:

Cadavers (from *cadere*, to fall) are to be found anywhere, at any time, in El Salvador—a standard feature in the landscape of fear, to remind the provisionally living that they too might fall at any moment. For everyone in El Salvador is, ineluctably, a hostage. Cadavers are produced by a government that is little more than a deranged killing machine. . . . The bodies are broken, disfigured, trussed and stuffed with their own organs, rearranged as if designed to carry a message. But the message is undecipherable, beyond anything that even Kafka's Harrow could inscribe in the flesh of the inmates of the Penal Colony. They are mere tokens that saturate the environment, suggesting that life at some point became the stuff of an obscure and debased coinage.[4]

Gomez and Corradi are clearly not on the same wave length as Kirkpatrick, for whom the election of 1982 transformed El Salvador's regime from "authoritarian" to "democratic." It is quite evident, however, that Kirkpatrick will make any condition of terror managed by "friends" into "authoritarianism," and any disfavored regime "totalitarian" independently of the substance to which those words relate. In short, with Kirkpatrick we are firmly anchored in the world of *1984.*

As another illustration of the continuous resort to manipulative word usage, we are said to seek a "political solution" rather than military victory in El Salvador. In President Reagan's words, "Bullets are no answer to economic inequities, social tensions or political disagreements. Democracy is."[5] Of course we are *using* bullets, and have used them directly or through proxies on a prodigious scale in Vietnam and El Salvador prior to appealing to "democracy," but we must not look too closely at such a magnificent rhetorical flourish. The Reagan usages are a modernized version of Lyndon Johnson's search for "negotiations" and "unconditional discussions" during the Vietnam War, which was strictly a public relations cover for an undeviating quest for military victory.[6] In both cases the political aims were incompatible with any compromises with the enemy and could thus be accomplished, if at all, only by the application of very large scale military force. Nevertheless, these leaders could claim to prefer a "political" to a "military" solution, in the sense that if all their political objectives were acceded to by the opposition they would no longer fire bullets. Thus a call for unconditional surrender is not an insistence on a "military victory," except in common and meaningful word usage.

The Reagan administration's main trick in obfuscating a wholly military route is its appeal for free and democratic elections as a means of accommodation. A main theme of this work, however, is that elections held under conditions of military occupation and extensive pre-election "pacification" are not free or democratic at all, but, on the contrary, serve to ratify power and display to some target audience an ability to gain nominal approval of the regime sponsored by the occupying forces. The deception and fallacy rest on the fact that in a state of armed conflict and military rule, elections are won by those possessing the most bullets and controlling the electoral machinery. Elections may therefore substitute the *form* of democracy and free choice for their *substance*, and provide an Orwellian inversion based on fear, ignorance, limited and meaningless choices, and a militarily assured voter turnout.

We show throughout this book how the staging process occurs and how "observers" and the media are mobilized to achieve a public relations hoax. They do this very naturally; cadavers are cleared off the streets before the reporters and observers arrive, people given a day off from work and going to the polls under military occupation do not *look* terrorized and do not complain to strangers in public, and the massive official propaganda is not only very upbeat, it is also the only food on the interpretive menu. We point to the ironic fact that in both Vietnam and El Salvador the United States actively opposed or was completely indifferent to elections until military occupation and state of siege conditions prevailed. Official observers and media analysts and commentators never note this oddity, nor suggest that elections held in such unpropitious circumstances are meaningless, nor hint—God forbid!—that the elections are held only after military occupation precisely *because* the desired results are thereby assured. On the contrary, the conventional view is one of wonderment that elections can be held at all under such adverse conditions. The fact is, however, that it is extremely easy to get people to the voting booths under conditions of military occupation and rule.

The success of staged elections and the new levels attained by Orwellian usage in recent decades have been contingent on mass media cooperation. It has been part of the recent conservative propaganda offensive in the United States to contend that the mass media are hotbeds of liberalism and radicalism, unfair and un-balanced critics of national policy, and constantly on the search for antiestablishment negatives. In fact, however, the mass media are truly "big business," often multinational, heavily dependent on corporate advertising for the bulk of their revenues, and interlocked extensively with other members of the corporate elite.[7] As integral parts of the business system the mass media can be expected to, and do, reflect in news and programming the major premises and demands of the business leadership and government.[8]

The conservative critique does contain a small germ of truth: namely, that the best media, even while following the national party line on all fundamentals, still allow a steady trickle of unpleasant details from which the careful reader could infer something of the policy reality of his or her state. The *purpose* of the conservative offensive, and the role of media critics like Accuracy in Media and Freedom House, is to keep this trickle to a minimum or suppress it altogether. The implicit standard from which the bias of the liberal media is inferred is that of a public relations arm of the government. Thus media that feature exclusively the corporate-government view are not "biased" or "unbalanced," only those that allow an occasional glimpse beyond the government press release. This steady assault on the media not only serves to reduce the flow of information distasteful to the powers-that-be, it also performs another role. If the general citizenry can be made to believe that the mass media are hostile to "the system," it will have been weaned away from elemental reality. Instead of looking at the mass media as reliable arms of the establishment, which they are, the public will tend to discount their already modest and carefully rationed flow of antiestablishment information and criticisms as reflecting bias!

The subservience of the media to government political and propaganda aims is illustrated throughout this book, as the staged elections which we examine have all been public relations triumphs only by virtue of a level of media cooperation that amounts to propaganda service. The more generalized deference of the media to government political goals can be seen in its treatment of a multitude of events that might embarrass the government. Take, for example, the murder of human rights workers and monitors in El Salvador. In October 1980 two officials of the independent Human Rights Commission of El Salvador (CDHES) were seized and murdered by the National Police. Between November 1980 and early March 1983 five more officials of CDHES were murdered or disappeared and may be presumed dead.[9] These seven murders were barely mentioned by the U.S. mass media. On March 15, 1983 the body of Marianela Garcia Villas, the successor head of the Human Rights Commission, was found near San Salvador; she had been shot through the chest and legs by high-calibre explosive bullets. Marianela Garcia had been compelled to flee El Salvador in April 1981 after her house had been ransacked and her name had appeared on a death list. She returned in January 1983 quite openly to investigate reports that government troops were using napalm and white phosphorus against the civilian population, a subject on which she was scheduled to give evidence before the UN Human Rights Commission in Geneva. According to an account of the British human rights publication *Index on Censorship*:

> Marianela Garcia was one of Latin America's best-known human rights workers, highly respected internationally for her testimony before bodies such as the United Nations Human Rights Commission, or the Parliamentary Human Rights Group of the British House of Commons, to which she gave evidence on her last visit to Britain in October 1981. She was a founder member of the CDHES in 1978, since when the Commission has twice been nominated for the Nobel Peace Prize and has consultative status with the UN. She was also Vice-President of the International Human Rights Federation in Paris, which she represented before the Organisation of American States in Washington.[10]

The governments of the Free World and the mass media of the West hardly noticed her murder any more than that of her predecessors. Insofar as the case was covered at all, the media passed on the propaganda line of the Salvadoran military junta. Thus, a UPI dispatch from San Salvador in the *Washington Post* reported a Defense Ministry claim that Marianela Garcia was "a former Salvadoran congresswoman turned guerilla commander."[11] Another statement the same day in another news item in the *Post*, also quoting the Defense Ministry, had Marianela Garcia killed with guerillas who were "trying to ambush a military patrol...."[12] A tiny Reuters dispatch appearing in the *New York Times* passed on the army's claim that she had died fighting with the guerillas and that CDHES was subversive, although Reuters generously provided balance by reporting a denial of these claims by her associates.[13] The *Index on Censorship* noted that "the armed forces press office at one stage during a confused and contradictory series of statements after her death claimed that she had been leading a guerilla attack. This was withdrawn, but not before the international news agencies had repeated it verbatim and without qualification."[14]

In brief, although the death of Marianela Garcia Villas was the eighth in a series of killings of human rights workers associated with a single agency in El Salvador,[15] the mass media of the United States and the West in general swallowed the foolish and implausible explanations of this death from a military regime that has regularly claimed its thousands of civilian victims to be "guerillas" killed in fighting or escaping arrest. The media failed to retract these lies even when they had been abandoned by the Salvadoran army's press office. After eight killings they still simply refused to look closely at the facts and saw no basis for moral indignation or any campaign or crusade against villainy. Why were Marianela Garcia Villas and her predecessors *unworthy* victims? Would it be unreasonable to suggest that if eight Helsinki Agreement monitors in Bulgaria or Poland were killed there would be a little more press attention, expressions of concern, and inferences about the quality of the offending states?

Let us take a case closer to home. Consider the media's handling of the rape-murder of four U.S. religious women in 1980 by the Salvadoran security forces. The action itself was close to the limit of human viciousness—a brutal, cowardly, and deadly attack on defenseless members of a religious order engaged in humanitarian work. From the standpoint of U.S. public and media interest, it is important that these victims were U.S. citizens as well. The act was one that clearly should have aroused the utmost degree of horror in the U.S. public and antipathy toward the Salvadoran government and security forces, whose reign of terror was showing its face in the most dramatic form.

But just as with the series of murders of human rights officials of the CDHES which culminated in the death of Marianela Garcia Villas, here also the threat posed by these murders to the U.S. policy of supporting the military regime was contained by media self-restraint. First, after an initial but small surge of publicity, the media quickly abandoned or muted their treatment of the subject. They did not, as with the Soviet downing of a Korean airliner, devote special sections of the newspaper to the event and maintain a high intensity of coverage and protest for weeks on end. The Soviet action, of course, involved 269 people instead of four; but it should be noted that the four women victims added to a cumulative Salvadoran total running into the thousands, including several individual episodes in which the number of deaths exceeded 269 without eliciting any noticeable western media indignation. Furthermore, the murder of the four women was unambiguous in viciousness of purpose and significance; the Soviet action was far more uncertain in meaning, given the fact that the plane had flown over Soviet military installations and given the context of active U.S. aerial spying efforts in the vicinity.[16]

Second, the mass media almost uniformly played down or suppressed altogether the planned nature of the murder of the four women and its tie-in with the military junta. A Pacific News Service release of July 3, 1981 reported that there had been discussions of the threat posed by the Church and the women religious workers and expressions of an intent to act against them by top military officials in El Salvador only shortly before the murders. The news report also provided evidence of detailed planning to intercept the women.[17] The original news article was carried by the *Washington Post, Los Angeles Times*, and some 15 other papers, but it was generally not featured prominently, nor were the tremendous opportunities for investigative journalism opened up by the report pursued by any major media enterprise. Again, the contrast with the Soviet downing of the Korean airliner is instructive; attention in that case had been quickly and aggressively focused on the role of the Kremlin versus the local authorities, and the question of Soviet government responsibility was immediately pushed front and center. In the Salvadoran case, it was barely evident in the mass media that the murderers were members of the armed forces and agents of the government.

Third, the inability of the Salvadoran system of justice to bring anybody to book for these crimes has not been dwelt upon by the media and did not cause its leading members to stick with the case and raise the intensity of protest; nor did it suggest to the media the greater likelihood of guilt at the top. The media also did not allow the case and the system of justice it displayed to influence their benign view of electoral processes held in El Salvador under the jurisdiction of the army and other security forces. The Soviet action, on the other hand, was the basis of immediate and widespread generalization about the quality of the Soviet system, long before all the facts were on the table.

Fourth, when Secretary of State Alexander Haig lied to Congress, suggesting that "the most prominent theory" of the case was that the women had been shot while trying to run a roadblock, and went on to *joke* about never having run into pistol-packing nuns,[18] the media did not assail him and make this combination of brazen lying and sneering at murdered U.S. citizens into an issue. Similarly, when Jeane Kirkpatrick hinted that the religious women were maybe subversives and perhaps got what they deserved[19]—a point which she also made in regard to the six murdered and mutilated rebel leaders[20]—she also suffered no negative repercussions. Lying about and smearing raped and murdered U.S. citizens victimized by agents of a nearby fascism under U.S. tutelage brings with it no political costs. The murder of the four women was "inconvenient" to the U.S. government, which served actively in the process of cover-up,[21] and a muted press treatment of this violence ensued. In striking contrast, the Soviet downing of the Korean airliner was serviceable to Reagan administration plans, and thus became the basis of a systematic and worldwide media campaign of great intensity and duration. The mass media support role of selective frenzied indignation was an essential ingredient of this propaganda effort.

Finally, it goes almost without saying that the media of the United States and Western Europe never suggested that the United States was actually *responsible* for the murders of the four religious women or the human rights monitors. These same media had no hesitancy in attributing blame for the martial-law crackdown on Solidarity in Poland to the Soviet Union, given its power and frequent bullying of its satellites in Eastern Europe. But there is no symmetrical allocation of blame to the United States for violence in its own backyard, although its interventions there have been large and continuous, it aids and protects the Salvadoran government doing the killing, and the relevant (and ugly) behavior patterns in a whole string of nearby clients followed a long-term and purposeful U.S. build-up and training of the local security forces.[22] Of course administration leaders appearing before Congress are always "deeply troubled" by the large-scale murder being carried out by the client governments which they are actively supporting, and they always claim to be doing their level best to inculcate a respect for human rights. But as these same leaders insist with respect to Soviet performance, we must look beyond self-serving propaganda statements to substantive actions. The western media patriotically attend carefully to the *words* of their own leaders, while focusing on the *deeds* of the leaders of enemy states.

This is an age of "elections" and "democracy," in an Orwellian sense. Rightwing regimes in Chile, Guatemala, Turkey, and elsewhere, talk about and plan for elections with great enthusiasm, although sometimes the plans are not expected to materialize until some years ahead, after the public becomes better imbued with true principles. The Chilean and Turkish military juntas speak of a coming "true democracy," which they will install when the time is ripe. The regimes seeking true democracy move cautiously, only a step at a time. In El Salvador we had only a small "step toward democracy" in the election of March 1982. In Turkey a member of the military regime concedes that the election in the fall of 1983 is only a *step toward a step*: "The upcoming election won't be a return to democracy, it will only be the *beginning of a transition* toward democracy."[23] Could it be that these regimes have seen the democratic light and are rushing toward increased public participation? Or do they perhaps understand that the Reagan administration will use any suitable words and gestures that express a commitment to democratic forms—a "beginning of a transition"—as a basis for providing them with more bullets? It is our hope that the present volume will contribute to an understanding of some of these seeming paradoxes.

As Orwellian usage is so central to the recent U.S. sponsorship of free elections, we provide a small glossary of Orwellian terms following chapter 6, with references to the appropriate words as they appear in the main text. As an illustration of our translations of contemporary propaganda clichés, we define "Step Toward Democracy" as follows: "In a friendly client state, any verbal assurance no matter how vague and remote and any formal act no matter how empty of substance."

The authors want to express their thanks to Phillip Berryman, Noam Chomsky, Colin Danby, Tran Van Dinh, Howard Friel, Eva Gold, George Kahin, Jack Malinowski, Jim O'Brien, James Petras, John Schall, and David Wurfel for valuable comments and suggestions that have helped improve this book. Special thanks are owing Professor Wurfel for allowing us to reprint as an appendix a part of his report made as an independent observer of the 1967 election in South Vietnam. We also want to acknowledge and thank W. H. and Carol Ferry, Dale Wiehoff and Ann H. Hess, and others whose financial support was important in helping bring this volume to completion. The authors alone are responsible for its content.

CHAPTER 1

The Rise of the Demonstration Election

Elections have been used by the United States as an instrument of management in Third World client states since the turn of the century. The *functions* which they have served, however, have changed in accordance with the shifting demands placed upon the managers. The aim in holding such elections has always been to ensure "stability."* In the first half of this century the threat to stability came almost exclusively from within the client states, which were subject to internal turmoil and thus threatened with a loss of "independence."* In recent decades, serious challenges have arisen from within the United States itself. It is this shift in functional need that has led to the emergence of elections oriented to influencing the home (U.S.) population, which we designate "demonstration elections."*

The occupation of Cuba in 1898 marked the beginning of a wave of U.S. interventions in the Caribbean and Central America, including, in addition to Cuba, invasions and occupations of Panama, the Dominican Republic, Haiti, Nicaragua, Costa Rica, and Mexico.[1] These interventions were often terminated only after constitutions were written, party organizations encouraged, and

---

*Words designated by an asterisk are defined in the Glossary of Orwellian Usage that follows the text.

1

electoral machinery established by the imperial authorities to provide for the orderly resolution of conflict in these client states. Elections allowed the local populations to work out their differences through electoral rules and processes rather than by resort to force. With appropriate restrictions on suffrage, and with splintered parties and poor communications, shared local elite rule and the maintenance of order were the hoped-for political outcome of the institutionalization of elections.

This internal political settlement was not an end in itself, however, but a prerequisite to the efficient control and management of a system of dependencies. While the acquisition of Puerto Rico, the Philippines, and Hawaii indicates that the United States shared the concerns that drove Europeans to scramble for colonies in the late nineteenth century, it was readily apparent that the administrative and political costs of a colonial system were high. Far preferable was an "informal empire,"[2] like that enjoyed by Britain in the mid-nineteenth century before it was challenged by Germany and other imperial rivals. While its colonial competitors forced Britain to formalize much of its world trading empire—to define its territories within the rules of international law and force other nations to recognize its claims—no similar rival emerged in the Western Hemisphere to press the United States toward a similar formalization of its domain. As long as the Monroe Doctrine, asserting a United States monopoly on hemispheric pickings, was recognized by the European powers, Washington policy makers found indirect rule far preferable to the burdens of formal empire.

"Free elections"* played an important part in providing the basis for indirect rule by the United States. They helped defuse the substantial anti-imperialist sentiment within the United States, thus playing an early "demonstration election" role. The United States could use the electoral machinery during an occupation to build up, legitimate, and ratify its own preferred electoral choice. Following the official U.S. departure, it was usually easy to influence election outcomes by a judicious use of money, sugar quotas, advice, credit, military missions, and other direct or sub rosa interventions. The continuing goal was a loosely knit system of dependents, open to U.S. investment, with support given by the colonial elites to the special needs of U.S. business—cheap labor, improved roads and communications, and laws protecting foreign capital and favoring the production of crops for export rather than for subsistence. "Open" means *economically* open. The regimes of Somoza, Batista, Pinochet, Stroessner, Ubico, and Rios Montt are or were "open." Cuba is "closed." The United States believes in open systems. With such a system in place the economic strength of the United States allows a strong U.S. economic presence and creates a structure of economic dependency, from which political dependency necessarily follows. The entire set of imperial inputs—economic, political, and military—strongly constrains the scope of policy by democratic processes within client states. As Jules Benjamin noted in reference to U.S. arrangements for Cuba from 1898 onward: "In effect, the Cubans were not to have politics; only elections."[3]

The Rise of the Demonstration Election

In recent decades U.S. concern over and sponsorship of elections in Third World countries has shifted markedly toward their use as propagandistic and public relations (PR) instruments. Most notably, "free elections" have been used to reassure the U.S. home population, defuse domestic opposition, and, in effect, ratify ongoing U.S. interventionary strategies.

The interventionary plans supported by a "free election" strategy have been consistently designed to oppose and defeat popular movements and to preserve and fortify elite structures often inherited from a colonial past. While the goals of U.S. intervention have remained constant, however, the world context in which the intervention strategy must work has greatly changed. The decolonisation of Asia and Africa in the post-World War II years created a powerful body of world opinion which would be aggravated by the cruder methods of gunboat diplomacy. The crumbling of the bloc system—the division of the world into U.S. and Soviet spheres—and the tentative emergence of a neutralist camp, increased the need to present U.S. intervention as something desirable, as a means of promoting "democracy" and "freedom."* Similarly, the growing domestic importance of black and Third World constituencies in the United States made it politically inexpedient for politicians and governments to openly advocate domination by force of Third World, nonwhite countries. Finally, the costly failure of the U.S. intervention in Vietnam created a still-powerful sentiment against foreign adventures, or at least those that would commit substantial numbers of U.S. troops.

Thus the ability to continue their intervention strategies in the post-World War II period has increasingly required Washington policy makers to persuade foreign and domestic opinion that such intervention is not merely to be tolerated, but is a good thing in itself. Where earlier interventions were carried out under the guise of spreading Christianity and Civilization, and shouldering the White Man's Burden, intervention is now justified by the obligation to protect freedom by stopping Communism. Communism is used loosely,[4] and is said to raise its ugly head whenever we are threatened with possible loss of control (e.g., if Juan Bosch returned to the Dominican Republic in 1965, contrary to our preference).[5] In a context of rationalizing imperial intervention, Orwellian usages quickly take over. The village is saved by destroying it; freedom is preserved by keeping nonelected regimes in power; "free elections" become the PR instrument serving to consolidate the rule of an army that has institutionalized SS-type violence.

The "free election" PR strategy operates at three levels.

First, popular and insurgent movements against existing governments are opposed by the United States on the ground of our devotion to "peaceful democratic change" (Secretary of State Shultz). The official rhetoric is that U.S. opposition to popular movements is not based on hostility to the *goals* of the revolutionaries, but rests entirely on our burning commitment to peaceful, democratic *means* of social change. It is true that the United States supported violent means in backing the overthrow of democratic regimes in Brazil, Chile, and Guatemala, but this was because "Communism" threatened, at which point anything goes. (We reserve the right to decide when Communism threatens.) We may also give unconditional support to regimes that will not allow peaceful democratic change, so that the approved *means* of change that we demand of revolutionaries is entirely foreclosed. At this point, we fall back on faith in the "quiet diplomacy"* of George Shultz and Jeane Kirkpatrick and their devotion to the long run welfare of Third World peasants. Or shall we introduce a modicum of honesty? Peasants, know thy place! God rewards toilers, perhaps in the hereafter.

The second level of the PR election strategy is to attack revolutionary regimes for their electoral failings. Castro's refusal to hold free elections in 1959 and 1960 was considered a very serious matter in Washington, even though this was the very time of escalating U.S. sponsorship of counterinsurgency and the proliferation of client military regimes that held no elections as a matter of course, generally without the slightest negative reaction by the Godfather.[6] In the same pattern, the failure of the Sandinistas to hold elections in Nicaragua in the early 1980s was put forward as a justification for open U.S. arming of external dissidents and mercenaries, and the attempted subversion of that country. According to Ambassador Kirkpatrick, the U.S. goal in organizing and arming the remnants of Somoza's National Guard was to pressure Nicaragua into holding elections. The hypocrisy of this gambit is apparent not only in the active and warm support given numerous rightwing "authoritarian"* regimes, but also in the nostalgia the Reagan team has expressed for the Somoza government,[7] which held no meaningful elections over a 40-year span and was undemocratic in the most basic senses of the word. But the Somoza regime, though not open to popular participation, was open to U.S. investment. The absence of "free elections" is pressed only upon insurgent regimes which fail the really substantive test of "openness." If they were open in the Somoza-Pinochet-Batista sense described earlier, the pressure for free elections would immediately cease. "Free elections" are the Washington moral and PR cover for its real agenda and interventionary strategies.

The third level on which "free elections" serves as an instrument of propaganda is in countries currently or recently occupied or under siege by U.S. forces or proxies. The present book is about this kind of election. Among the most prominent instances were the June 1, 1966 election held in the Dominican Republic, the September 3, 1967 election in Vietnam, and the March 28, 1982 election in El Salvador. Each was characterized by the presence of numerous foreign "observers," extraordinary press interest, and thus exceptional publicity. These elections were also distinguished by the fact that they were sponsored by the U.S. government to "prove something" to the world, and especially to its home population.

The central theme of this book is that these were "demonstration elections," which may be defined as elections organized and staged by a foreign power primarily to pacify a restive home population, reassuring it that ongoing interventionary processes are legitimate and appreciated by their foreign objects. The demonstration election emerged in full flower in the second half of the 1960s, paralleling the growing opposition to the Vietnam war and to U.S. interventions elsewhere during the post-"Castro-shock" years. It was (and is) designed to neutralize this opposition by means of a symbolic act.

Demonstration Elections as Patriotic Dramaturgy

In his *Symbolic Uses of Politics*, Murray Edelman notes that the public responds "to currently conspicuous political symbols...gestures and speeches that make up the drama of the state."[8] Elections are a positive and heartening symbol; communism and terrorism* are threatening. A skilled manipulation of such symbols allows the public to be reassured and rendered quiescent, especially where its understanding is vague and information sparse. The success of a demonstration election therefore depends on how the mass media treat the government's attempt to "manage" the public. The second major theme of this book is that the national media of the United States have been highly cooperative, accepting the government's manipulation of symbols, its agenda of relevant information and questions, and its formulation of the election as a drama between the forces of good and evil.

In the positive demonstration election dramaturgy, the staged election is meritorious, the good guys are those favoring the election and trying to make it work. This makes the "security forces"* of El Salvador good guys. The bad guys are those who criticize and refuse to participate in these elections staged by the United States. This makes those who refuse to participate because they would surely be murdered by the "security forces," and those who see its objective as clearing the ground for further warfare, bad guys. The drama is structured as follows: will the good guys be able to hold this marvelous illustration of democracy in action and get a good turnout,* or will the baddies successfully boycott or disrupt it? Following the government's lead, the media accept the election at face value, focusing on the personalities of candidates, the surface mechanics of election day procedure, and other secondary matters and propaganda gambits, the most important being the alleged efforts to disrupt the election by the bad guys. They carefully avoid or downgrade issues such as the prior decimation of a political opposition, death squads as an institutionalized phenomenon, and the exclusion of major political opposition groups from participation.

When the *enemy* stages a demonstration election, as in the election managed by the Soviet Union in Poland in January 1947, the dramaturgical cast is reversed and the set of relevant facts is turned upside down. The good guys are the dissidents and the opposition party, who are harassed and encumbered by the power staging the election. (It should be noted that in the Polish election of January 1947, the mass opposition party was at least allowed to run; whereas in Vietnam and El Salvador they were completely excluded from the ballot by law and/or very real threats of murder.) The prior and ongoing terror against the dissident parties and the unequal access to the media move front and center. Given the unsatisfactory electoral conditions, the baddies are both those who stage an election in the first place and the candidates supported by the staging authority. In this case the election can be condemned beforehand as a staged fraud, the electoral idea corrupted. The drama is structured as follows: given the coercion and harassment of the opposition, a Greek tragedy is unfolding as the forces of decency must inevitably lose in the face of superior power. A large turnout in *this* case is a demonstration of the cynical tactic of *using state power to get out the vote.* The dichotomy is complete, and it is not based on different levels of fraud and terror.[9] It is a compelling testimonial to the propagandistic service rendered by the mass media in making *our* demonstration elections credible.

Demonstration Election Staging Props: The "Observers"

As demonstration elections are pseudoevents designed to manipulate a distant (home) population, they need proper staging. "Observers" are now an institutionalized part of demonstration election props, just as prompters and scene designers are part of a theatrical production. The functions of the observers are to attract media attention and to assure the home population that the election was both "fair" and a valid reflection of the will of the population under siege. The attention follows from the fact that the observers are more or less famous people from abroad, and the U.S. government and its military junta try hard to publicize the efforts of the observers.

The observers invariably find demonstration elections good, whether held in Rhodesia under conditions of intense civil warfare, in Vietnam under the rule of generals openly admitting to no popular base whatsoever, or in El Salvador under a state of siege with the murder of unarmed civilians proceeding at the rate of over 100 per week during the immediate pre-election period. The observers' conclusions result, first, from their composition and bias. They are usually carefully chosen from members of the establishment, and they recognize that their own government is sponsoring the election and supports the military junta directly staging the event. Third country observers are almost always supplied by client states or are invited because they are supporters of the ongoing pacification effort, to which the election is the PR complement. As the point of the election is to show popular support for the junta, and to display its newly discovered dedication to democratic processes, for observers to find the election unfair would be a slap in the face of their host, and unpatriotic to boot.

There has even emerged a body of professional observers, associated mainly with establishment and rightwing propaganda agencies like Freedom House* and the American Enterprise Institute (AEI), who travel from one demonstration election to the next to give their approval. Bayard Rustin and Leonard Sussman of Freedom

House and Howard Penniman of the AEI even traveled to Rhodesia to give their imprimatur to the 1979 demonstration election held there under extreme conditions of civil war violence. The Patriotic Front of rebel groups refused to participate in that election, which strove for "turnout" to prove black acceptance of a new constitution which had been voted upon by the white minority but had not even been submitted to the black majority. The voters were never told that the regime was publicizing the election abroad as proof of black support of the constitution. The substance of the constitution was never addressed by any candidate in the election. Voting was urged on grounds of citizen responsibility and as an important step toward "peace." Coercion, both subtle and direct, was enormous.[10] The black candidate put forward by the Smith regime, Bishop Muzorewa, got 67% of the sizable vote. In an election held one year later, with an international supervisory presence, and the Patriotic Front now included, Robert Mugabe got 63% of the vote, the Patriotic Front altogether got 87%, and Bishop Muzorewa got 8%. The Freedom House observers found the 1979 election fair, the 1980 election questionable. We feel that the Freedom House reports on the Rhodesian elections of 1979 and 1980 are such model illustrations of observer bias and corruption, by individuals regularly serving as observers in U.S.-sponsored demonstration elections, that we examine them in detail in Appendix 1.

A second reason why observers find elections fair is that they are in no position to evaluate them at all. Some observers come to realize this and end up with qualified negative propositions—that they saw no solid evidence of unfairness but couldn't really see very much.[11] Even this conclusion serves an apologetic function, because the media always fail to note that the negative proves not fairness but incapacity to observe. The most important limit is that the observers cannot observe at all the larger parameters of fairness: pre-election day freedom of institutional organization and activities, the overall climate of coercion and fear, freedom of speech, media freedom and access, and the right to form parties, put up candidates, and campaign. But even on election day, observers are guided by government forces, with armed guards to "protect" them. They suffer from language barriers, can almost never speak confidentially with even a token number of voters, and observe only a tiny fraction of polling places. What they can reasonably testify to is that nobody was beaten and ballot boxes were not stuffed *in their presence*. This is entirely compatible with massive coercion and ballot box stuffing. Some professional observers like Richard Scammon claim that while they can't observe a large part of the relevant universe, they can see that the "mechanics" of the election are sound. This is fraudulent. Honest mechanics includes honest watching at each polling place, which Scammon can't assess, and total privacy in casting the vote. It is notable that Scammon and company failed to observe even those elements of the voting mechanics in El Salvador that had a potential for aiding coercion—among others, the use of transparent plastic ballot boxes which allowed the observation of voting by interested officials. Furthermore, Scammon and the other observers also have no way of evaluating the integrity of the final disposition and counting of votes, done by machine but with human assistance. As we describe in Chapter 4, the El Salvador vote was inflated by the election officials after the observers had completed their work.

The efforts of election observers, in fact, have a negative relationship to election validity. Their approval, based on a combination of bias and inability to observe, serves to validate a PR spectacle. The role of the observers is addressed in each of the chapters that follow, but we explore their bias more systematically in Appendices 1 and 2.

Demonstration Elections as Ratification of Minority Rule and State Terrorism

Although elections can be useful means of allowing public participation in the political arena, they often provide form without substance. Especially when countries are under military control, voting numbers and choices may reflect fear, coercion, and manipulated information and symbols. Elections in such cases are put on and managed to ratify power. The U.S. government has resorted to such elections in Third World countries only when it wishes to provide a PR gloss to obscure an ugly reality. A third major theme of this book is that the demonstration election has been antidemocratic in intent and effect, both in the United States and within the client state itself.

As regards the *home population*, in a demonstration election the government uses the symbolic value of an "election" to mobilize home support for its preferred policies. In the case studies which follow, we will see that each election was intended to mislead the home populace about both the situation in the occupied country and the intentions of the U.S. government. The demonstration election was thus designed to win approval of external policy by deception.

Abroad, the United States has used the election to ratify its support of a rapacious and violent minority that would never have survived elections in an "unpacified" state. In the cases of El Salvador and South Vietnam, the real election victors were the security forces, who had opposed or subverted all prior elections. In the Dominican Republic, the United States supported a former puppet of Trujillo, after rebuilding the same police-military establishment which had overturned the first freely elected government in Dominican history only three years previously. In Vietnam the generals supported by the United States never tired of explaining that "we are very weak politically and without the strong political support of the population which the NLF have. Thus, now even if we defeat them militarily, they can come into power because of their greater political strength."[12] The United States had to convince the Saigon generals that even though they were "very weak politically" it was easy to win an election which we stage and manage! The generals were finally convinced, the election was held, and the United States was able to demonstrate that the South Vietnamese wanted what the generals and the United States had in store for them.

The El Salvador election of March 1982 was intended to consolidate the power of the ruling unelected military junta, which had been murdering unarmed civilians at the rate of over 150 per week for the three prior years. The administration likes to focus on the rebels as an "armed minority"* unwilling to submit to the test of the ballot box. This is an Orwellian inversion. The military junta is an armed minority that has so abused an *unarmed majority* that important elements of the majority have been driven to armed struggle in self-defense. The rebel armed resistance was an *effect*, not a *cause* of violence. The cause was the long, consistent, and total refusal of the oligarchy and its military arm to allow democratic elections or reform.[13] The administration thus distorts the causal sequence, while glossing over the fact that its preferred faction is not only a minority, but (in the words of former U.S. Ambassador to El Salvador Robert White) "one of the most out-of-control bloodthirsty groups of men in the world." The administration pretends that this same group that precipitated the insurgency, and which has never shown a proclivity to do anything but kill and steal, is deserving of support as a vehicle of progressive change. This is as plausible as the view that meaningful elections can be held under the auspices of the El Salvador security forces, or that these elections are *intended* to bring about democracy or reform.

We stress throughout this book that it has been standard procedure for U.S. authorities to occupy a country militarily (Dominican Republic, Vietnam) and/or arm a military junta to the teeth (El Salvador), pursue or encourage an extended pacification program, and then, after army and police control has been established and an adequate climate of "understanding realities" has been created, to call for "free elections." This process, which transforms elections into dramatic farce, was carried to an extreme in El Salvador in March 1982.

Six Criteria of Election Integrity
and their Application to El Salvador 1982

Another way of looking at the validity of elections is to examine the conditions making for a free election and see how the actual electoral case conforms to these criteria. The U.S. mass media never do this in reference to U.S.-sponsored elections, consistent with their dramatic and propaganda role. It is our view that the distance between the realities of U.S.-sponsored demonstration elections and the requirements for meaningful elections has widened, even since 1966, and that in El Salvador in March 1982 the gap attained truly Orwellian levels. To show this discrepancy more graphically, we list here six widely acknowledged core requirements for a *real* election, and consider in summary form their application to El Salvador in 1982.[14]

1. **Freedom of speech**. An obvious requirement for a free election is that individuals be able to speak their minds. They should be able to criticize their leaders, their police and army, national economic and foreign policies, and even raise questions about the role of the Godfather. This condition was clearly not met in El Salvador in the years 1980-83, either in law or in the realities of daily life. Basic issues were not debatable, and there were no real choices capable of being verbalized or offered for vote. Neither the case for nonmilitary options, nor serious or radical reform, nor information or views objectionable to the security forces, could be safely expressed in public. Only the representatives of the extreme rightwing parties could move around with relative freedom in the countryside.

By law a state of siege was in effect, in which questioning authority in any way was treated as subversion and could lead to arrest, immediate assault, rape, and murder, all without legal recourse. While this law was officially suspended for the participating political parties in the months immediately preceding the March 1982 election, there was no slackening of official murder. Over 1,500 unarmed civilians were murdered by the security forces in the three months of January-March 1982, and perhaps 30,000 from the time of the coup of 1979. This is impressive testimony to the high risk of speaking out. There is no recorded case of the criminal prosecution of any member of the security forces or death squads for murder, even in the instances of the rape-murder of four U.S. women or the killing of two U.S. citizens involved in the land reform program. Although the U.S. government put pressure on the Salvadoran authorities because of the publicity given these killings and the negative image which they conveyed about the system of justice in El Salvador, that pressure was not effective. The threat of extreme violence carried out by the state against individuals expressing dissident opinions was far greater in El Salvador in 1982 than in the Soviet Union during that year or in Poland at the time of the January 1947 election.

2. **Freedom of the media**. A free election requires a free press—a variety of media organs under noncentralized control, open to a wide range of opinion, and uncensored either directly or by threats. In El Salvador in 1982 the press, radio, and TV were under government control. Independent papers had been gradually closed down; those still in existence carefully toed a progovernment line either by choice, direct censorship, or fear of retribution. There were only three substantial newspapers in San Salvador in the mid-1970s that were not controlled by the oligarchy. One, the Church paper, was bombed in 1977 and has been repeatedly closed down by attacks and threats ever since. The second, *La Cronica*, terminated its existence in 1980 when its editor-in-chief and two employees were kidnapped, killed, and mutilated. The third, *El Independiente*, was closed down in 1981 after the army arrested its personnel and destroyed its physical plant. Its editor fled the country. The only independent radio station, owned by the Church, suffered five bombings after the 1979 coup and was shut down for an extended period in 1981 after its transmitter was destroyed. At least 26 journalists, domestic and foreign, have been murdered. A death list of 35 journalists was circulated by the security forces in the spring of 1982, just prior to the murder of four Dutch journalists. These efforts put the final touches on a media environment incompatible with a free election.

3. **Freedom of organization of intermediate groups**. Perhaps the most important political fact about El Salvador in March 1982 was the prior decimation of popular and private organizations. Political sociologists from Durkheim onward have stressed the importance of independent intermediate organizations and groups as essential to democracy. Such intermediate bodies interest and protect individuals in political activity, allow organized pressure on the state, and restrain state power. The decimation of these groups, leaving the individual isolated, powerless, and manipulable, is one of the main characteristics of totalitarian states, which "search out all

independent forms of organizations in order to transform them or destroy them."[15] As we describe in detail in Chapters 4 and 5, the undermining of intermediate groups in El Salvador by state-sponsored terrorism occurred on a massive scale. Several thousand leaders were murdered, and numerous organizations were destroyed, driven underground, or brought under government control. For example, from the 1979 coup to the 1982 election more than 100 officials and organizers of the peasant union sponsored by an arm of the AFL-CIO were murdered. A report of July 1982 by a Salvadoran teachers union indicated that 292 teachers had been murdered, 16 disappeared, 52 were arrested, and 1,200 schools had been closed by government repression following the 1979 coup. An earlier Amnesty International report on teacher murders showed that most of those killed had been active as organizers or union officials. The toll of officials and organizers of other trade unions and professional organizations was also very high. The demonstration election of March 1982 followed several years of assault on such mediating groups. The people were then mobilized to vote under conditions of atomization, government control of the media, and a state of siege.

4. The absence of highly developed and pervasive instruments of state-sponsored terror. In evolving totalitarian societies there is a steady enlargement of the secret police, the army, and other elements of state-organized terror. In El Salvador, the official instruments of state coercion—the army, the National Guard, the Treasury Police, and the National Police—have increased in size, resources, and training. Equally important, from 1966-67 onward there emerged a large terrorist organization, ORDEN, sponsored by the army and security establishment, and with scores of thousands of members. ORDEN was officially outlawed in 1980, but this act was nominal only. From ORDEN the security forces obtain information about dissidents and organizers of potentially threatening groups like peasant unions; and together the official forces and ORDEN man "death squads" that have murdered thousands. In turn, ORDEN members receive favorable treatment from land reform officials and protection from the death squads. Particularly in isolated rural areas, the mere existence (or rumored existence) of ORDEN members would have a chilling effect on the voicing of dissenting opinions, let alone organizing and campaigning for opponents of the government.

Under U.S. sponsorship, ORDEN is being integrated into a new and more sophisticated counterinsurgency program. In a plan for the "Well-Being for San Vicente," being put in place with 17 U.S.

advisers, thousands of U.S.-trained Salvadoran troops, and $1 million a month in AID funds, a *Boston Globe* news report of July 17, 1983 states that the army "plans to train and arm up to 1000 village-based civil defense forces to stop the guerillas from slipping back into their old positions." Who are the "civil defense" personnel who will "defend" the populace against the terrorists? The report indicates that many villagers were worried that the army was simply revitalizing ORDEN, and "in one nearby town, Raul Alvarenga, 55, a civil defense leader, said that all the new unit's members had once been in Orden." This program closely resembles the Phoenix program in Vietnam, under which thousands of Vietnamese civilians were assassinated to root out a radical "infrastructure."

5. **Freedom of party organization and ability to field candidates.** For a *real* free election various interest groups must be able to organize and maintain political parties. This has not been possible in El Salvador. Even Duarte's Christian Democratic Party (PDC), strongly supported by the United States, has suffered numerous casualties from the army and death squads. An April 1981 report recorded the death by assassination of 40 Christian Democratic mayors and scores of other PDC party functionaries.[16] In a three week period in May 1982, six more PDC mayors and a number of other party activists were killed. The Democratic Revolutionary Front (FDR) was subjected to a wholesale slaughter—combined with torture and mutilation— of its six top leaders in San Salvador on November 27, 1980. In 1982, 12 more FDR leaders were seized and disappeared; only six have been released, and the whereabouts of the others, if still alive, is unknown. In April 1981 the army published in a prominent newspaper a death list of 138 names that covered the leadership "establishment" of the left and center. In short, not only radical but even pro-U.S., only mildly reformist parties cannot escape decimation by political murder in El Salvador. This defines a system of terror of such ferocity and magnitude that if it existed within an enemy state it would immediately be seen as ruling out the possibility of a meaningful election.

6. **Absence of coercion and fear on the part of the general population.** A free election requires a population free of coercion, fear, and threats of violence. In an environment of no legal rights for the individual, and 150 security force murders of civilians per week, fear and coercion were an important part of everyday life in the El Salvador of 1980-83. There is abundant and uncontested evidence that this fear has been produced overwhelmingly by government and

government-sponsored forces.

In El Salvador in March 1982 voting was required by law, and the effective head of state, General José Guillermo Garcia, warned Salvadorans just prior to the election that nonvoting was treasonable. Those failing to vote would be identifiable by the absence of a mark placed on their hand at the voting stations, and by the absence of the appropriate stamp on their identity card. The specific vote itself was also potentially identifiable under the procedures employed in El Salvador in March 1982.[17] The announced aim of the United States and the Salvadoran army and other security forces was to get out the vote, to produce a large turnout. If, being given a day off to meet their legal voting obligation, Salvadorans trek long distances, stand patiently in long lines to vote and to have their identity card marked, what do we infer from this? The plausible inference in this environment of daily murder and endemic fear is that the security forces can "get out the vote."

Not one of the six basic conditions just described was addressed by the U.S. mass media in depth and with prominence during El Salvador's election. The administration and media focused on the election-day details, not on the framework that makes elections meaningful. But even conservative theorists stress that the significance of voting "depends upon the degree to which the other parts of the process have operated *before* voting takes place."[18] A secret of the success of demonstration elections is that the media disregard the fundamental processes that operate before voting takes place in U.S.-sponsored elections. We will show in Chapter 5 that such processes and the specific conditions enumerated earlier *were* featured by the media during the *Polish* election of 1947, where they provided the basis for the (accurate) conclusion that the election was a fraud. But the Polish election was no more fraudulent than the El Salvador election of 1982. The difference in media treatment can only be explained in terms of the patriotic service of the U.S. mass media in aiding the policies of their own government.

In the chapters that follow we present case studies of the background, organization, and media treatment of three major demonstration elections—those of the Dominican Republic, Vietnam, and El Salvador. We also describe briefly the sequels to these elections. This allows us to see that in each case the results deviated radically from the claims of the sponsors—instead of peace and reconciliation, the elections provided a cover for escalated warfare and/or internal repression. We can also see that the mass media, which had swallowed the government's forecasts of good things to come, failed to follow up and analyse the real denouement. In chapter 5 we also examine more systematically the media's treatment of the El Salvador election of 1982 and the full gamut of mechanisms of selective focus and suppression that make the mass media a vehicle of national propaganda. In the final chapter, we present some thoughts on the future of the demonstration election, and, more specifically, on the electoral and other PR ploys that the Reagan administration is already putting into place as it attempts to gain support for its strategies of intervention.

CHAPTER 2

The Dominican Republic

The first U.S.-sponsored election in which the "demonstration effect" on the U.S. home population was of major importance was held in the Dominican Republic on June 1, 1966. The need for such an election arose out of the U.S. invasion and military occupation, which began in late April 1965, and from the circumstances surrounding that intervention. The Vietnam War then underway had already led to vocal protest at home and abroad. The Dominican invasion provided another illustration of U.S. willingness to use force to impose its authority on smaller countries in defiance of international law.[1] What is more, the surface facts were more compromising of the image of U.S. beneficence and defense of the higher values than in the Indochinese case, where Red China, Ho Chi Minh, and a Communist-led insurgency could be invoked. Although the Johnson administration made much of an alleged Communist threat in the Dominican Republic, and the frightening spectre of Fidel Castro stood in the wings threatening U.S. "national security," the Dominican invasion seemed to have had the immediate aim of preventing victory by "Constitutionalists" and the return to power of the last democratically elected president of that country, Juan Bosch. The United States appeared to be—and in fact, *was*—intervening to protect a reactionary oligarchy and military establishment from the

17

threat of popular and democratic government. The situation was exacerbated by the fact that the Johnson administration lied frequently about "atrocities" allegedly perpetrated by the Constitutionalists and about the Communist presence in the pro-Bosch camp. What is more remarkable, the liberal mass media exposed these lies rather prominently, featuring with unusual generosity the harshly critical remarks of people like Senator William Fulbright and the journalist Theodore Draper.

The Fulbright-Draper-media response to the Dominican invasion was one of the last audible protests of the liberal establishment to the interment of the youthful but moribund Alliance for Progress.[2] Designed with liberal fanfare to combat Castroism by aid that would facilitate reform and structural change, the Alliance quickly receded, leaving the field to counterinsurgency and repression, as Latin oligarchs and generals saw that the presence—real or contrived—of "Communist guerillas in the hills" would control any reformist tendencies in Washington. Bosch in the Dominican Republic was a test case that cast the gravest doubts on the willingness and *capacity* of Washington to give strong support to real reform. Unwilling to protect Bosch from overthrow by the military in 1963, Washington was prepared to absorb the public-relations costs of an armed invasion to prevent his return in 1965. This was too much for those like Fulbright and Draper who believed that the United States should (and could) support serious reform to achieve its long term ends. Although these liberals had already lost this war during the Kennedy administration, with its stress on counterinsurgency and its almost pathological fear of Communism,[3] they were still doing battle. To them the Dominican invasion of 1965 seemed a regression and a violation of liberal fundamentals, and the reaction was strong.

It was in this context that the Johnson administration saw the need to proclaim its commitment to a free election. Theodore Draper noted that to "repress a popular movement to restore [constitutional government] and then to promise new elections and a new constitution is a travesty of constitutionalism and an insult to the intelligence."[4] This "insult to the intelligence," of which a major component was the demonstration election of June 1, 1966, was nonetheless effective. With the aid of a gradually more understanding press, and a contingent of observers and intellectual apologists, the government was able in the end to convey the impression that even if we had been a bit hasty, we quickly saw the error of our ways and were prepared to put power back into the hands of the Dominican "people." This impression was false, however. As we will show below, the election merely put a public relations gloss on the preservation of power in the hands of a small set of people whose continued rule was the goal of the original decision to intervene.

The Trujillo Era

The United States had assumed the natural right to intervene in the Dominican Republic in the nineteenth century, based simply on its power and obvious cultural and moral superiority. Secretary of State Olney asserted in 1895 that "today the United States is practically sovereign on this continent, and its fiat is law upon the subjects to which it confines its interposition."[5] This assumption of the right to define the internal arrangements of the small powers in its sphere of influence was aided by the racism that pervaded U.S. policymakers, steeped in the background of slavery, Jim Crow, and wars of Indian extermination. Poverty, illiteracy, and *caudillismo* in our backyard reinforced the racism and made it easier to bully our smaller neighbors with good conscience.

The U.S. occupation of the Dominican Republic from 1916 to 1924 set the stage for the 30-year Trujillo dictatorship. The occupation was in no serious way constructive. Several roads and some schools were built, and some public health advances were achieved, but school reform was modest and political reform was stifled. The government was headed by a U.S. military officer, the Dominican Congress was suspended, elections were postponed indefinitely, and the press was heavily censored under a martial law regime.[6] Protesters were treated as agitators and punished; genuine rebels were hunted down mercilessly. Piero Gleijeses says that

> The Military Government was led by officers who could not speak the language of the people, who felt contempt for their color, and who had no idea of their history or national psychology. If the occupation brought a degree of peace and stability, it was the crushing peace and stability of dictatorship. In the end, the occupation made the possibility of democracy on Dominican soil more remote.[7]

The military regime did have a profound effect on the economic structure of the Dominican Republic, changing the land ownership law in 1920 to allow U.S. sugar interests to obtain legal title to land. Under the new law vast tracts of land were taken over and thousands of Dominican peasants were driven out, their villages burned. By the time U.S. troops withdrew in 1924, sugar companies owned a quarter of the agricultural area of the Dominican Republic. U.S. companies owned 81% of this total, Dominican companies only 3%.[8]

The main contribution of the occupation to the Dominican future, however, came from the disarming of the general populace, the neutralization of the *caudillos*, and the building up and training of a strong national police force, which opened up new possibilities for centralization of a formerly dispersed power.[9] Raphael Leonidas Trujillo joined the military force of the occupying power and "made a considerable impression upon a series of his Marine superiors," who described him as "calm, even-tempered, forceful, active, bold and painstaking,...one of the best in the service."[10] He rose quickly through the ranks. This "bastard son of the occupation forces"[11] assumed full power in 1930, and a 30-year reign of terror ensued.

By force and fraud Trujillo gradually accumulated in his own hands as much as two-thirds of the assets of the country, including half of all the arable land.[12] He could perhaps have said with more justice than Louis XIV, "L'État, c'est moi." He took control of the salt business in 1932 by using state power to abrogate some prior concessions and tax others into submission, and it was estimated in 1940 that Trujillo was making $400,000 a year from this concession alone.[13] By similar methods Trujillo gradually came to dominate the milk, meat, sugar, tobacco, cement, paper, paint, wheat and flour, airline, newspaper, radio, and television industries. As the expatriate Dominican intellectual Jésus de Galindez noted, perhaps ironically, "Trujillo is the first businessman of the Dominican Republic."[14] He was astute enough so that when he decided to take over the sugar industry, in which U.S. interests were important, he compensated reasonably; and he maintained openings for U.S. investment in bauxite (Alcoa), bananas (United Fruit), hotels (Intercontinental Hotels), oil (Esso and Texaco), and in other areas.[15]

Trujillo also used systematic terror to maintain political and economic control over the Dominican Republic. As Dan Kurzman pointed out:

> If Trujillo ran the country like a huge private enterprise to be exploited for the sole purpose of enriching himself and his family, this was the least of his crimes. Thousands of his political enemies, automatically called "Communists," died in secret police dungeons, many of them after suffering hideous tortures perpetrated with electrical devices, nail extractors, decapitation collars, and leather-thonged whips. Young ladies who spurned his advances were found dead in "accidents." Even those who fled abroad lived in constant dread of kidnapping and death at the hands of Trujillo

agents who, after performing their murderous tasks were themselves marked for extinction. In 1937 he supervised the massacre of from 15,000 to 35,000 Haitian squatters in two days.[16]

U.S. relations with Trujillo through most of his 30-year term were nonetheless satisfactory. Wiarda characterizes their evolution as from acquiescence to "enthusiastic support," up to the very late falling out.[17] The U.S. minister to the Dominican Republic, Charles Curtis, strongly opposed Trujillo's takeover in 1930, but his position was overridden by more powerful forces. Trujillo could count on the support of the U.S. Army and Marine Corps, he had strong support in the State Department, and he played his cards well. In contrast with Bosch in 1963, Trujillo pretended to be subservient and eager for U.S. guidance;[18] while Bosch was more assertive of nominal independence, he was, in fact, more friendly to the United States. Subsequently, Trujillo maintained a nice balance, offsetting his internal extreme terroristic violence, and the gradual absorption of Dominican resources into his own portfolio, with a number of devices. One was a loudly trumpeted anticommunism, which he saw would carry him very far in dominant U.S. political circles.[19] Second, he was carefully subservient to larger U.S. political-military strategies, exemplified by his prompt entry into World War II on the side of the western allies and his facile adoption of Cold War rhetoric. Third, as noted, he avoided major provocation of U.S. economic interests, and cultivated some of them, who were pleased with the extremely low wages and nonstrike environment maintained by Trujillo. Fourth, he forced the Dominican Catholic Church into submission and mobilized its support for his regime, partly through terror, partly by bribing its most reactionary elements. Also helpful were a Concordat with the Vatican, friendship with Franco, and his deep devotion to the Christian faith. Cardinal Spellman, on a visit to the Dominican Republic, publicly embraced Trujillo and referred to him as a "Benefactor of the Church."[20]

Finally, like his friend Somoza, Trujillo engaged in a major lobbying and favor-buying campaign in the United States, and succeeded in building and maintaining a strong congressional faction that served his interests. Numerous U.S. leaders were taken on guided tours of the Dominican Republic and witnessed for themselves the great works that The Benefactor had wrought, the stability of the country, and the deference and love which the citizenry felt for him. A "rock of stability" (Senator Johnston), a "builder greater than all the Spanish conquistadores" (Rep. Fish), author of "broad humanitarian policies" (Rep. McCormack), ruler of "one of the most truly democratic nations of South America" (Rep. Dorn), "a splendid President, who is outstanding among all those in the American nations" (Secretary of State Cordell Hull)[21]—there were few complimentary adjectives not applied to Trujillo by U.S. political and religious leaders. They came from people who were the recipients of his favors or, in some cases, were merely ideologically pleased with his blend of anticommunism and repression. The strength of the pro-Trujillo faction in the United States was impressive testimonial to the U.S. establishment's capacity to support the most outlandish terroristic violence and totalitarianism, as long as it had the appropriate rightwing accoutrements.[22]

Trujillo's downfall was a consequence of his overreaching and bad luck. He had encroached too heavily on Dominican economic opportunities, leaving too little for foreign enterprise and too small a business support base in the United States. In the short term, his abduction and murder of Jésus de Galindez and Gerald Murphy[23] and the attempted assassination of Roman Betancourt, the President of Venezuela, had major political repercussions. His bad luck was in the fall of export prices and the liberalized political environment in Latin America in the 1950s. Trujillo lost his closest allies, dictators Batista and Jiminez, in the late 1950s, and from his increasingly isolated position he lashed out blindly. His failed attempt to assassinate the liberal successor to Jiminez, Betancourt, in June 1960 led to sanctions by the OAS, stronger U.S. hostility, and frantic internal repression and arms buying by Trujillo. With sugar, cacao, and tobacco prices falling, Trujillo's policies were now generating internal Dominican opposition among the well-to-do. In a show of democratic reform he put forward a puppet president—Joaquin Balaguer, a loyal servant of the regime—and he offered "free elections," but nothing availed. With CIA assistance, he was murdered on May 30, 1961.[24]

From the Fall of Trujillo to the Overthrow of Bosch

The death of Trujillo ushered in a period of considerable turmoil: a *trujillista* reaction, a democratic organizational upheaval, the ouster of the Trujillo family, rule by a Council, and eventually the organization of an election in 1962. The U.S. role in this maneuvering toward a new equilibrium was enormous. Without a U.S. presence, the power vacuum would have been quickly filled by the family heirs of Trujillo, the Trujillo military-police establishment, and the economic elite, although the potential for violence and breakdown in the jockeying for power would have been great. The long-submerged masses might have been able to assume some political role in a period of elite confusion and struggle, but this is not clear. The Kennedy administration threw its weight against both a Trujillo family succession and a seizure of power by the *trujillista* military. Its bargaining and coercive resources were great, as it held both much needed aid and the suspended Dominican sugar quota as a club over the elements seeking power. The United States also brandished a military threat at strategic moments to help persuade Dominican intransigents to relinquish power.[25] The U.S. strategy was to keep the *trujillista* old guard at bay, and to allow freedom of organization and the genesis of a civil power to parallel the *trujillista* military power. An element in this strategy was an election, a means of institutionalizing and stabilizing a democratic regime.

It is important to recognize that the framework sponsored by the United States allowed greater freedom without disbanding—in fact, while building up further—the Trujillo police and military establishment, and the economic power structure. These interests were corrupt, reactionary, and potent, and they posed a dire threat to even the mildest democratic order, which would of necessity try to limit their powers. The preservation and strengthening of this tainted *trujillista* structure as a parallel base of power was not accidental, but reflected a fatal flaw and contradiction in Kennedy-Cold War liberalism; one which foredoomed a democratic order in the Dominican Republic. Cold War liberalism feared Communism far more than it feared the destruction of democracy in Third World client states.[26] The "insurance policy" strategy, supporting and building up anti-communist military and police establishments to reduce any leftwing threat—in full flower in 1962—increased the *rightwing* threat and weakened the power of liberal democracy. The refurbished *trujillista* military would assure that democratic "excesses" did not yield any openings to "Communism"—but in fact it assured that democracy had no chance at all.

Thus, instead of clearing out a military establishment that had been "the blind tool of the Trujillo dictatorship—hired assassins in uniform, their hands bloodied by countless crimes...a hotbed of corruption, an occupation force in their own country,"[27] the Kennedy plan was to build up and, of course, "democratize" the Dominican military-police establishment. Wiarda notes that "the indoctrination of the armed forces, under the direction of Colonel Elias Wessin y Wessin...concentrated primarily on simple anticommunism to the exclusion of almost all else."[28] Besides indoctrination, civic action programs were carried out to buttress the image of the military, and counterinsurgency training was inaugurated under a Pentagon-sponsored program. Ambassador Martin noted that "by the end of the year, despite Castro-Communist outcry, we had trained three companies of counterinsurgency troops."[29] This was clearly what was needed in the Dominican Republic.

On the basis of an alleged concern for the "defense capability" of the budding Dominican democracy the national police force also was increased in size from 3,000 to 10,000, at the insistence of the United States. Under its new chief, General Belisario Peguero Guerrero, the police became "the most oppressive, most corrupt, and most *trujillista* of all the armed forces."[30] Gleijeses notes ironically that, while it "proved uncommonly efficient at maintaining order against defenseless crowds," it did not do so well at the moment of truth on April 25, 1965.[31]

It was within this framework that an election was organized and held in the Dominican Republic in 1962, the first free election ever held in that country. What made it unique in its freedom was the disarray of the old elites and the *trujillista* military and police; the U.S. presence and commitment to an election; the holdover prestige of the Social Democratic Alliance of Latin leaders, who included Juan Bosch; and the presence of Bosch and his Dominican Revolutionary Party (PRD), their organizational freedom and campaign of 1962. The *substance* of the freedom of the 1962 elections was not merely an uncoerced vote on election day but: (1) the ability of Bosch and other party leaders to communicate often to the mass of the population; (2) the extension of *organization* into the countryside, affording a long-oppressed peasantry a source of information and a sense of solidarity and protection; and (3) the belief of the masses, suddenly released from extreme tyranny, and in a state of optimism and euphoria, that their role in an election might be meaningful.

Bosch went into the countryside by jeep every day, talking to the peasants in a language they understood. Although his message was unreported in the press, he saw many people personally and communicated to the countryside twice a day by radio. His Secretary General, Angel Miolan, was a good organizer, and PRD cadres ranged through the countryside. They created a peasant affiliate of the PRD, a grassroots organization of some 300,000 members called the Federacion Nacional de Hermandades Campesinas (FENHERCA).[32]

Bosch was a spokesman of the masses, whose "language was so common that even a peasant could understand him," speaking to them about "'beans' and 'papayas,' compared with Fiallo's concern over the 'noble and long-suffering Dominican people' and Jimines Grullon's outrage at the 'betrayal of the revolutionary ethic.'[33] He gave the peasants hope that they might have rights—that actions might really be taken directed toward their interests! Late in the 1962 campaign, when the *gentes de primera* realized that Bosch might actually win, a wild campaign of defamation was unleashed in which Bosch was alleged to be a Communist, a latifundist, a Trujillist—but mostly a Communist.[34] Though the frenzy was great, the accusations were so crude and contradictory that the campaign failed, but it was an ominous warning of the uncompromising quality of the forces of the old regime.

On December 20, 1962 Bosch swept the national election with 59% of the vote, and he was sworn in as President in February 1963. Seven months later he was deposed in a coup only mildly opposed by the United States. His term was short, first, because he represented "a segment of the Dominican population that previously had never played a role in the political life of the nation: the peasants, the urban unemployed, the working class poor."[35] Bosch was not overthrown because he was arrogant and vain. Nor was he overthrown because of mistakes he made during his short administration. It was his program and the threat of his program that did him in. A fiscal conservative, Bosch moved very cautiously in carrying out his reforms, beginning first with cutting down the massive thievery of the bureaucracy and military. As Ambassador Martin noted, "his brief administration may well have been the most honest in Dominican history, if not in Latin America";[36] but honesty, fiscal conservatism, devotion to democratic principle, and cautious reformism were not "strategic assets." Bosch quickly lost Martin's confidence, and the military representatives of the United States regarded him as an enemy. Crucial here was his "passivity" toward Communists and failure to recognize the threat of "Castro-Communism." That the Communists were a small and ineffective lot was irrelevant; giving them great attention was a symbolic act of assurance and subservience to a higher interest. Rounding them up, torturing, killing, or deporting them, would have been acts of good faith, genuflexions, like the willingness to "name names." Jerome Slater pointed out that

...in the course of Bosch's brief administration, [U.S. Ambassador] Martin, the lifelong liberal and devoted admirer of Adlai Stevenson, pressed the following measures on the Dominican President: the elimination of agrarian reform measures involving land confiscation; a major effort to control "subversion" through the training of an anti-subversive force; the closing of leftist schools; the illegal harassment or detention of Dominicans traveling to Cuba; and finally, as rightist pressures mounted, the "wholesale roundup," imprisonment, or deportation of both the extreme right and left![37]

Bosch was not able to meet the high standards set by liberal democracy, and quickly lost favor in Washington.

The role of the United States in Bosch's overthrow was thus critical in two senses: it left intact and even built up the *trujillista* elements that made democracy impossible; and it was quickly "disappointed" in Bosch for his alleged ineffectiveness and insensitivity to the touchstone test of reliability—active anticommunism. Thus, while it is not clear that any U.S. officials except those affiliated with the AFL-CIO played an *active* role in the coup,[38] their *passivity* was of great importance. As Gleijeses points out, "Dominican officers needed no prodding to perpetrate a coup. On the contrary, they needed strong pressure to check their urge to strike, and the pressure was missing."[39]

The Triumvirate and the Revolution of 1965

The overthrow of Bosch ushered in a new minority government dominated by the military, which quickly installed a three-member civilian front known as The Triumvirate. This trio represented six rightwing parties, five of which had amassed an aggregate of under 6% of the vote in the 1962 election. U.S. aid was immediately suspended, but it was quickly renewed when the new government promised "elections" and signaled its recognition of the primacy of the Red Threat. No threat of military intervention was ever posed for this overthrow of a democratic regime. The Triumvirate was helped in its relations with Washington by a tiny radical faction which took to the hills to emulate Fidel Castro. Quickly hunted down and captured, all the prisoners—15 in number—were murdered in cold blood. These murders led to the resignation of one member of the Triumvirate. He was replaced by Donald Reid Cabral, who quickly emerged as the dominant individual among the civil trio.

Under the new regime Bosch and scores of other democratic political leaders were deported without judicial process, constitutional guarantees against arbitrary imprisonment were suspended, special permits were required for political meetings, and long distance phone calls were monitored by the police. Beatings and torture in prison again became commonplace, and the Dominican Republic once again became a country of fear and intimidation.

Perhaps the most striking feature of the era of the Triumvirate was the return and enlargement of corruption. As Howard Wiarda noted:

> As if trying to make up for the seven months lost during his [Bosch's] administration, government servants engaged in a rash of corrupt practices that had not been employed since the Trujillo regime. Bribes to administration officials, for example, occurred on a scale almost matching that of the former era. Government offices became so overstaffed that many were receiving salaries without rendering any services. More importantly, the spirit of fraud which characterized every aspect of government under the slain Generalissimo again was rampant in the public service—the enrichment of favored individuals through the expenditure of funds for public projects, self-aggrandizement through one's knowledge of pending government programs, the receipt of goods, favor or money through the performance of an official duty.[40]

Even more important, perhaps, was the aggressive pursuit of private gain by the police and military establishments. Peguero Guerrero, head of the police, took advantage of a 1962 autonomy law that gave him absolute control over police resources, using policemen as construction laborers to build "a large and luxurious home near the fashionable Embajedor Hotel and across the street from the residence of [General] Imbert."[41] Gleijeses observes that after the overthrow of Bosch,

> ...the top brass were free to resume their true calling—as thieves: "Through their mushrooming canteens the military imported food, liquor and all kinds of household goods duty-free and went into the wholesale business. U.S. cigarettes, for example, which sell 80 cents for a pack in the cities' stores were purchased by the Armed Forces at prices as low as 20 cents and resold to retailers at enormous profits."[42]

The process reached its pinnacle when a National Police Canteen Company was set up to formalize the looting. Business protest was strong, and the company was discontinued; but as with Trujillo, "the military's 'business' vocation was too strong and their desire for gain too tenacious."[43] Smuggling boomed, and the leading ports of illegal entry were the major naval and airforce bases.[44]

The downfall of the Triumvirate resulted in part from the fact that their looting and terror were not alleviated by any overall economic gains. "Extreme corruption and mismanagement were responsible for the country's economic collapse after the incipient recovery brought about by the Bosch government."[45] Furthermore, the terror was not sufficient to eliminate all opposition, partly because of military-police factionalism, partly because of the desire to maintain an aura of moderation after the Trujillo reign of terror, and partly also because of complacency. With Bosch and the majority of the population easily routed in September 1963, and with no uprising at home or really threatening response from the United States, the elite underestimated the potential for unrest and revolt. While the Triumvirate kept Bosch and other PRD leaders in exile and used its power to propagandize and buy support, the PRD was still legal and gradually regained some strength. The masses, who had been disappointed by Bosch's performance in office, came to regard that era as a golden age, and Bosch became a happy memory and a national symbol, "his lost popularity unwittingly restored by Reid Cabral and the government's supporters."[46] Not only the peasants and urban masses, but some elements of the lower and "middle" middle class also became attracted to Bosch in the wake of a return to extreme corruption, incompetence, and fear. Even more important, a significant element in the military establishment began to question the status quo and show an interest in a return to constitutional government.

By 1965 the Triumvirate—by then essentially the Reid Cabral government—had the complete backing of the United States. The Johnson administration had quickly recognized the new police state and gradually increased aid and support. It was concerned with abuses only as an element weakening the Triumvirate's grip on the country. The fact that Cabral "had no popular support,"[47] according to U.S. secret polls, was irrelevant, as was the fact that Bosch and the PRD were the legally constituted authority. The Cabral government received some $100 million in direct and guaranteed loans from the United States between January 1964 and April 1965, a historically unique input for the Dominican Republic. The U.S. Ambassador to that country, a "courtly southern gentleman," struck up a "cordial" relationship with the smooth "Donny" Cabral. His contacts with the majority party, the PRD, were sparse and cold. He never received the black leader Pena Gomez, nor did his deputy. The Mann-Johnson policy with respect to Bosch was to refuse to recognize his existence. Their view, in Gleijeses' words, was that U.S. interests "dictated that in the future this dangerous figure be kept out of Dominican politics."[48] This the United States obviously had the power to do, and it did it.

The revolt of 1965 rested on a mass base plus a constitutionalist faction within the military willing to take risks in the interest of the search for a democratic order. The great majority of the military conspirators wanted no popular revolt—no armed civilian body— although they counted on the PRD and the populace to demonstrate in the streets in support of a military countercoup. When it began, on April 24, 1965, the outpouring by the public was extraordinary. The anti-Boschist Danilo Brugal Alfau noted that "the movement won, from the outset, unanimous approval."[49] Frank Moya Pons wrote in his diary that "quite literally the entire population of the capital rushed into the streets."[50] The rebels took over Santo Domingo on April 25 without opposition. The conservative elements of the military and police were cautiously "awaiting developments," some even turning constitutionalist in expectation that the tide was too overwhelming to stem.

At that point the revolution would have been over, no lives would have been lost, and Bosch would have returned to resume his constitutional position as head of state, if the United States government had given a modicum of support to this movement. Instead it reacted with fear and panic and actively opposed the revolt. PRD leaders going to the U.S. Embassy on April 25 were not even received by the higher U.S. officials. A low-level functionary, extremely hostile, told them that their movement was Communist and could receive no U.S. support.[51] The telegram sent by the Embassy to the State Department on April 25 noted:

> The Air Force has decided to fight to block return of Bosch and Wessin y Wessin has agreed to support the Air Force. . . . All members of the country team feel Bosch's return and resumption of control of the government is against U.S. interests in view of extremists in the coup and Communist advocacy [sic] of Bosch return.[52]

In an earlier communication the Deputy Ambassador expressed "our strong feelings everything possible should be done to prevent a Communist takeover."[53] These U.S. Embassy representatives knew almost nothing about the constituency of the Constitutionalist revolt; but their class-nationalist reactions to movements from below, with people who were poorly attired, dark, unpolished, and sometimes expressing threatening slogans, were intense. They were also suffering from the U.S. disease of anticommunism, then in one of its virulent phases. If the Communists "advocate" Bosch's return that is enough. The right of the United States to shape the politics of the Dominican Republic is unquestioned. Although the people of that country were speaking, the U.S. Embassy represented a higher authority. As Gleijeses expresses it, "The court had passed sentence. No appeal could be made. The Constitutionalist movement had to be crushed even if it meant more bloodshed."[54]

We will not recount here the details of the civil war that ensued.[55] The U.S. Embassy assumed that the local military establishment could suppress the rebellion. In pursuit of this end it aided the "loyalist"* generals in their effort to reestablish control by all means available, supporting even the large-scale bombing of a defenceless population. But this means of pacification failed. In order to prevent an imminent victory of the Constitutionalists the United States had to dispatch a large military force, all in the name of a "humanitarian intervention."

The U.S. Invasion and Occupation

On April 28, 1965, the Johnson administration ordered the first landing of Marines in the Dominican Republic, in response to a frantic appeal from the U.S. Embassy that the forces of Law and Order were in jeopardy. The landings were justified on the grounds of a threat to U.S. lives—U.S. authorities, in fact, instructed the Dominicans to phrase their appeal for U.S. intervention accordingly.[56] It was hoped initially that a small U.S. contingent would sufficiently encourage the "loyalists"—and discourage the popular forces—to turn the tide without massive U.S. involvement. This was not to be. The continued disintegration of the official military establishment required a more massive U.S. presence, and eventually 23,000 U.S. troops went ashore to pacify and occupy the Dominican Republic.

To justify the larger force a larger threat had to be invoked. President Johnson and his associates therefore shifted quickly to the Communist threat and Constitutionalist "atrocities." The atrocities charge was not merely a complete fabrication, it was a familiar Orwellian inversion, as the only large-scale massacres were carried out by the loyalist military with the logistical assistance and quiet military and diplomatic support of the Johnson administration.[57]

The "Communist menace" was objectively slight, but in the fevered moral environment of U.S. politics following the "Castro shock" anything was subjectively believable. Some U.S. officials no doubt "really believed," although it was (and is) *so* convenient to rationalize fear of popular revolt, reformism, radicalism, and most importantly, *loss of control*, as a manifestation of "Communism." Anything can be done—any goons of convenience supported—if we are fighting the forces of evil.

A popular revolt led by persons of imperfect or unknown reliability means an uncertain outcome. The probability of "Castro-Communism" emerging out of developments in the Dominican Republic had increased in late April 1965 from a probability level of zero to something like 5% or even higher. Even if it was only 5%, why should the United States have to accept any such finite probability of injury or inconvenience to itself, or political damage to the party in power, when U.S. power would easily allow it to snuff out any such unpleasant possibilities by preventive intervention? These are imperial premises that come easily to the leaders and officials of imperial states.

The political left in the Dominican Republic was extremely weak and divided in April 1965, although fairly vocal. It had no representation within the military faction that led the revolt, which was strongly anticommunist, and it had virtually no representation or influence within the Bosch party. If the United States had supported the uprising, there almost surely would have been a return to the constitutional regime of 1963 with Bosch and the PRD in power, supported by an anticommunist military group that believed in liberal democracy and objected to a system of institutionalized corruption and violence. U.S. Embassy contacts within the Dominican Republic were exclusively with the military and economic elite, i.e., the forces of corruption, privilege, and moderate terror. About the politics of the majority and dissident groups, the Embassy was both fearful and comprehensively ignorant. They (and the CIA) completely failed to anticipate the liberal military movement, which catalyzed the deep dissatisfaction of the population. Even as regards their *betes noires*, the Communists, they knew nothing. The Embassy telegram to the State Department that the Communists "supported" Bosch and the coup was inaccurate—some of the extreme left thought the military counter-coup was a CIA plot and gave it no support whatever.[58]

In the world of the U.S. Embassy, reflecting local elite opinion as well as anticommunist ideology, Bosch was hard to distinguish from a Communist. Communism is used loosely in Latin America, often indistinguishably from "objecting to the status quo." As the status quo is often undemocratic in the most elemental political (as well as economic and social) sense, advocating constitutional government, not to speak of unions, or tax reform, is very often adequate proof of Communism. Cold War liberals, of course, rarely engage in such crudities. Instead, they maintain that people like Bosch are not Communists, but they "play into the hands of" Communists by demagogic appeals, class warfare, and "provoking" the military and oligarchy. Of course, Alliance for Progress rhetoric about the need for "structural change" as a means of defusing radicalism would appear to call for actions that will inevitably "provoke" the elite. But multinational corporations and the U.S. security establishment don't really like structural reforms. They prefer highly amenable clients and a strike-free and low-wage environment. How is the apparent contradiction to be reconciled? By recognizing that the liberal rhetoric is a cloak of second or third order values that invariably gives way to the primary values—investment climate, anticommunism, and political subserviency.

Bosch was a superb test case for Cold War liberalism, as he represented the *nominal* values—democracy, civil liberties, integrity, and reformism—to a high degree. He represented the *real* values imperfectly, however. He was strongly anticommunist but was prepared to tolerate communists as long as they stayed within the law; he was politically independent, although initially warmly attached to the United States; and he was ready to welcome foreign investment, but as a social democrat and reformer he was not prepared to create the investment climate offered by a Marcos or Suharto. As noted by Gleijeses:

> His nationalism and particularly his deep belief in political democracy cost him the support of the Kennedy adminis-tration. The Americans were unable to accept real, rather than formal Dominican independence. Above all, they wanted Bosch to persecute the "Castro-Communists." He refused. This was a capital sin.[59]

Bosch was quickly found to be a poor administrator and lacking in practical realism. Trujillo was acceptable for almost 30 years; ditto Donnie Cabral, mismanaging a system of corruption and benign terror that was known by U.S. officials to have stripped him of any popular support. But Juan Bosch was not acceptable. In April 1965 the U.S. government was determined to prevent Bosch's return to power. In this important test case *it was not Juan Bosch who failed*; it was that the enduring values in U.S. foreign policy revealed themselves with a stark clarity.

The small contingent of 536 U.S. Marines who disembarked on April 28, 1965 failed to stem the Constitutionalist tide. The forces of law and order, valiant in assaulting defenceless civilians, were quite incapable of handling an armed populace. The United States was therefore compelled to intervene more actively, throwing its over-whelming military and political weight behind the heirs of Trujillo. Even before the actual invasion, the United States had given extensive aid to the loyalist military, both material and advisory. Following the invasion, after a brief period of mere positioning, the U.S. forces attacked the Constitutionalists directly, capturing a key bridge and then creating a corridor through Santo Domingo which split the Constitutionalist forces in two. Although a comprehensive truce was in effect, on May 14 the loyalist forces, rearmed and financed by the United States, began an extensive attack on the Santo Domingo slums, moving freely through the corridor occupied by U.S. troops. This assault lasted eight days and involved numerous casualties and major atrocities. "Scores of prisoners were tortured and murdered," and an investigation of the Inter-American Commission on Human Rights found that the official military and police were engaging in widespread murder as part of a "policy of seeking to eliminate adversaries."[60] The Constitutionalists held on but were militarily bottled up and isolated in a sector of Santo Domingo. In another classic of great power hypocrisy, the United States claimed it could not interfere with the eight-day offensive and massacres as this would be a violation of U.S. "neutrality"![61]

The United States and its official military-police ally then carried out a policy of attrition, feasible with vastly superior resources. The military aim was to reestablish the hegemony of a traditional military-police establishment, which had been able to contain the popular forces for the prior 40 years; to provide the arms, training, and other elements of support, and to kill and deport enough Constitutionalists to restore the Old Regime of elite rule and general citizen passivity.

Politically, the U.S. aim was in exact parallel—to use a series of transitory regimes under which a final cleansing could take place, then holding a ratifying and demonstration election. A Government of National Reconstruction (GNR) was quickly installed, made up mainly of military personnel. The only civilian of real credibility who would serve in this dirty job, one Julio Postigo, a Bosch supporter, did so on grounds that are of interest in assessing the meaning of "elections": he felt that the alternative to such a government was a U.S. military offensive against the remaining Constitutionalist forces![62] The GNR was a stop-gap pending the installation of a "negotiated" government acceptable to all the relevant parties— which would, in its turn, govern till an election. After a brief flurry of negotiations that would have made some concessions to the Constitutionalists, the dominant faction in Washington decided to hold out for total victory. By protracted bargaining the virtually helpless Constitutionalists were forced to give up on every important issue.[63] The United States succeeded in achieving its central goals: the old guard military and police establishment was restored without any substantive concession to the Constitutionalists, thereby giving full guarantees for a "stable future" for the Dominican Republic. The U.S. and associated foreign military forces were to stay in the Dominican Republic through the election of June 1966. The Constitutionalists had to be satisfied with verbal assurances of protection and nondiscrimination in the future, none of which were realized in fact. Defeated militarily, the Constitutionalists were now defeated politically. Both facts were manifested even prior to the election of June 1966 in Constitutionalist officer murders, deportations, and exclusion from advancement or power within the military establishment. Many scores were settled by the elite reestablished in power by the United States, both before and after the 1966 election. The election was to be held in a repacified and militarily occupied country.

The Election of June 1, 1966

The election held in the Dominican Republic on June 1, 1966 was a huge success from the official U.S. viewpoint. Bosch was persuaded to run, and lost; the administration's preferred and sponsored candidate won handily. The old regime—including a large and omnipresent military and police establishment—had been restored to power by classic legitimizing processes. The election had demonstrated to doubting U.S citizens the enduring commitment of the United States to democracy and self-determination—that, in the unctuous words of Under Secretary of State Thomas C. Mann, our actions had been "for the purpose of helping to preserve for the people of [the Dominican Republic] their right to choose their own government free of outside interference."[64] Observers from abroad, many sympathetic to Bosch and social democracy, had been present in the Dominican Republic at the time of the election, and testified that it was generally fair.

An election, however, is a complex phenomenon that has to be examined closely to establish "fairness" and meaning; its qualities and significance cannot be understood by a small sample of observations on election day. This would seem obviously true when the election is arranged for a small country by a nearby superpower that has just intervened to achieve certain definite political objectives. Our simple and obvious theme is that the superpower intrusion, carried out with serious purpose and involving large resources, must itself sharply alter the parameters affecting an election. The ways in which those parameters are affected is susceptible to scientific examination. The secret of a demonstration election is that *the relevant questions are never addressed before the home populace.* The election is portrayed as if carried out in a political vacuum by an informed and secure population—with the only possible threats coming from insurgents and radicals who perversely question the integrity of the election process. The neutrality of the invader and his dedication to preparing the ground for a truly free election is patriotically assumed.[65] The absurdities to which the pretense of a meaningful election environment can be carried reached far greater heights in South Vietnam and El Salvador, as we shall see, but they abounded in the Dominican Republic as well.

Consider the basic anomaly—that Bosch won a landslide election victory in 1962, and that at the time of the revolt of April 1965 it was generally understood that he had even greater indigenous support. Presumably he would have won an election overwhelmingly in April 1965. The United States did not like the prospect, invaded and occupied the country—and 14 months later organized an election in which, *mirabile dictu*, Bosch lost decisively. It would appear that the "people" of the Dominican Republic had spoken earlier; and their preference not being acceptable to the United States it intervened to rectify the situation. If the "election" which followed the intervention turned things around in ways allowing the U.S aims to be realized in detail, it should immediately occur to a small child that the invasion and subsequent deployment of power by the invader must surely have been crucial to the turnaround.

As noted, the mass media play dumb. One position taken is that the United States, having made a mistake, and now having assured itself that "Communism" did not really threaten, quickly and submissively sought the true will of the Dominican masses. Or it is argued that the invasion and occupation, and all events prior to the election are "history." In the words of Frances Grant, while "a series of incidents had occurred on Dominican soil which altered the climate of the country," including the "inexplicable error" by the United States in invading and occupying the country, the selection of Godoy as Provisional President till the election was "a solution apparently acceptable to all parties to the conflict."[66] It was "apparently acceptable" apparently because it *happened*. The idea that a negotiated solution in the occupied Dominican Republic might have reflected the balance of power—the power of the United States versus that of the militarily defeated, isolated, and gradually weakening Constitutionalists—apparently never occurred to Grant. By removing history from the analysis—even very recent history directly explaining the constellation of power and the expectations and hopes of, and threats to, the Dominican majority—a free and fair election is defined as one in which people are allowed (or are forced) to vote, are not obviously coerced in casting their votes, and the ballot boxes are not stuffed. But these conditions can be met in elections which are meaningless in the sense of reflecting democratic choices. If massive power has been deployed the parameters of an election shift and the choices no longer reflect indigenous forces alone. We will also show that the June 1966 election failed to meet minimal election day conditions of fairness as well, but we regard this as a secondary point.

Dominican politics from April 28, 1965 through June 1, 1966 was decisively shaped by the military actions, presence, and obvious political intent of the United States. The Dominican Republic was an occupied country in which the invader was free to take actions rewarding friends and damaging enemies. Under the cover of this occupying force, the loyalist military of the Dominican Republic was rearmed, reorganized, and protected in its reoccupation of the country and dismantlement of the threat that had erupted in April 1965. An important plank in the initial bargaining agenda of the Constitutionalists, trying to salvage something in their negotiations with the representatives of the invaders, was that elections be held only *after* the exit of the occupying foreign armies. On this point, as well as all others, the Constitutionalists were defeated. Elections were held under the conditions of military occupation.

The altered parameters of political power. Let us enumerate and describe briefly some of the ways in which the invasion-occupation altered the terms of the election of June 1, 1966 and assured that the outcome would be in keeping with U.S. objectives:

1. The Bosch party suffered the stigma of military defeat. It could not reasonably have been expected to cope with the armed

forces of the United States; nonetheless, it was a loser and suffered defections from this fact alone.

2. As a defeated group the Bosch party and Constitutionalists were unable to protect their supporters and cadres from retaliation. The Constitutionalists were disarmed, the United States and its dependent Inter-American Peace Force were well armed, and the United States hastened to rehabilitate the military-police establishment of the old regime. *These were the central political facts of the invasion-occupation.* Many commentators on the Dominican revolt and its aftermath have noted that turmoil and violence continued and even escalated *after* the U.S. occupation and disarming of the Bosch-Constitutionalist forces. With rare exception they fail to ask why the United States could so easily disarm the "enemy," the rebels, and yet not contain the "excesses" of the old regime's military and police, our "friends" and dependents, whom the invasion had saved from defeat and whom the United States had armed and financed. These rightwing forces are patriotically assumed to be "out of control";[67] the more cogent assumption, that the rehabilitated loyalists were doing precisely what the United States wanted them to do—just as the South Vietnamese loyalists at the very same time were helping us "pacify" the indigenous population of that distant country—is not even entertained as a possibility. This was a Dominican pacification program, however, needed to set the stage for a demonstration election—and thereafter "stability."

According to Wiarda,

> Especially in the countryside and interior towns, where the local military post constituted about the only authority and where Garcia-Godoy's well-intentioned compromises could be easily ignored, thousands of PRD organizers, local leaders, and members were killed, jailed, and/or beaten. At the same time, the rural population generally was cowed into submission.[68]

Confirmation of this point is strewn throughout the local press and in the reports of the Inter-American Commission on Human Rights. In Barahona, for example, "when the Commission endeavored to verify in that city the facts denounced [a disappearance], it found that a climate of terror under the local military authorities prevailed, and that it was difficult to obtain information from them."[69] Thus to the disillusioning effect of defeat was added the reality and omnipresent threat of physical violence, and widespread fear.

3. Between April 1965 and the election of June 1, 1966 the number of casualties suffered by the popular forces in the course of

U.S. and loyalist pacification was very substantial and had obvious political significance in weakening the leadership cadres of the Bosch-Constitutionalist group. There are no reliable numbers on political killings during this period. Donald Keys, an observer at the 1966 election, states that political assassinations by Balaguer supporters during the election campaign numbered about 300; Wiarda speaks of "several hundred" Constitutionalists murdered.[70] Estimates of total political killings for the period from the invasion of April 28, 1965 through 1972 run from hundreds up to 2,000 or more.[71] In addition to deaths many were deported or fled. Eleven prominent Constitutionalist officers left the country under pressure in January 1966, including their premier leader Francisco Caamano. "Deprived of their leaders, demoralized, some of their numbers assassinated in the streets of the capital—and yet still hoping against hope—the Constitutionalist military placed their faith in promises that would never be respected."[72]

4. The invasion-occupation also caused serious—in fact, insoluble—strategic problems for the Bosch-Constitutionalist forces, as the conditions for attaining power and for affecting the well-being of the Dominican populace were sharply changed. Should the party take a strenuous anti-U.S. stance or should it be accommodating, stressing its ability to do business with the invader? If it took the first position, would this not display its powerlessness? If the second, would it not have abandoned principle? And could it "deliver" if the United States was strongly opposed to Bosch and the Constitutionalists? The key point is that the strategic confusion weakening the Bosch forces was strictly a function of the U.S. intervention itself, which greatly attenuated indigenous power and eroded the Dominican capacity for self-determination.

5. Looked at another way, the invasion-occupation made the United States a huge factor in Dominican politics. The Dominican Republic became a U.S. dependency. This was most obviously true while U.S. troops remained on Dominican soil. If U.S. troops had left early, the tremendous hostility to the invader might have had political expression. But the United States would not leave till after the election; and, as we saw, it quickly rearmed the loyalist military and allowed it to reestablish the traditional climate of fear. Under these conditions, Bosch's handicaps were overwhelming. Unable to organize effectively or protect his supporters, he could not promise voters that, if reelected, he would not be removed by a further coup with a further outburst of terror. Nor could he promise that he could

bargain effectively with the invader looking toward the end of occupation or economic aid. A peasant or urban slum-dweller believing deeply in Bosch and in Bosch's program might rationally have voted for Balaguer as a means of assuring personal safety and out of a reasonable perception that Bosch's program could not be implemented in the new order.

Dependency and occupation created a correspondingly great opportunity for a local politician who could claim to be both a patriot and unobjectionable to the United States. Joaquin Balaguer played this role to perfection. His faction had secretly opposed the revolt of April 1965 and had encouraged the counterrevolution and invasion.[73] This enormously important fact was not publicized during the 1966 election campaign. The United States quietly supported Balaguer. Having served as agent of The Benefactor, Balaguer was now prepared to play a similar role for another Benefactor. In this capacity he could suggest that he alone could intercede effectively to assure the exit of the invader, and to induce him to aid in reconstruction. In short, U.S. intervention shifted the balance of power away from a popular independent to a clever collaborator, acceptable to—and semi-secretly sponsored by—the occupying power.

6. Military defeat, strategic confusion, the death and deportation of leaders and organizers, and the climate of fear led to organizational failures on the part of the Bosch-Constitutionalist forces. An important feature of the 1962 election had been the successful mobilization of the peasants. The peasant organization FENHERCA was a protective and mobilizing body that had helped bring the agrarian masses back into political life. Under the Triumvirate it had disintegrated and the peasants had been returned to their traditional atomized condition and political passivity. Following the revolt of 1965, the invasion-occupation served to return them to apathy once again.

7. A major effect of the invasion and occupation was polarization and fragmentation. Wiarda stresses that "the Revolution, the U.S. intervention, and succeeding events tore apart and nearly destroyed whatever there was of social and political solidarity and integration in the country [which has become]. . .a highly 'dysfunctional' system."[74] In the context of disintegration, the dominant power forces became the United States and the refurbished Dominican military and police establishment.

All of the above factors, which were a consequence of the U.S. invasion and occupation, constitute what we may call "unnatural inputs," shifting the weight of political forces in the Dominican Republic in ways that interfered drastically with the power of self-determination of the local inhabitants. They had a necessary and powerful impact on the election of 1966, and any analyses which fail to take these factors into account cannot be taken seriously.

The election. Bosch ran a perfunctory campaign, hardly venturing forth from his home in Santo Domingo. One of his bodyguards was killed and his son was shot, and he apparently feared for his life. But more important was his demoralization and vacillation stemming from a sense of betrayal and dim recognition that larger forces would not let him take or maintain power. He was going through the motions, but without confidence or hope. His organizational support and media access were poor. He could promise nothing in a dependency environment, and his potential supporters were neither mobilized nor free of fear and intimidation. As the agent of the United States and the U.S.-supported local oligarchy, Balaguer *could* promise things, was well financed, could move around freely, and had no reason to be pessimistic or strategically confused. He carried out a clever campaign stressing his ability to bring peace and deal effectively with the Invader.

Balaguer won easily, almost equalling Bosch's margin of victory in 1962. As this was an affair staged by an occupying power following a lengthy pacification program, the election was contaminated at its very root. But it was also subject to massive direct election-day fraud, which followed automatically from the restoration of a corrupt and brutal military-police collective. The military and police were everywhere; according to election observer Donald Keys, in Santo Domingo "soldiers and police stood on nearly every corner in the old quarter, each loaded down with pistol, automatic rifle and extra ammunition." Out in the countryside "every sizable town contained a large number of Dominican troops." The first town Keys observed had about 50 police, 150 soldiers, and four U.S. military personnel stationed there. Keys asked a leader of the Bosch party "if they were ever threatened or harassed by the military. 'Siempre,' he said, 'siempre.'"[75]

Howard Wiarda's conclusion was that "despite the presence of a number of foreign observers, there is little doubt of widespread fraud in the election—although probably not enough to change the outcome."[76] Journalist Norman Gall, however, made a powerful case that the level of fraud and direct intimidation was sufficiently massive to have reversed the results of an honest count:

For the fact is that the electoral procedures of at least the all-important military authorities—claimed to be "perfectly correct...free...fair," etc.—included: widespread commandeering and switching of ballot boxes; conniving at mass forgery of identification cards; seizing and beating up a Boschist congressional candidate; murdering Boschist supporters and preventing investigation or punishment of the offenders; importing, in defiance of Dominican law, Cuban experts in vote fraud formerly high in Fulgencio Batista's dictatorship; general intimidation of the peasantry; and a series of mendacious campaign practices, among them the distribution from Air Force planes of spliced photos showing Bosch and Fidel Castro embracing.[77]

Gall provided impressive detail on the influx of hundreds of pro-Batista Cubans, a number of them experts in electoral manipulation. The computers used in the headquarters of the National Electoral Board "were operated by Cuban exile employees of IBM."[78] Gall observed that these Cuban inputs, plus Balaguer's winning the same 60% majority Bosch won in 1962, reminded one of Batista's fraudulent 1940 election victory over Ramon Grau San Martin— which was marked by much military intimidation of voters in peasant areas, the use of phantom polling places to produce huge Batista majorities, substitution of ballot boxes after the polls closed, and multiple voting through mass forgery of voters' identification cards.[79] In the 1966 election Dominicans could vote anywhere in the country, not just in their place of residence; and Gall and several reporter colleagues observed "the organized way in which the voters were transported from one place to another." Gall also noted the inflated vote totals, and the delays in getting vote counts to the central office. The results of the June 1 election came in much more slowly than the *hand-counted* results of the 1962 election, which were available the day after the vote; "this year [1966] they were still being counted and the results were being revised five days after the election." In the urban zone of Salcedo, for example, the ballots from three of the seven voting places, once in the hands of the army and police, took 22 hours after the closing of the polls to reach an Electoral Board office three blocks away. The law had protections against this type of abuse, but in a great many cases these protections were disregarded.[80]

There were 25% more votes cast in June 1966 than in 1962, 87% more in Santo Domingo, where Bosch's 80% avalanche of 1962 was cut to 63%. Balaguer's winning margin of 237,000 votes corresponded almost exactly to the huge increase in the officially reported vote. In San Cristobal where Bosch had won by 7-1 in 1962, Balaguer won by a 3-2 margin in 1966. Balaguer even beat Bosch in Bosch's own birthplace, La Vega, reversing the proportions between 1962 and 1966. The increase in the vote total, and the result in many places, were implausible, given the increased turbulence, disillusionment, and the fear. Gall and two Canadian reporters visited the countryside to see whether the welcome for the great victory of Balaguer equalled that for Bosch in 1962:

> The towns we visited seemed under martial law. There was no sign of the celebrations a foreigner would expect after a leading politician had received an overwhelming popular mandate in a critical election. Passing through La Vega after midnight, two nights after the voting, we found that the Army had set up sandbagged strongpoints in the streets, guarded by barbed wire and .50 caliber machine guns. There were sentries inside and outside the cemetery guarding against desecration of graves where discarded Bosch votes had been found and were reportedly buried.[81]

Gall gave a number of further illustrations of literal coercion and ballot box stuffing that added up to a formidable indictment of the election as fraudulent even in the simple mechanical sense.

The Demonstration

An important part of a demonstration election is a special public relations effort to show that a major event is taking place as well as to prove our devotion to the higher values. This is done by encouraging media attention, providing it with the "relevant" information, and helping to make the event into a spectacle.

Observers. "Observers" were encouraged to go to the Dominican Republic and to give close attention to electoral arrangements and conditions in order to show that everything was fair and square, and to provide a focus for media attention. The Provisional Government invited the OAS to send observers, and a Committee on Free Elections in the Dominican Republic was organized in the United States to unofficially oversee the elections and help keep them honest. Both of these efforts were sponsored by the Johnson administration and its organizational affiliates such as the CIA.[82] In contrast with Vietnam and El Salvador, it was easy to get an impressive group of U.S. liberals to go to the Dominican Republic, as many Bosch sympathizers were persuaded that they would help him by helping to keep the election clean. Their presence was important, but in a way contrary to the intent of a number of them.

That the observers made the elections more honest is very doubtful. They never visited over four-fifths of the polling places;[83] their relatively brief visits would usually be known in advance via police-military communications networks;[84] they were escorted by official military forces; they suffered barriers of language and culture, and negatives could not easily be communicated to them in an environment of fear; and they had no way of evaluating vote-counting procedures and practices. As very few people would be beaten up or threatened with the observers present, their replies to the inevitable question of what evidence of cheating they observed—that they saw no evidence of coercion—was about as useful as similar statements they might have made without leaving New York City. Some of them actually made fairly cautionary—even negative—statements, which were duly ignored. Others recognized their insignificant capacities to "observe" and retreated to vacuities such as that their role was "a moral symbol of solidarity with the Dominican people."[85]

The real impact of the observers was in enhancing the credibility of the election as a meaningful expression of democratic choice. They achieved this, first, by the very premise of their activity, which presupposed that an election in a militarily occupied and pacified country was not inherently a travesty of the democratic idea, with the decks stacked in advance. By focusing on election day coercion and ballot-box stuffing—that is, by centering attention on secondary parameters—the observers legitimized the election.

Second, the Committee on Free Elections was especially valuable to the staging process in that its social democratic leaders, headed by Norman Thomas, succeeded in persuading Juan Bosch to run, despite the occupation, pacification, and stacked deck. As Thomas said in a retrospective,

> The fact that our observers would be present during the election period was an important element in persuading Dr. Juan Bosch not to withdraw from the campaign. Had Dr. Bosch not continued his candidacy, there could not have been a meaningful election.[86]

Thomas does not say in what sense the election was thereby rendered "meaningful," but we must assume that he believed he had observed an uncoerced and unbiased indigenous choice. In our view, getting

Bosch to run made the election a more effective *demonstration* election.

Finally, because the observers were in no position to evaluate the fairness of the election, they were "set up" to give it a clean bill of health. It was inevitable that nothing they saw provided substantial evidence of fraud. There were dissenters among the observers, and some had serious qualifications, but the leaders of the teams performed their functions well, lauding the election as a masterpiece of the democratic process, on the basis of negligible evidence not yet all in!

The media. The demonstration election requires that the home media take it very seriously, ask the right questions and eschew the wrong ones, and strip it of historic and power context. The position which the U.S. government wants to get across is that the election is a major event, fairly run, and provides the basis for establishing a truly democratic and stable regime. The U.S. mass media cooperated fully in establishing these truths in May and June of 1966.

The election was made a media event, with literally hundreds of correspondents on the scene to report on this historic occasion. It was given front-page treatment in the major newspapers and rated attention on the major TV networks on June 1 and June 2, and it received fairly extensive coverage on the immediately preceding and succeeding days. The observers from the OAS and United States contributed to the PR value of the election, some of them being notables, and their visit, attention, and opinions added to its newsworthiness.

In keeping with demonstration election criteria, the mass media concentrated heavily on the mechanics of voting, the turnout, the personalities and chances of the candidates and minor squabbles among them, speculation about possible outcomes, and the badmouthing and "threats" from the "left." While continually referring to the extremists present among the voters, and the dangers which they posed, the media all expressed patronizing approval of the silent majority, going to the polls with quiet dignity, uncoerced, choosing "stability." Except for the leftist extremists, and sorehead Juan Bosch, everybody from Lyndon Johnson on down was pleased with the Dominican results. Hopes were therefore high that reconciliation and stability would follow this meritorious event, which had brought democracy and peace to this land torn by civil strife, and a semivindication of the invasion. In short, the mass media, which had raised serious questions, briefly, during the U.S. invasion of April-May 1965, had returned to the vacuities and distortions of patriotic apologetics by June 1966.

The mass media consistently deflated the image of Juan Bosch in their election commentary. They did this by a series of devices: he was a "Leftist," "erratic" if honest, "widely accused of being a Communist," and "supported by Leftists and Communist troublemakers" (all from *Time*, May 27 and June 10, 1966). The *New York Times* stressed that while Bosch was "maligned as a pro-Communist" and "erroneously confused" with the Communists, he was not a Communist, but rather a "left-of-center liberal." Bosch was also a complainer and crybaby, threatening to withdraw from the election unless rightwing military elements stopped terrorizing PRD supporters in the countryside. *Newsweek* referred to this as a "ploy" (May 30, 1966). After the election, Bosch continued to fail to be a good sport by suggesting fraud. One thing the media never did, of course, was examine seriously Bosch's allegations and the "unnatural inputs" we discussed earlier.

How did the media explain the "surprising" and "puzzling" election results? *Newsweek*'s answer was "that the lamb simply outfought the lion" (June 13, 1966). It mentions, however, that the "lion" felt able to leave his house only twice; that Balaguer was able to wage "an American-style campaign, largely financed by U.S. businessmen with interests in the Republic"; and that one voter expressed the position, "What is the sense of electing a president who'll get thrown out before the year is over?" *Newsweek* failed to discuss the terror of the prior 14 months, the impact of an omni-present military, or the relevance to the election outcome of the presence of the rather larger, occupying "lion"—the United States—hostile to Bosch. For *Time* magazine it was simpler still—a triumph of Moderation and a Vote for Peace—with never a hint that military occupation, pacification, and restored military-police hegemony could influence the election outcome. Furthermore, there were the "observers": "In the end, all the visitors—including even [sic] Norman Thomas himself—agreed that last week's election was fair" (*Time*, June 10, 1966). The *New York Times* proposed "two theories" about the transformed countryside vote: one was the peasants' desire to return to "the ordered life that was imposed on them under Trujillo. The other is that the Balaguer vote was a vote of weariness...for security and stability instead of change" (June 5, 1966). Note the total exclusion of fear, the organizational collapse of the PRD and its inability to protect its supporters, coercion, and ballotbox fraud as even *possible* explanations.

The counterpart of this completely propagandistic portrayal of the election as totally "fair" was the stress on "leftist and Communist troublemakers [who] took to the streets, jeering 'A gigantic fraud,' throwing rocks..." (*Time*, June 10, 1966). The *New York Times* listed as the two "most pressing" problems of Balaguer, first, whether Bosch would accept the election, and second, the military threat of "the small, left, extremist and Communist parties" that supported Bosch (June 5, 1966). This focus on the alleged left threat served several propaganda objectives: it associated criticism of the election with a rock-throwing, "sore-loser" left, thereby turning aside the substantive issues of fraud; and it deflected attention from the fact that it was the rightwing military-police-oligarchy, now returned to power by the United States, which had collaborated with Trujillo and had liquidated democracy in the Dominican Republic as soon as it reared its ugly head in 1962-63. In a delightful gambit the *Philadelphia Inquirer* sternly admonished Bosch: "Already street corner gangs are threatening...we suggest it is up to Bosch to restrain them if he truly values democracy as he has often proclaimed" (editorial, June 4, 1966). Bosch, the last freely elected President, honest, tolerant—quickly ousted without significant U.S. response—was now threatening "democracy," so successfully brought to the Dominican Republic, compliments of Lyndon Johnson, Tom Mann, and the U.S. Marines.

The U.S. role in the election was portrayed by the U.S. mass media in staunchly patriotic fashion. First, the context was stripped clear. The 1965 invasion, if mentioned at all, was attributed to the fear of a Communist takeover, which obviously justified our unilateral invasion and occupation of another country. The illegality of the invasion, the Dominican casualties, the 100% support and buildup of the loyalist (Trujillista) army and police, and the U.S. role in the 14-month pacification-terror campaign were completely suppressed. Second, the possible relevance of military occupation to the election results was never addressed. Third, the fact that the United States was strongly backing Balaguer was played down or suppressed. *Time* ignored the fact altogether. *Newsweek* suggested that the Johnson administration preferred Balaguer, but hastens to add that its *real* concern was a free and fair election. The *New York Times* sometimes acknowledged a preference, at one point making it only a "marginal preference" for Balaguer.[87] By contrast, we may note CIA officer Ray Cline's description of his encounter with President Johnson—in which he gave Johnson a rundown on the available non-Communist candidates to put in place in the Dominican Republic, with a strong recommendation of Balaguer. Johnson responded: "That's it. That's our policy. Get this guy in office down there!"[88] Finally, the media never suggested at any point that the election was being staged by the U.S. government for the benefit of the home population. It was taken at the nominal and patriotic value desired by the administration. In short, the mass media were an important component of the staging process.

The Sequel

The observers, the Johnson administration, and the U.S. mass media all concluded their election congratulations and summings-up with expressions of hope for a future of democracy, reconciliation, and reform. These hopes were not realized, but for the public the chapter had been closed. What followed in the Dominican Republic was: (1) a new wave of terror which reached a high crescendo of "death squad" murders in 1970-71; (2) a consolidation of the dependency status of the country, with a massive presence of U.S. advisers, military and economic aid, and a widely "opened door" allowing a further takeover of the economy by U.S. interests; (3) a consolidation of the power of the local oligarchy and military elite, as under the Triumvirate, with widespread corruption; (4) increased inequality and a continuation of the traditional policy of malign neglect of the majority; and (5) massive emigration.

1. The terror. Once the PR fervor and self-congratulations surrounding the election had died down and the U.S. media had departed, the forces of the old order quietly resumed the pacification program. The refurbished police and military, given additional weapons and training by the United States,[89] stepped up their attacks on dissidents and allowed and/or sponsored the formation in the late 1960s of a "death squad," La Banda, that terrorized the slums of Santo Domingo and murdered freely. The tempo of political killings reached new heights in 1970 when a murdered body was appearing on the Santo Domingo streets every 34 hours.[90] Norman Gall claimed that there was a higher rate of political murders in the Dominican Republic in the years 1969-71 than in any comparable period under Trujillo. Gall stated that

> The Santo Domingo newspaper *El Nacional* last December 30 filled a page and a half of newsprint with the details of 186 political murders and thirty disappearances during 1970. The Dominican terror resembles the current wave of political killings in Guatemala...in that the paramilitary death squads are organized by the armed forces and police, which in both cases over the years have been given heavy US material and advisory support.[91]

The total number of political murders in the period between the election of June 1966 and the end of 1971 was well over a thousand.[92] Large numbers were also imprisoned, and torture became institutionalized in the Dominican Republic.

In a study of Balaguer's political methods, Michael Kryzanek concludes that "since the PRD assumed opposition status in June 1966, the party has fallen prey to perhaps the most systematic and widespread program of political repression in modern day Latin America."[93] The elections of 1970 and 1974 were won by Balaguer under conditions of repression and fraud so severe that the mass opposition party (PRD) did not even try to field a candidate. The 1978 election marked an easing of repression and a return to democratic forms, but under sharp constraint and with no prospect of serious reform. We will return to this late development at the conclusion of this chapter.

   2. The new dependency. The invasion, occupation, and election of 1966 returned the Dominican Republic more firmly to the status of a satellite of the United States, occupied first politically and militarily, but then integrated more thoroughly into the U.S. and world economy by further economic penetration. U.S. aid and advisers flooded into the country following the invasion, with over $100 million allocated during the occupation alone, and another $110 million in grant aid and loans contributed through the balance of the 1960s. For some years AID financed virtually all conventional public investment projects—roads, water, light, and housing—providing 20% or more of the Dominican national budget. The Ministry of Agriculture had 45 U.S. technicians, all paid by AID.[94] The U.S. Embassy, with 900 employees in 1967, was exceeded in size in Latin America only in Brazil.

   Economic penetration followed quickly. The Bosch Constitution of 1963 had limited foreign ownership of land and the size of land holdings. This was quickly modified by Balaguer, who provided major tax benefits and guarantees to foreign capital. Union organization was made difficult, key unions were forcibly dismantled, and labor costs were kept low by the familiar combination of repression and policies that maintained high rates of unemployment. A program of denationalization also followed, transferring Trujillo property to the private sector. Foreign capital poured into mineral extraction, the sugar industry, and light manufacturing in the newly formed "free trade zones." Foreign companies also moved into the tourism trade, building hotels and resort projects. These developments permitted some degree of recovery from the chaos of civil war, but not much. In

1971 the unemployment rate was estimated to be about 33%, and hunger and malnutrition were widespread.

The consolidation of the counterrevolution under Balaguer terminated the hope of major reform, leaving the semi-feudal land ownership structures intact, and the great majority of the population—the Bosch constituency—uncared for. The U.S. economic intrusion transformed much of the already concentrated land and mining interests into foreign holdings, and made the Dominican Republic more closely integrated with and dependent on the United States and world economy.

The United States also brought into the Dominican Republic a large Military Aid and Advisory Group of 65-70 members, new police training programs, and other military aid to enhance the power and image of the forces of law and order. U.S. officials alleged that the "police activity target" was to make the Dominican National police "an effective force to preserve internal security and maintain law and order by using modern humane [sic] enforcement methods."[95] The word "humane" was also used in a U.S. government statement about police training in Guatemala in 1974. In both cases, humane police training was followed by a significant escalation of torture and disappearances.

    3. Consolidation of oligarchic-military control, and corruption. The purpose of the U.S. invasion was to preserve the status quo, maintain a friendly oligarchy and associated military enforcers in power, and keep the masses quiet. This was done. Regrettably, as in other U.S. client states, the enforcers tend to be corrupt. Thus Jon Nordheimer pointed out in 1978 that

> Corruption among the generals is almost as legendary as their ineptitude. . . . It is common knowledge that Lieut. Gen. Juan Beauchamps Javier, Secretary of State for the Armed Forces, owns a $300,000 yacht in partnership with a Dominican businessman and that Maj. Gen. Neit Nivar Siejas, the commander of the national police, is part owner of a major Santo Domingo hotel and gambling casino.[96]

This "legendary corruption" might have been overcome in the rebellion of April 1965, but that would have "endangered American lives," as President Lyndon Johnson pointed out.

    4. Increased inequality. The consolidation of elite and military power during the U.S. occupation and postelection period led to a sharp attrition of the strength of peasant and urban worker organizations, increased corruption, a shift of government budget priorities toward the elite and the provision of infrastructure for foreign capital, and denationalization. All of these sharply altered the distribution of income away from the majority. Moreover, the new economic strategy—encouraging "development" by making things attractive for foreign capital—failed to reduce unemployment below the high rates of 1966. A *Wall Street Journal* article of 1971 noted that

> The economy has recovered, in a sense, from the chaos of the 1965 uprising. The middle and upper classes are better off, as are the lower classes lucky enough to have jobs. But work is scarce; the poor are poorer and are more numerous. "Per-capita income is about the same as before 1965, but it's less equitably distributed," a foreign economic expert says. He estimates per capita income at $240—three times that of Haiti but half that of Cuba. . . . Most Dominican children don't go beyond the third grade; only one in five reaches the sixth grade. . . . Malnutrition is widespread. Says George B. Mathues, director of CARE in the Dominican Republic: "You see kids with swollen bellies all over the country, even here in Santo Domingo.". . . Food production is hampered by semifeudal land tenure. At last count, less than 1% of the farmers owned 47.5% of the land, while 82% farmed fewer than 10 acres. Many small subsistence farmers don't have legal title to their plots, and landless peasants who try to squat on idle land risk being evicted by the army.[97]

By 1983, little had changed. An attempted diversification in agriculture failed because of soil conditions and the elite-oriented strategies emphasizing exports. The industrial free zones employed a meagre 9,000 workers in manufacturing operations, which were largely packaging and subassembly with no useful technological spinoff, and ready to leave at the drop of a wage level elsewhere. A *Wall Street Journal* survey of 1983 notes that,

> Stripped of its imported goods, the Dominican Republic is essentially what it was 100 years ago—a plantation society with thousands of acres of sugar cane, some bananas and cocoa, and several gold and silver mines. Today, in this plantation society, about 6% of the population owns 40% of the wealth. Most of the people are peasants, living in rural areas where unemployment is 50%, illiteracy is 80% and many of the adults and children are malnourished. The

impoverished population spills over into urban barrios, and in the city streets children beg for money, contorting their arms and legs to appear as cripples.

In the sugar fields, wages average $3.50 a day, at least during the six-month cutting season when work is available. Much of the cutting is done by Haitians, trucked into the country under contracts arranged by the Dominican and Haitian governments. Many of the Haitians never return to their impoverished homeland, however, and Dominican officials concede that some half million of them roam the Dominican countryside, often working in conditions approaching slavery.[98]

5. Emigration. Although not attended to by the U.S. media with the diligence applied to the exodus from Cuba, the number of emigres from the Dominican Republic since 1966 has run into the scores of thousands, and a significant fraction have been political refugees. Bosch estimated in 1971 that 150,000-200,000 fled the country after the revolt. The *Wall Street Journal* claimed in early 1983 that 10% of the Dominican citizenry resides in the United States, which would amount to 500,000-600,000 people.[99]

Final Note

The Dominican Republic's demonstration election of 1966 was a great public relations triumph for the United States. After invading, decimating the democratic forces, and re-creating a climate of fear, the United States was able to follow President Johnson's order to "Get this guy [Balaguer] in office down there!"—*and simultaneously prove its devotion to self-determination and the democratic process!* This required an elaborate staging effort, at the center of which was a compliant press, asking the right questions, avoiding negatives, and mobilizing the dramatic symbols according to government plan.

The 1966 success also required that the press ignore the followup, which Michael Kryzanek described as a strategy of "Diversion, Subversion and Repression . . . in Balaguer's Dominican Republic." As an illustration of this media coverup, we may note that during the period from June 1966 through 1972, which saw over 1,000 political murders and was characterized by Kryzanek as "perhaps the most systematic and widespread program of political repression in modern day Latin America," *Time* magazine, in a total of six articles on that country, never once mentioned La Banda, torture, death squads, or systematic repression. It referred in article after article to the "left" being "splintered," to a "leadership gap" on the left, and to "eroding support for Bosch's party," but it never mentioned that people were being killed or that anything unpleasant was contributing to the erosion of Bosch's support. At the height of the terror, in April and May 1970, *Time* finally mentioned violence, but the language is instructive:

> The leftist, urban-oriented P.R.D., Balaguer's chief opposition, has been making headway with charges that Balaguer's police and troops—who he admits are difficult to control—have been reviving old-style political killings and repression. Last week police machine-gunned striking dock workers in Puerto Plata, killing four and wounding 18.

> [In the election of 1970 just concluded] as usual, violence played a leading role. In the three weeks before the balloting, 29 people died and 47 were wounded in political killings, victims of the extreme right and the extreme left.

Note first the frame of the first quote: the "leftists" are making headway with *charges* of violence. The violence itself is not front and center, nor the victims, but rather the possibility that violence may be put to use by the "leftists." Can you imagine *Time* saying that Poland's Solidarity is making headway by charges of violence? Note also the lack of specificity. Are the charges valid? How extensive have these "old-style political killings" been? Note also the distancing of Balaguer from the violence, the accepting on his say-so that he is trying but is somehow unable to restrain his own military and police. Note the lack of reflection on the police using *machine guns* on striking workers.

The second quote is equally revealing: the statement about violence being "usual" in Dominican elections contradicts *Time*'s version not only of 1966 but of local elections in 1968, which *Time* reported as quite peaceful. The equating of killings of extreme left and right contains a double deception: first, the killings of the "extreme left" in the years 1966-70 were tiny relative to those of the right; and the killings by the right during these years were in fact killings by the Balaguer government or one of its sub rosa death squad affiliates. In short, *Time* magazine's coverage of the Dominican Republic sequel was unqualified propaganda.

The return to some kind of democratic order with enhanced personal freedoms in 1978 and thereafter has provided a further justification for the U.S. invasion-pacification-election strategy. By preserving the Dominican Republic for the Free World, we kept open its "options," finally realized after more than a decade of severe repression. There are several problems with this apologetic. One is that if we *hadn't* intervened, the most probable outcome would have been a Bosch-Constitutionalist reestablishment of a liberal democracy, a sharp reduction in corruption, a beginning of real reform, and the avoidance of 2,000-5,000 deaths and over a decade of terror. A second problem is that the reestablishment of the old regime may have closed off real structural change—and an alleviation of the severe deprivation of the Dominican masses—indefinitely. The tentative political democracy reasserting itself in the post-Balaguer era is now structured into the world market and has little room for maneuver. Social and economic democracy are now hostages to the "confidence" of foreign business and finance, and they are still constrained by the oligarchy, military-police establishment, and the ever-alert forces of the Godfather.

CHAPTER 3

Vietnam

A classic demonstration election was held under U.S. auspices in South Vietnam on September 3, 1967. Conditions in Vietnam were even less favorable for meaningful elections than they had been in the Dominican Republic, with intense ongoing warfare, a limited electoral tradition, and with institutional structures other than the army and police actually weakened during the 12 years of sponsorship of an "independent" South Vietnam by the United States. But antiwar sentiment and activity were mounting rapidly in the United States in response to the bombing of the North, the escalation of U.S. attacks on South Vietnam, the troop buildup, and the evidence trickling back to this country of widespread South Vietnamese opposition to the war and to the ruling military junta. Administration leaders had enjoyed great success with the June 1966 election in the Dominican Republic. With a new set of "observers," a proper focus on election personalities and superficial mechanics, and vindication of the election by evidence of opposition by the Vietnamese Communists, the Johnson administration felt that even in Vietnam elections might be turned into a PR coup.

The U.S. record in Vietnam had not been notable for concern with free choice and self-determination. During the first phase of U.S. involvement, between 1945 and 1954, the United States was only an indirect participant, siding unequivocally with the French while they attempted to reestablish colonial rule. The French repacification effort was then taken over directly and continued on the basis of durable U.S. strategic principles. A key one applied to Indochina, as expressed by a Presidential Review Committee, was that "defeat of the Viet Minh in Indo-China is essential if the spread of Communist influence in Southeast Asia is to be halted."[1] The Review Committee's derivative conclusion was that "it [should] be U.S. policy to accept nothing short of a military victory in Indo-China."[2] It should be noted that discussions of these policy principles in internal U.S. documents made no reference to what the Indo-Chinese might choose of their own free will. Vietnam was a pawn to be won or lost by larger forces; free choice of the local population could not have been further from the minds of Truman, Acheson, Eisenhower, and Dulles. But the proper symbols, like democracy and self-determination, were nonetheless employed often and effectively in explaining and justifying U.S. intervention.

The French failure had led to a Geneva Conference in 1954, at which a temporary settlement was arranged: the French and their "loyalist" forces were to regroup south of the 17th parallel in Vietnam; the Communist-led anticolonial forces, the Vietminh, north of that parallel; and a future political settlement was to be achieved by a free election in July 1956 to unify the country. The Final Declaration at Geneva stated categorically that the 17th parallel was "provisional and should not in any way be interpreted as constituting a political or territorial boundary."

There has been much debate concerning the binding character and "seriousness" of the Final Declaration, despite its clear assertion that Vietnam is one country, and its specification, with a definite date and mode of organization, of elections as the mechanism for reunification.[3] The debate itself is a reflection of the power of the West, and especially the United States, to maintain and rationalize purely imperial "rights." The only indigenous power in Vietnam in 1954 was the Vietminh, which every serious observer recognized as the sole bearer of the flag of Vietnamese national aspirations, having proportionally far greater support among Vietnamese than that commanded in colonial America by George Washington in 1776.[4] That Ho Chi Minh did not rule a unified Vietnam in 1954 was solely a result of foreign intervention. The United States, by sheer assertion of imperial power, thrust itself into this distant country in place of a colonial power now ousted. It imported a puppet ruler from the United States, armed and financed his proxy occupation, and attempted to build him up as a legitimate representative of the South Vietnamese, a product of their "free choice." If the Soviet Union marches into Czechoslovakia and rearranges the government according to its own preferences, even though the puppet is Czech and might eventually build up enough power to "control" the population, this is seen in the West (properly) as imperialism and a blatant violation of the Czech right to self-determination. But when the United States does this in Vietnam (and elsewhere), organizing its own client government which is admitted to have no popular base, the imperialism and blatant violation of the Vietnamese right to self-determination is hidden by the power of nationalistic blinders. We were not "bound" by the Geneva Conference. Somehow our refusal to sign the agreement gave us the "right" to intervene and impose a government of our choice in a country 10,000 miles away.

From the standpoint of this study, which is concerned with the U.S. commitment to and use of elections, it is of great pertinence that the United States was instrumental in the failure to hold the unifying election provided for in the Geneva Accords. Whatever the legally binding character of the election proviso, it furnished a mode of settlement of a serious political dispute. The United States rejected this vehicle out of hand, for two main reasons. One was that it would not have been in a position to "stage" the election, as it could in the Dominican Republic or in other occupied or otherwise-dominated client states. The Geneva Accord had established an International Control Commission which was charged with the specific task of organizing the July 1956 elections. Furthermore, the Vietminh controlled the north of the country, and the people there could not be educated and disciplined as the peasants of the Dominican Republic had been during the year before the June 1, 1966 election. The second reason was that without the right to stage the election the U.S.-installed import would have lost decisively, as every informed observer understood at the time. The conservative reporter Joseph Alsop asserted that "in the area I visited [which was in *South* Vietnam], the Communists have scored a whole series of political, organizational, military and one has to say it—moral triumphs. . . . What impressed me most, alas, was the moral fervor they had inspired among the non-Communist cadres and the strong support they had obtained from the peasantry."[5] President Eisenhower stated in his autobiography that "I have never talked or corresponded with a person knowledgeable in Indochinese affairs who did not agree that had elections been held at the time of the fighting, possibly 80 per cent of the population would have voted for the Communist Ho Chi Minh as their leader rather than Chief of State Bao Dai."[6] Even Diem supporter Leo Cherne acknowledged that "if elections were held today, the overwhelming majority of Vietnamese would vote Communist."[7] What follows clearly from such a circumstance? The answer is—don't allow elections to be held. With a sufficiently compliant press, you can continue to assert blandly and without challenge that the Communists have "never succeeded in winning a free election"!

So much for the commitment to "free elections," "self-determination," and "international law." (We shall see later, however, that U.S. faith in free elections revived in South Vietnam in direct proportion to the militarization of the country under its own armed supervision.) Having refused to settle the Vietnam dispute by the electoral route specified in the Geneva Accords, the United States opted for pacification by force, through a proxy. This was in direct violation of the part of the Geneva Agreements signed by the French and Vietminh (in contrast with the Final Declaration which was unsigned). Article 17 prohibited the introduction into Vietnam "of all types of arms, munitions and other war materials." Article 14(c) prohibited "individual or collective reprisals against persons who have collaborated in any way with one of the parties during the war, . . ." These articles were violated by the United States and its sponsored government on a scale that resulted in the virtual annihilation of the Vietminh forces in the South, prior to any "infiltration" from the North. The latter also occurred only long after it was entirely clear that the United States had no intention of adhering to the electoral mode of settlement.

Pacification Without Free Elections

The U.S. route in Vietnam was in some respects analogous to its procedure in the Dominican Republic between April 28, 1965 (the date of the U.S. invasion landing) and the election of June 1, 1966. In both cases a crisis, threatening the loss of U.S. control, precipitated the deployment of U.S. power designed to establish an acceptable political environment. Because of the great publicity associated with the Dominican invasion, and the U.S. support of forces hostile to the well-known Bosch and the "Constitutionalists," an election was needed to prove U.S. good intentions. In Vietnam in the first years of the U.S. occupation, 1954-56, by contrast, in the midst of the McCarthy era, and with the conflict at a great distance, there was no substantial pressure at home for U.S. adherence to the Geneva proviso for unifying elections. Conservatives and liberals alike, such as publisher Henry Luce, columnist Max Lerner, Cardinal Spellman, and Senator Mike Mansfield, all agreed that Diem represented "freedom"—and the U.S. right to impose its preferred government on South Vietnam was an "imperial implicit" that flowed from imperial (U.S.) virtue, neutrality, and God-given police power.

The newly imposed government held a "referendum" in 1955 to consolidate its rule. Diem ran against the former French puppet Bao Dai, who was not even living in Vietnam but had already settled on the Riviera. Diem won 98.2% of the vote. There were no issues, much fraud, and of course the Vietminh was excluded from the referendum, although it was the largest indigenous force in the South. Elements of the model for demonstration elections were already in place.

The United States made a large investment in Diem, spending almost $2 billion in economic aid alone between 1955 and 1960. As usual, enormous stress was placed on building up Diem's "security forces." Diem started out with a tiny support base of military forces who had fought under the French, plus a small landed and comprador elite. The vast bulk of the population were peasants who had been won over by the Vietminh. By the time Diem was overthrown and murdered in 1963, after eight years of U.S. intervention and guidance, his support base was somewhat narrower than it was in 1955, and South Vietnam had become even less democratic than under the French. Local rule that had prevailed under the colonial regime in the rural areas was terminated by Diem's centralizing policies,[8] and Diem established a terroristic regime that weakened or destroyed all mediating groups threatening his total power. (The same degenerative processes occurred in Guatemala and El Salvador. The former was more democratic in every respect in 1953, prior to U.S. intervention, than in 1983; El Salvador, while hardly democratic in 1979, was even less so in the polarized and disorganized police state of 1983.) David Hotham, a Vietnam correspondent for the *London Times* and *The Economist*, wrote in 1959 that

> [Diem] has crushed all opposition of every kind, however anti-Communist it might be. He has been able to do this, simply and solely because of the massive dollar aid he has had from across the Pacific, which kept in power a man who, by all the laws of human and political affairs, would long ago have fallen. Diem's main supporters are to be found in North America, not in Free Vietnam,...[9]

The United States encouraged Diem to "pacify" the countryside. Nominally, this was to be by both "reform" and repression—but the reform, like the Alliance for Progress in later years, unaccountably and quickly got lost. In this peasant-dominated country, already swept up in revolutionary fervor, with land reform understood by all observers to be essential to social stability, 1.4% of U.S. aid between 1955 and 1960 went into the agricultural sector.[10] The *Pentagon Papers* historians noted that "by the end of 1956, the civic action component of the GVN pacification program had been cut back severely."[11] According to Joseph Buttinger, an early Diem supporter and adviser, in 1956 Diem organized two massive military expeditions against regions in which the population supported the Vietminh:

His soldiers arrested tens of thousands of people.... Hundreds, perhaps thousands of peasants were killed. Whole villages whose populations were not friendly to the government were destroyed by artillery. These facts were kept secret from the American people.[12]

This terror, while killing large numbers of Vietminh cadres and successfully reducing many to quiescence, solidified the peasant attachment to the Communists. The *Pentagon Papers* refer to "Diem's nearly paranoid preoccupation with security," which led to policies that "thoroughly terrified the Vietnamese peasants, and detracted significantly from the regime's popularity."[13]

The U.S. public was led to believe that "terror" was being carried out by rebels during the Diem era, when in fact such killings were relatively very small, less indiscriminate, *and* a lagged reaction to prior Diem terror. The public version was sustained, first, by the suppression referred to by Buttinger: "These facts were kept secret from the American people." It was also partly a consequence of patriotic redefinitions of reality, in which official violence under our auspices, no matter how extensive and unjust, is never "terror" and is always responsive. This standard media usage was grotesque in application to Vietnam.[14]

In the period 1955-59, the Vietminh was deliberately on the defensive. This was partly based on its continuing (though flagging) hope that the Final Declaration of the Geneva Accords, and peaceful reunification by elections, might still be implemented. It was also based on the reluctance of Ho Chi Minh and his North Vietnamese associates to lend support to their southern compatriots, thereby interrupting their development processes north of the 17th parallel and entering into serious conflict with the great power provoking and threatening them from the south. The Vietminh forces in the south were thus badly mauled and decimated in the Diemist reaction, doing nothing much of a retaliatory nature until 1958. The Democratic Republic of Vietnam (DRV) commitment to the southern resistance only began in May 1959.[15] Diem, on the other hand, from 1955 onward, financed and unstintingly supported by the United States, engaged in terroristic violence of such scope and ferocity as to generate a new and higher level of revolutionary consciousness and pressure in the countryside, literally pushing the Vietminh into armed struggle as a condition of survival. This counterproductive proclivity to kill continued into the 1960s. Jeffrey Race, a former U.S. Army adviser in South Vietnam, concluded that it was Diem's tactics "that led to the constantly increasing strength of the revolutionary movement in [the province of] Long An from 1960 to 1965."[16]

Thus, the U.S.-Diem attempt at pacification by force not only failed, it actively provoked revolution and rejuvenated the support base of the Vietminh. Even U.S. officials in Saigon in the early 1960s conceded that about half the population of South Vietnam supported the Vietminh,[17] which was widely recognized as the largest political force in the South and the principal representative of the peasant majority. Douglas Pike, the leading U.S. government authority on the rebel movement in South Vietnam, stated in 1966 that "aside from the NLF [the National Liberation Front, the name of the successor organization to the Vietminh in South Vietnam], there has never been a truly mass-based political party in South Vietnam."[18] Pike's view was that negotiations were unfeasible precisely because the NLF had mass support and the Saigon government had virtually none—his metaphor was that the U.S. clients were reluctant to enter into a coalition that reflected a balance of indigenous forces "fearing that if they did the whale would swallow the minnow."[19] The "minnows," Diem and the generals who followed him as rulers of South Vietnam, had a tiny internal support base that consisted mainly, and increasingly, of those on the U.S. dole.

In an internal document circulated within the army in 1965, the experienced and high ranking "pacification" officer John P. Vann repeatedly acknowledged that in 1965, when the United States invaded Vietnam, it did so in support of a government with a record of "a continued failure...to win its own people," whose popular political base "does not now exist." It was a government "oriented toward the exploitation of the rural and lower-class urban populations," a "continuation of the French colonial system of government with upper class Vietnamese replacing the French," and whose members and minority base are "intrinsically opposed to the social revolution in progress." This upheaval, with mass support in the deeply dissatisfied agrarian population, "is largely expressed through alliance with the NLF."[20] No more explicit admission could be made that the U.S. effort in Vietnam was to *oppose* self-determination and to support a minority and reactionary clique known to be a barrier to needed social change.

In the early 1960s the United States decided upon a three-pronged strategy designed to avoid giving any voice whatever to the only mass-based political party in South Vietnam. First, it would refuse to negotiate a political settlement that fell short of total victory for a U.S.-chosen client. In accordance with this objective, the United States turned down a long succession of NLF, UN, and French proposals for negotiation or mediation, a stance maintained steadfastly until the discussions leading to the Paris treaty of 1973.[21] The United States nevertheless pretended throughout this period that it was anxious to negotiate, especially during the great U.S. invasion and escalation years of 1965-67. The numerous peace moves of this era were in every instance strictly for PR effect. It was made perfectly clear to Hanoi and the NLF in private or by clear signals that the peace offer had a hidden "surrender" agenda attached. These moves, however, were extremely important and effective devices for quieting the public, assuring them that the United States sought peace but was unable to get an intransigent enemy to come to the conference table. The mass media invariably took each of these PR moves at face value—"The problem of peace lies now not in Washington but in Hanoi," stated the *New York Times*' James Reston after Lyndon Johnson's "peace offer" of April 7, 1965—thus clearing the ground for the next planned escalation.

The second and active arm of the U.S. strategy from 1961 onward was an intensified military effort, including more direct U.S. participation and a greater resource input. In 1962, U.S.-flown air sorties became very important, and the United States began to use chemical warfare against the countryside and installed the "strategic hamlet" program. New emphasis was placed on counterinsurgency warfare, with substantial Green Beret inputs. The U.S. answer to the lack of indigenous support for Diem and his successors of U.S. choice was to repress or kill enough of the rural NLF cadres and populace, and later the North Vietnamese, to alter the balance of power by the application of superior force. Perhaps after enough pacification the enemy might be willing to "come to the conference table" and "nego-tiate," and we might then be able to hold a free election and show that we were aiming all along at self-determination.

It is interesting to note, in examining the *Pentagon Papers*, how regularly U.S. authorities in the 1950s and 1960s refer to the problem in Vietnam as one of "control" of the population. They normally did not use this kind of language in speaking to the U.S. public, for whose benefit we were "winning hearts and minds." It was a natural and suitable usage in describing a policy that viewed the population as the enemy, to be beaten and cowed into submission. The United States shared the chronic inability of its allies, an extremely reactionary landed and military elite, to generate any positive program oriented to the problems of the agrarian masses, and their tendency to focus exclusively on "security." Hearts and minds, antiterrorism, self-determination: these words and phrases concealed the reality of U.S. acts and purposes.

The Vietnam War was a U.S.-sponsored war from 1954 to 1960 in terms of where the strategic decisions (political and military) were made and how the Diemist policies of aggressive pacification were finan-ced. It became a U.S. war in a more direct sense in 1961-62, with the larger commitment of resources and prestige and a significantly larger direct participation. The new military tactics of the Kennedy years, with an intensive use of new helicopters flown by U.S. pilots, tempor-arily turned the military tide, but the NLF soon learned how to cope with the new weaponry and escalated its own level of violence against Saigon forces and supporters. As the United States would reject any political solution that threatened its client state in the South, escala-tion moved steadily forward.

A third element of the new strategy was a more active manipula-tion of the Vietnamese political process. The U.S. aim was to place in power and protect a leader who would meet two conditions: he must show an ability to "control" the population (maintain "stability") and a determination to pursue military victory at any national cost. Diem was viewed as a failure by 1962. His violence against the rural population and ruthless crackdown on dissent had not been bother-some, but Diem succeeded in alienating a large number of elite and military factions, threatening a complete breakdown of solidarity among the forces of the "haves." He was also showing unexpected resistance to a more complete U.S. takeover of the war and internal Vietnamese affairs and was even rumored to be flirting with negotia-tions. Diem was murdered in a coup of November 1963. There followed what historian Jean Lacouture called the "coup season," with a series of juntas appearing in November 1963, January 1964, August 1964, December 1964, January 1965, February 1965, and May 1965. The U.S. presence was decisive in shaping this pattern. The only civilian cabinet, that of Dr. Quat, was overthrown in May 1965 in part because Quat was believed to harbor "neutralist" sentiments and possibly favored a negotiated settlement.[22]

To find an adequate instrument to serve as the local agent and handyman for a full-scale U.S. invasion and assault on the rural population, the United States had to sink low. Nguyen Cao Ky, who displaced Dr. Quat in May-June 1965, was a playboy airforce officer, a French-trained mercenary, a dope smuggler, and an ignoramus. Twice he referred in public to Adolf Hitler as a model for himself and his country.[23] His close relations with his own people may be illustrated by the following news report of early May 1966:

> Ky made an unscheduled flight to this northern province [Quang Ngai] to have a look at war-battered villages wrested recently from Viet Cong control. He made his tour in a U.S. Marine helicopter.
>
> He was greeted by silent crowds of men and women gathered near shell-smashed homes surrounded by fields sprayed by crop-killing chemicals. In the fortified village of Duc Phung, Ky distributed American blankets and cooking oil to silent, expressionless women.
>
> "I am satisfied with the work being done in this region," Ky said. "The population works with the army. We are isolating the Viet Cong. The Americans are behind us. All we have to do is to continue."
>
> "Pacification is progressing," Ky said. "In this area alone, 2,000 Viet Cong were killed in the past two months. This is great progress."[24]

But Ky was a consistent advocate of an "Invasion of the North" (by the United States Army!) and of no compromise short of victory over Communism. For the United States this was the litmus test, the one that Bosch failed so egregiously. Thus the United States worked hard to refurbish the Ky image as a "Nation-Builder" and reformer. As noted by Kahin and Lewis:

> To this end, the premier was persuaded to deliver a series of speeches in which he voiced a new-found concern with social justice, the needs of the peasantry, and unification of

the conflicting religious interests of his country. . .[Under the tutelage of General Edward Lansdale] the Air Vice-Marshal made more frequent references to reforms for correcting social and economic injustices. By November, one correspondent could report that the remarks of both Ambassador Lodge and Premier Ky on the need for a social revolution "are virtually interchangeable—a statement by one sounds like a statement by the other."[25]

Two great reformist traditions were merging into one, although there had been and continued to be a slight delay in implementation.

The Buddhist Revolt and the Election of September 1966

The U.S. occupation of South Vietnam proceeded rapidly in 1965 and 1966, with over 375,000 American personnel in the South by the end of the latter year. Ground and air attacks and civilian casualties reached staggering proportions, as the United States was using B-52s for bombing attacks on wide-area targets in populated parts of South Vietnam by June 1965. More than a million refugees from napalm and fragmentation bombs came into Saigon-controlled cities by the end of 1966.[26] Economic life in the rural areas was badly disrupted, and the influx of U.S. troops added to economic and social pressures. In addition to the agrarian population under direct and massive assault, many urban Vietnamese saw that their country was being thrust involuntarily into a situation of unparalleled disaster and violence and that the fate of South Vietnam was now in the hands of U.S. decision makers. Their fears were reinforced in May 1965 when the Quat regime was overthrown by a military coup and Marshal Ky was installed as premier. The Quat government was the last civilian government during the U.S. occupation, although the elections of 1966 and 1967 were purportedly a preliminary to constitutional and civilian rule.

Ky shared the local satrapy with the other members of a ten-man military junta, the National Leadership Committee. The United States worked hard to keep this military collective unified and in power, and Ky served as its interim leader. Much effort was expended in strengthening his prestige and instructing him on public relations strategies. Ambassador Lodge advised him even on the details of speechmaking, telling him to use cue cards so as not to bob his head up and down.[27] He was brought to the Honolulu Conference of February 1966, along with General Thieu, as another image enhancer. Lyndon Johnson, Marshal Ky, and General Thieu issued a joint declaration on the need to defeat aggression from the North and stop the Communist plan for the conquest of all Southeast Asia. They also agreed on the need to struggle against the economic poverty of South Vietnam!

Opposition to military rule in South Vietnam was expressed most vocally in 1965-66 among the organized Buddhist groups in Danang and Hué. They became the focal point of mass sentiment for getting South Vietnam out from under the conspiracy of the French-trained military officers and the United States, and for an effort to achieve peace by political means. The organized Buddhists, the "Struggle Movement," sponsored massive demonstrations in Hué and Danang in March and April of 1966. The protestors worried the Johnson administration, which openly assailed one of the main Buddhist leaders as power hungry and divisive. The Johnson position was made clear when Ambassador Lodge openly avowed a strong preference for military rule in South Vietnam.[28]

To firm up military control of South Vietnam, the Ky regime, with constant advice and tutelage from the United States, carried out a dual strategy of repression and constitutional-electoral-"reform" promises. The repression was real and massive; the constitutional-electoral-reform promises were gradually watered down, drained of meaning, and carried out in such a manner as to assure preservation of military rule.

With the Buddhist crisis at a peak in April 1966, the Ky regime agreed to hold elections for a Constituent Assembly in three to five months. This quieted the opposition temporarily. On May 14 the Ky government then began a full-scale military campaign, occupying Danang and then Hué by force, with the aid of U.S. airplanes. gasoline, and airbases. There were hundreds of Buddhist casualties and arrests, and in succeeding months Buddhist organization and activity suffered a major setback. Douglas Pike had mentioned the Buddhists as the only group in South Vietnam who would have considered entering into political competition with the NLF "whale." Having disorganized by force and threat the one remaining mass group capable of putting up any political opposition to the military regime, Ky then proceeded to whittle down his election promises in preparation for elections.

The Buddhists had called for elections to be held under an interim civilian government. They recognized that with the military government in power the election result was a foregone conclusion. Buddhist and other reformers also wanted the Constituent Assembly to be given continuing status and legislative powers, not merely to formulate a constitution. The Ky government rejected these suggestions and structured the election sequence as follows: First, full governmental powers were retained by the military junta through the election, thereby ensuring durable junta authority. Second, while allowing the proposed Constituent Assembly to continue in existence after promulgating the constitution, its role was confined to election overseer. Third, it reduced the power of the Constituent Assembly in preparing the constitution by an important decree which allowed the chairman of the military junta to redraft the constitution without restriction if he could muster 40 of the 117 members' votes. That is, a two-thirds vote was necessary to override modifications of the constitution by military fiat. A fourth proviso forbade the use of "any familiar religious emblem," which denied the Buddhists the use of their easily recognized lotus symbol. A fifth and very important limit affecting the membership of the Assembly allowed exclusion of any candidates "who work directly or indirectly [sic] for Communism or neutralism [sic]." This provided the grounds for ruling off the list of candidates anybody deemed to favor a negotiated settlement of the war. This was a major basis for the removal of 200 of 735 candidates who filed to run for election. There were other tricks employed also, such as structuring the electoral districts so as to weaken Buddhist electoral power.[29] This package, put together by Saigon with the advice and support of U.S. authorities, gave the military junta "total control of drafting the new constitution."[30]

The organized Buddhists decided to boycott the September 1966 elections for the Constituent Assembly, given the enormous built-in bias. Nevertheless, 80.8% of the registered voters of South Vietnam went to the polls. Note that with the only mass-based party off the ballot and underground (the NLF), and the second largest and most popular grouping in South Vietnam, the organized Buddhists, boycotting the election, the military junta, representing the United States government and, at the outside limit, perhaps 15% of the South Vietnamese population, was still able to get a very nice "turnout."

The September 1966 election led to a Constituent Assembly with a heavy representation of military personnel, civil servants, businessmen, landlords, and Catholic refugees from the North. It assured the military junta control of the 40 votes they needed to dominate the Assembly. By the same token, it foreclosed the possibility that the views of the majority would be taken into account in writing the constitution and in organizing the presidential election of September 1967. It was, however, a very successful affair for the Johnson administration. It guaranteed a semi-martial law constitution and a favorable outcome for the 1967 election. It was also a useful demonstration election in its own right, serving the Johnson administration in the forthcoming U.S. congressional elections of November 1966. As Kahin and Lewis point out,

> The Johnson administration on the eve of the Congressional elections could tell the American public that Saigon's elections and the President's meetings with Asian leaders at Manila provided assurance that the reason the United States was in Vietnam was to protect and promote freedom and democracy there.[31]

The Demonstration Election of September 3, 1967

Between the elections of September 1966 and September 1967 the Johnson administration sharply escalated the scope and intensity of the war in Vietnam. The number of U.S. participants increased rapidly, reaching 385,000 by the end of 1966 and 535,000 by the time of the Tet offensive of February 1968. More than 8,000 U.S. participants were dead and 50,000 wounded by April 1967. The amount of U.S. ordnance expended rose from 300,000 tons in 1965 to over two million tons in 1967; and South Vietnamese civilian casualties increased from 72,000 killed and 144,000 wounded in 1965 to some 300,000 killed and 600,000 wounded in 1967. South Vietnamese refugees poured into Saigon and other major cities to escape the assault on their rural land and villages.[32]

Moreover, while enemy soldiers were being killed at a very high rate, the press reported regularly that they fought well and that their numbers were replenished by a steady supply of new "Communists" generated by "search and destroy." At the same time, it was widely reported that Saigon's soldiers fought poorly, seemed badly motivated, and were deserting at the rate of 10,000-12,000 per month in mid-1966.[33] While the U.S. public might not recognize that their leaders were fighting against self-determination in a very literal sense, they could see that the South Vietnamese seemed unenthusiastic about our "helping them" to fight for "freedom."

Johnson's popularity sagged as the U.S. involvement escalated. It rose with each "peace move" and in response to enemy actions that caused U.S. casualties and military setbacks, but the popularity advances fell back quickly and reached successive new lows. By August 1967, for the first time in his presidency, over 50% of Gallup Poll respondents disapproved of Johnson's conduct of his office and only 33% approved his handling of the war, while 54% disapproved.[34] The antiwar movement grew steadily and became increasingly aggressive. Draft resistance and elite opposition to the war were also substantial and very disturbing to the administration.

The election of September 1967 was a further attempt to show that the South Vietnamese really wanted us there, and that our aims were honorable as evidenced by our support of another great symbol of freedom. The election was held, however, under conditions of military occupation, intense warfare, and a constitution and legal structure that allowed the arrest, incarceration, and even killing of individuals alleged by the security forces to be subversive. In spite of frequent expressions of admiration that elections were held at all in such an unfavorable environment, it is not difficult to hold a formal election under military occupation and to get the controlled population to the voting booths. The question is: how do these special and unfavorable conditions affect the substance of elections? Let us take a brief look at these conditions essential to a free election in Vietnam in 1967.

1. Free speech. Was there free speech in South Vietnam in 1967? Were candidates and ordinary citizens allowed to advocate a wide range of policy alternatives? "Neutralism" and "indirectly aiding" Communists were explicit (though vague) bases for ruling out election candidates and were also grounds for arrest and further violence. These terms were never defined. Communism, of course, was advocated at the risk of immediate arrest, torture, and death. As the Communists represented a larger number of people than the Saigon generals, by the admission of the generals themselves, the situation could be compared to an election under Soviet military occupation of the United States in 1983 where advocacy of the private ownership of capital was treasonable. But within that small constraint everybody could engage in more or less free speech. The analogy is, of course, inappropriate because we know that private ownership is good and Communism is bad, and Communists use coercion and guns, etc. In short, national prejudices can obscure just about anything.

2. Freedom of the press. The radio and TV were government controlled in South Vietnam. Conservative election observer Howard Penniman noted that each candidate was allowed "only one or two 15-minute radio broadcasts" and "some TV time for the Saigon area."[35] The candidates also had government funding totalling about $46,000 for posters and pamphlets, although how this would allow a meaningful outreach to an illiterate peasantry is not clear. These speeches and posters were precluded by law from expressing anything that was "neutralist" or which could be construed as aiding the Communists directly or indirectly.

Government control over the press occurred via censorship, the threat of cutting off of government-controlled newsprint supplies, and closure by government fiat. According to David Wurfel, a well-informed independent observer of the 1967 election:

> Throughout the campaign "freedom of the press," though greater than before, continued to be compromised by closure, censorship and differential subsidy. Government control of the allocation of subsidized newsprint amount to covert grants of as much as $2,000 dollars per month to newspapers which received more newsprint than their own circulation required and could thus resell. The tell-tale mark of the censor, blank columns, appeared from time to time in Vietnamese dailies, for instance in *Song* on August 23rd, even though the Saigon government had announced that this practice would stop when the campaign officially opened on August 3rd. Shortly after the campaign began, one of the leading political dailies, *Dan Chu*, was closed. *Dan Chu* is published by the immediate past president of the Saigon Newspaper Publishers Association, Vu Ngoc Cac. The ostensible reason for closure was the *Dan Chu* had Communist reporters on its staff, but the men in question had both recently received Vietnamese Government grants for travel abroad, which is always preceded by a careful police check. The real reason was apparently sharp criticism by *Dan Chu* of a senatorial ticket supported by the Minister of Information.[36]

The United States put on pressure for a relaxation of censorship in the months before the election, which shouldn't have been necessary anyway as the constitution promulgated on April 1, 1966 prohibited newspaper censorship; but as R. W. Apple noted, "the Ky regime had chosen to ignore the Constitution on this point" (NYT, July 20, 1967). The Ky government never did relinquish the right to harass and close newspapers. The result, as noted by one observer, was that "very little appeared in the press about the positions or even the identity of opposition candidates, while the papers were constantly filled with the statements and activities of the existing government."[37]

3. Organizational freedom. There were two major groupings in South Vietnam that could be said to have an indigenous mass base: the NLF and the organized Buddhist movement. The former had gone underground in 1955 in order to survive, as described earlier.

The Buddhists, the only other sizable base of potential civil opposition to the takeover of their country by the United States and its chosen military vehicle, were initially somewhat protected by their religious and traditional status and role. In this respect they served, as did the Protestant Churches in Nazi Germany and the Catholic Churches in Latin America since World War II, as a last refuge of an abused and terrorized majority.[38] As we noted above, however, with U.S. moral support and military backing, the South Vietnamese military regime attacked the strongholds of the Buddhists, Danang and Hué by military force, disbanding their struggle committees and arresting, imprisoning, and physically maltreating large numbers. At least 20 Buddhist leaders were kept under multi-year arrest.

Student movements were also repressed by extreme force, with many student leaders arrested, tortured, subjected to early punitive draft, or killed. Destroying, driving underground, terrorizing into silence, or bringing under government control mediating organizations that threatened totalitarian power was an integral feature of the Ky regime. In the U.S. press and rightwing propaganda, however, the Buddhists and students were creating "disorder" and "stirring up trouble," while General Ky was restoring "stability." The real issues being addressed by the Buddhists and the students—the agony of a people under furious attack by the U.S. war machine and its local agents, and the right of the United States to impose its policies and its puppets on the Vietnamese people—were never at issue in the U.S. press.

4. Freedom to organize parties and run candidates. A key feature of the South Vietnam electoral process was the inability of the NLF to run. This was of course by plan, and was justified by patriotic clichés and a rewriting of history (see Appendix 2). The time was ripe for an election by September 1967, as military occupation and pacification had made it possible for a military junta with minimal public support to get a "turnout" and win with only a modest level of further manipulation; that is, to win a "fair election."* "Procommunist neutralists" were also ruled out, with this to be determined by the military junta and the Constituent Assembly which it dominated. This made the election a complete farce, resulting in the barring of all serious peace candidates beforehand and making it impossible to test out support for either the war or the war party in power.

A semi-peace candidate did eventually emerge in the election, Truong Dinh Dzu, who campaigned with a white dove symbol, which he wisely chose to announce only after he had already been approved as a candidate. It is an interesting question why Dzu was allowed to run. On the legal criteria used by the junta, he could have been removed from the ballot list of candidates and barred as a "neutralist." It is our belief that he was spared this treatment for the following reasons: he could be pointed to as a "peace option," thereby allowing it to be said that the people could have voted for peace. On the other hand, he was an unknown, with a dubious background and no organization, and he was not even consistently or strenuously for peace. In the early days of the campaign he was quoted as opposing negotiations with the NLF, though favoring a 24-hour bombing halt to see if Hanoi would come to terms. He also said: "Six more months of bombing and the North Vietnamese people will start to revolt against the Hanoi Government..." (NYT, August 6, 1967). This was the peace candidate. Actually, Dzu was hemmed in, for if he had taken a really strong and consistent peace position he would have been ousted from candidacy. With all these handicaps and constraints Dzu could be allowed to run, especially in competition with nine other civilians, without posing a serious threat to the military ticket. If by any miracle he had come in first, the generals had already stated publicly that a "neutralist" would not be allowed to take office.[39] Anybody voting for Dzu might have known that such a vote was, at best, a protest vote. Dzu's 17% vote was impressive in the circumstances. In a real election he might have done quite well!

Apart from excluding the left and anybody else presenting a serious peace option, the Thieu-Ky team made the election a total "laugher" by preventing the candidacy of two establishment candidates likely to pose a strong challenge to the military ticket, General Duong Van Minh and Au Truong Thanh. Only the most extreme propagandists have attempted to rationalize these exclusions (see Appendix 2).

Finally, all the Senate tickets allied with the militant Buddhists were disallowed. Thus, representatives of all mass groupings in South Vietnam were prevented from running, plus all seriously competitive and popular individuals. The U.S. media treated these maneuverings as slightly naughty peccadillos, regrettable, but perfectly compatible with a fair election.

5. State terror and general level of intimidation. The U.S. occupation and imposition of the Thieu-Ky military faction was associated with a steady increase in the number of soldiers, police, interrogations by torture, and political prisoners. The National Police Force rose in size from 16,000 in 1963 to 88,000 in 1969, and the police intelligence network was pervasive. Arrests for alleged subversion, without legal recourse, were solidly institutionalized in 1966-67.

So was torture, carried out in Provincial Interrogation Centers, in over 200 national prisons, hundreds of local jails, and in the field.[40] Former military intelligence officer Michael Uhl testified in 1969 that large numbers of detainees, the majority women and children, were "captured in repeated dragnet operations" in the rural areas, "and whatever looked good in the catch, regardless of the evidence, was classified as VCI [Vietcong Infrastructure]. . . . Not only was there no due process" applied to these prisoners, according to Uhl "all the detainees were brutalized and many were literally tortured."[41] The political prisons were also filling up rapidly in 1966-67, requiring additional allocation of U.S. "aid" money to new construction of "infrastructure" to further South Vietnamese advances toward democracy. The number of political prisoners in South Vietnam at the time of the election may be judged from the fact that the Saigon government announced shortly before the election that it was releasing 6,270 prisoners. A "ranking official" described this number as only a "tiny fraction" of the total.[42]

State terror was even an omnipresent threat to establishment figures and members of the respectable classes who got out of line. David Wurfel described a case relevant to the election process:

> One important incident not heretofore publicized was the assassination of the private secretary of the president of the Bar Association. The Bar's president was a member of the Central Election Council established by the Election Law to evaluate candidates' qualifications and to report their findings to the Constituent Assembly. He was reputed to be the only independent mind in that official-dominated body. His secretary was murdered the night before the Council recommended Dr. Thanh's disqualification. In this context, implied threats were sufficiently effective against Constituent Assembly members.[43]

Prior to this incident, one of the most progressive members of the Constituent Assembly, Tran Van Van, was assassinated on December 7, 1966. This killing was immediately blamed on the NLF by the government, but nobody in Saigon believed this. Van, a strong opponent of Ky, had been trying to push through a 40-year age limitation on candidates for the presidency (Ky was 37), and he had planned to run for President in 1967 on a ticket of accommodation with the NLF. Another progressive member of the Constituent Assembly, Dr. Phan Quang Dan, narrowly escaped death by an assassin's bomb on December 27, 1966.[44] These incidents reinforced the effect of the conspicuous presence of the Ky-dominated security police on potential establishment dissidents in the Constituent Assembly and elsewhere in Free Vietnam.

In sum, state terror was pervasive in South Vietnam and the rule of law under the new constitution was as effective as it had been under the superb Stalinist constitution of 1936. The analogy with Guatemala and El Salvador is once again striking. "Security" in the pursuit of anticommunism and military victory—goals foisted on a hostage population by the United States and its sponsored armed minority that was not an "armed minority"*—were achieved at the expense of insecurity and pervasive fear for the peasant majority and, increasingly, any urban and elite dissenters.

6. Obligation or pressure to vote. It was not legally obligatory to vote in South Vietnam in 1966 and 1967, but the pressures to do so in the countryside were great. In elections in the 1950s it was always a striking fact that Diem did much better in the small villages and rural areas of South Vietnam than in the big cities like Saigon. The stronger the hold of the Vietminh, the larger the vote for Diem! Even Howard Penniman recognizes that this may have reflected coercion in the past, but the large turnout to vote for the Thieu-Ky and other war party options in 1967 in the "pacified" rural areas he does not regard in the same light, for no credible reason.[45] In 1966-67, while voting was not legally required, registering to vote was nonvoluntary and voting cards were stamped after voting. And the United States and its junta strove to get out the vote. Karl Purnell wrote in 1967 that:

> The recent history of rural Vietnam has taught the peasant farmer that respect and obedience to the local authority can spell the difference between life and death. Since the province, district and most hamlet chiefs have been appointed by the Saigon government, it takes little imagination to determine which ticket these officials were supporting. Most peasants, who neither knew the candidates nor had any conception of what the election was about, were easily susceptible to the subtle suggestions of their superiors.[46]

At a press conference held in Saigon on August 22, 1967, the head of the South Vietnamese National Police stated that "National Policemen will be stationed *inside* and outside booths all over the country. As the National Police are the people in closest contact with the lowest echelon, there will be police telling them where to vote, how to vote and when to vote."[47] William Corson was told by a former Saigon official that

"The National Police at their thousands of check points routinely search the people and in the case of the presidential election, as in past elections, if an individual was found without the election-day stamp on his registration card it meant prison and in some cases even death. The real meaning of the election was not lost on the people. *They voted to stay out of jail.* They also knew from past performance that the government-picked candidates would win regardless of how they voted."[48]

7. Did the Vietnamese public have any real options? The majority of South Vietnamese were peasants interested first in peace, second in some kind of land reform. As John P. Vann pointed out in 1965, "The dissatisfaction of the agrarian population...today is largely expressed through alliance with the NLF," given the fact that "the existing government is oriented toward the exploitation of the rural and lower class urban populations."[49] But this representative of the "agrarian population" was excluded from the election, and nobody expressing a radical position on land reform was eligible to run. Anybody who was pro-peace even to the point of urging a negotiated compromise with the only mass-based political party in South Vietnam was—or could have been—thrown off the ballot.

South Vietnam was an occupied country in 1967. The occupying power wanted somebody in Saigon who would devote himself to serving the U.S. war aims. Thieu and Ky had been chosen. The election was designed to give the appearance of legitimacy and popularity to these agents of U.S. power. They were sure to win. In the extremely unlikely event of an electoral defeat, this would have been followed by either a military coup or an arrangement with a Duarte-type figurehead who would have served as the civilian front. There were no options for the South Vietnamese majority.

Managing the Election

The preliminary deck-stacking, as described above, was accomplished first by the mere retention of governmental power by the military junta throughout the entire period of voting in a Constituent Assembly, establishing a constitution, and then holding the election for executive and legislative office. This gave the generals control over a massive army, the police, an intelligence network, radio and TV, transportation, and vast budgetary resources (provided by the

U.S. taxpayer). Their control over the constitution-making process also left nice loopholes that allowed the junta to operate with state-of-siege powers.

Several other major legal maneuvers should also be mentioned. First, the original electoral rules held that active military officers were ineligible to run. Eventually, however, the Constituent Assembly was persuaded to make an exception for Thieu and Ky. It had been contended, with extreme cogency, that the top generals might have both conflicts of interest with the civil society and an advantage from military incumbency and power. Furthermore, the Johnson administration had claimed the election to be a step toward civil and democratic rule—a fraudulent pretense, of course, but the Thieu-Ky candidacy flew in the face of any kind of democratic purpose. The combining of these two heirs of French colonialism in a single ticket was done under U.S. pressure,[50] to assure the victory of the "democratic forces."

Another deck-stacking effort, already mentioned, was disallowing the candidacies of Minh and Thanh. This blatant exercise of power to throw out strong candidacies was paralleled by a deliberate encouragement of numerous civilian candidates, who received a nice government subsidy and some free publicity. Proliferated civilian candidacies, with one consolidated military ticket, would disperse the civilian vote and assure the military ticket a winning plurality.

A still further element of manipulation was to provide that the presidential election would be decided by a plurality rather than by a majority. This assured that the diffused civilian vote would not be consolidated in a runoff.

Given these formal deck-stacking maneuvers, all the military ticket had to do was win a modest plurality. Thieu and Ky were well known, and used their control over radio and TV, military authority, and political incumbency to call attention to themselves. They were strongly supported by the U.S. government, whose huge payroll and large resources underwriting the Saigon government's budget were important advantages to the military junta. The United States participated more directly in the election with advice on electoral strategies, informational services, and other inputs. The direct service to the military regime in its propaganda and staging effort is illustrated by Table 3-1, which reproduces a part of a larger table put out by the U.S. Embassy in Saigon in 1967, showing its printing and distribution plans for an extensive body of propaganda and voting aids. Frank Snepp and Seymour Hersh have shown that U.S. resources were directly available for bribery in the 1971 election,[51] and it

Table 3-1: Media Production and Distribution Schedule of the U.S. Embassy in Saigon, in Aid of the 1967 Election Campaign in South Vietnam (part of a larger schedule)

Annex 'E' MEDIA PRODUCTION AND DISSEMINATION SCHEDULE
Annex 'F' AREA DISTRIBUTION SCHEDULE

L-Leaflet C- Comic Book
I - Photo Insert R- Ruler
P- Poster A- Adhesive material
S- Slogan

NO	ITEM		QUANTITY	NAVY	SAIGON	GIADINH	QUANG NAM	QUANG NGAI	QUANG TIN	QUANG TRI	THUA THIEN	DA NANG	BINH DINH	BINH THUAN	DALAT	DARLAC	
1	L-ELECTION LAW	SP-2040	800,000	24	60	70	21	25	14	14	28	14	42	14	10	105	21
2	L-REQUIREMENTS	SP-2041	2,000,000	70	66	180	55	74	37	37	93	37	III	37	10	25	55
3	L-HOW TO VOTE	SP-2042	2,000,000	70	66	180	55	74	37	37	93	37	III	37	10	25	55
4	L-BALLOTS	SP-2043	2,000,000	70	66	180	55	74	37	37	95	37	III	37	10	25	55
5	L-VOTER CARD	SP-2044	2,000,000	70	66	180	55	74	37	37	93	37	III	37	10	25	55
6	L-VC		3,000,000	WILL	BE	AIR	DELIVERED	THROUGH	MAC								
7	L-VC		6,000,000														
8	L-VC		6,000,000														
9	I-VOTE	SP-2045	500,000	10	35	42	14	18	9	9	21	9	26	9	4	7	14
10	I-ELECTIONS	SP-2046B	150,000	13	15	12	3.6	4.5	2.4	2.4	6.0	2.4	7.2	2.4	1	1.5	8.4
11	I-DO'S & DONT'S	SP-2047B	150,000	.	15	.	.	.	.	.	.	.	.	.	.	.	.
12	I-IMPORTANCE	SP-2048B	150,000	.	15	.	.	.	.	.	.	.	.	.	.	.	.
13	I-WHAT YOU SHOULD KNOW	SP-2049B	150,000	.	15	.	.	.	.	.	.	.	.	.	.	.	.
14	I-REQUIREMENTS	SP-2050B	150,000	.	15	.	.	.	.	.	.	.	.	.	.	.	.
15	P-ELECTIONS	SP-2046A	150,000	.	15	.	.	.	.	.	.	.	.	.	.	.	.
16	P-DO'S DONT'S'	SP-2047A	150,000	.	15	.	.	.	.	.	.	.	.	.	.	.	.
17	P-IMPORTANCE	SP-2048A	150,000	.	15	.	.	.	.	.	.	.	.	.	.	.	.
18	P-WHAT SHOULD KNOW	SP-2049A	150,000	.	15	.	.	.	.	.	.	.	.	.	.	.	.
19	P-REQUIREMENTS	SP-2050A	150,000	.	15	.	.	.	.	.	.	.	.	.	.	.	.
20	P-HOW TO VOTE	SP-2042A	150,000	.	15	.	.	.	.	.	.	.	.	.	.	.	.
21	S-PARTICIPATE	SP-2051	1,000,000	55	30	90	27	37	19	19	46	19	55	19	5	14	25
22	S-BUILD DEMOCRACY	SP-2052	1,000,000	.	30	.	.	.	.	.	.	.	.	.	.	.	.
23	S-WIN	SP-2053	1,000,000	.	30	.	.	.	.	.	.	.	.	.	.	.	.
24	S-HONOR	SP-2054	1,000,000	.	30	.	.	.	.	.	.	.	.	.	.	.	.
25	C-COMIC BOOK	SP-2055	50,000	SPECIAL		DISTRIBUTION											
26	R-RULER	SP-2056	1,000,000	35	30	90	27	37	19	19	46	19	55	19	5	14	25
27	A-ADHESIVE SYMBOL		30,000	SPECIAL		DISTRIBUTION											
28	A- " SLOGAN		10,000														
29	BANNER MIX SP-2069 SP-2070		500,000	10	35	42	14	18	9	9	21	9	26	9	4	7	14
30	L- DAI DOAN KET		50,000	SPECIAL		DISTRIBUTION											

Source: Given to Professor George Kahin by an official of the U.S. Embassy in Saigon.

seems likely that this was true in 1967 as well. (We point out below that large bribes were offered to members of the Election Committee and Constituent Assembly in 1967, but the exact source is unclear.)

Some small fraction of South Vietnamese voters undoubtedly liked Thieu and Ky and their policies; others voted for brand name and power; still others were bought, by pre-election bonuses to military personnel and deals with various power groups. Another large bloc of Thieu and Ky votes was "delivered" by their political agents in the countryside, as in the Diem years. The military ticket could also count on a large fraction of the one million votes of the military and police, a base larger than the 817,120 vote total obtained by the first-ranking civilian candidate Dzu.

With all of their advantages, along with the inability of their rivals to campaign extensively or on the most fundamental issues, the military ticket still got only 35% of a restricted registration. If we add to the number of registered voters the three million adults in the NLF-controlled areas, the generals were only able to obtain the votes of about 16% of the potential electorate.

Fraud. What is more, some unknown but probably sizable fraction of the Thieu-Ky total was fraudulent. The coerced rural vote was probably accompanied by massive ballot box stuffing. R. W. Apple reported in the *New York Times* (Sept. 3, 1967) that a highly respected South Vietnamese group of civilians circulated a list of 54 districts (of a total of 334) "where government officials were said to have been ordered to tamper with the vote." It was also pointed out that important areas ran out of ballots, which allowed ballot stuffing to make up for those deprived of ballots. There was also a very large increase in registration in the months before the election in areas where Thieu and Ky did remarkably well. Penniman attributes this to the success of pacification, bringing new registered voters into the orbit of government control. He fails to explain why these new registered voters would bother to vote, and why any of them would vote for Ky and Thieu. It was also acknowledged by the military junta that soldiers had sometimes been given more than one ballot. General Thieu was very sorry about this mistake and called upon all recipients of more than one ballot to return them.

In short, there is spotty but strong evidence of coerced votes, multiple voting by military personnel, ballot box stuffing, and even fraudulent vote counts. An informed summary of the extensive evidence of fraud, and some of the mechanisms employed, is provided in Appendix 3, taken from a report by David Wurfel. Some further analysis of these issues appears in the critique of Penniman's defense of the 1967 election in Appendix 2. Wurfel estimated that fraud was extensive, producing 300,000-500,000 completely manufactured votes, several hundred thousand more via pressure on the military forces and civil service, and a coerced vote of unknown but probably large size in the pacified rural areas. Without these fraudulent and coerced sources we believe that Thieu and Ky would have received under 10% of the vote of the South Vietnamese population of voting age and would have lost the election to Dzu, even with the stacked deck.

The evidence of fraud was so great that the Election Committee of the Constituent Assembly voted by 16 to two to invalidate the 1967 election results. The Chairman of the Election Committee, Nguyen Thanh Vinh, told George Kahin that the reports from 2,539 of the 8,954 polling places, 28% of the total, failed to conform to regulations, and that several hundred other reports looked "suspicious."[52] These irregular or suspicious reports covered polling places that accounted for about 35% of the total vote. The decision to invalidate was based only on the documents submitted to the Election Committee, although Vinh claimed that the Committee members were convinced that only a small proportion of irregularities were recorded in the documents they received. The Constituent Assembly initially supported the recommendation of the Election Committee, but eventually changed its position. The reason for the change, according to Vinh, was a wide array of inducements and pressures. Bribery was a large factor, with as much as one to two million piasters going to Assembly members, and Vinh himself receiving an offer of 10 million piasters. A second factor and major form of pressure was the threat of change in draft status of members of the Assembly and their sons. Ten vote switches in the Assembly were by draft-age members. Vinh reported, also, that the head of the National Police had surrounded the Assembly building and refused to permit his Committee access to additional data from the outside. During the Committee's deliberations, he and other members were visited by representatives of the U.S. Embassy and urged to validate the election. In short, the evidence of massive fraud was eventually submerged by the determined mobilization of massive power.

The observers. Having had a great success with observers in the Dominican election of 1966, President Johnson arranged for a panel of 22 U.S. notables and three experts to go to South Vietnam to watch over that election. In contrast with the Dominican case, Johnson was unable to get a substantial number of authentic liberals. His real "catches" were Whitney Young of the Urban League and publisher John Knight. Otherwise, the contingent included second-line politicians and government officials and a number of conservative business, labor, and religious representatives. The observers were in Vietnam for only a few days, moving around relatively freely in Saigon, but under military guard. They visited the more remote towns only with prior notice. They never saw, even through a limousine window, over 90% of the polling places outside of Saigon. None of them spoke Vietnamese. They talked to some Saigon officials and a very small number of ordinary citizens through translators and under military observation. They saw nobody beaten up in their presence. There were a few minor reservations, mainly by John Knight. But in general the observers were once again impressed with what a "beautiful and wonderful people" we were protecting (Werner Gullander of the National Association of Manufacturers), and that the election was fair, even terrific ("As good as any election in the United States," according to Gov. McCall of Oregon).

One of the three expert-advisers, Richard Scammon, described the election as "reasonably efficient, reasonably fair, reasonably honest." If 90% of the rural polling places were unobserved, there was no way in which Scammon could generalize on "honesty" based on *evidence*. The secret of the observer-expert in the demonstration election is to stress "form." One establishes that the "forms" and technical details seem to conform to the rules on getting up registration lists, checking voters against registration rolls, maintaining voter privacy, and providing mechanisms for a final vote count. With a stress on form rather than substance, it is easy to find staged elections "reasonably fair." This is greatly aided by the fact that demonstration election "experts" are all good patriots, who are quite prepared to make the further assumption that in the client state the form is translated into substance. With this patriotic assumption, the nominal becomes the real; an election with good form has substantive quality. In a classic illustration of this important step, another of the three expert advisers in 1967, Professor Donald Hertzberg of Rutgers, "added that irregularities were unlikely since the election law forbade them" (NYT, Sept. 5, 1967). The third expert, Howard Penniman, claimed that fraud was improbable by noting that the election officials in South Vietnam were provided a handbook of rules that was 40-50 pages long![53] The other main element in finding demonstration elections fair—in translating good form into electoral substance—is ignoring or distorting the fundamental parameters that determine beforehand whether an election has any real meaning.

In Appendix 2 we will examine how Howard Penniman manages to avoid or misrepresent these basic factors.

In sum, the observers sent by President Johnson for several days of escorted visits to a country whose language they didn't understand and of whose culture, history, and politics they were largely ignorant, found the election fair. Going to Vietnam was of absolutely no relevance in their reaching this conclusion, but going there was part of the staging process and a basis for a great deal of media insight into the facts about Vietnam.

The Mass Media and the Vietnam Election

Mass media coverage of the election of 1967 was perhaps a bit more sophisticated and less perfectly integrated into the government's dramatic format than in either the Dominican or El Salvador elections. This was partly a result of the fact that the Dominican election gave the superficial appearance of fairness, with Bosch at least able to run, which helped soften up the media to patriotic subservience. The Vietnam election was more blatantly fraudulent, and the national audience was already restive and suspicious of government trickery. In the case of El Salvador in March 1982, the tremendous media subservience, which we detail in Chapter 5, seems to have been a result of a much more aggressive government propaganda campaign, carried out in a more conservative environment.

Even in the case of the Vietnam election, however, while the careful reader and listener could arrive at a negative view of the election, most of the media portrayed the election on the government's terms. In the best media the same was true but with reservations which often showed up in back-page articles in juxtaposition with government propaganda clichés never reconciled with the negative facts nor subjected to serious and sustained analysis. And the reservations were never allowed to produce categorical rejections of government positions or deny front page space to the government for the further dissemination of proven fabrications.

Even in back-page critiques, the analysts never quite let go of the government propaganda line, even if it rendered their articles incoherent. Thus Charles Mohr, writing in the *New York Times* on September 11, 1966, noted that the United States had been unenthusiastic about elections for a while because of fears that they might lead to a government determined to end the war. But during 1966, after the crushing of the Buddhist movement by force, U.S. officials came to recognize that in such an unpleasant case the army would always overthrow the threatening government! Thus relieved, U.S. officials recognized that "elections" would either provide a government that would be legitimized to fight, or it would be deposed. Furthermore, elections in South Vietnam really tested control, not popularity. But after having said all of this, Mohr then asserts that the importance of the election "will lie in the fact that a small, but vital step has been taken in giving South Vietnam a popular government." This is a propaganda cliché incompatible with the main body of Mohr's argument, and it was repudiated by succeeding events.

In an article written at the height of the Buddhist crisis, Max Frankel explained that the U.S. aim is "the survival of the 10-man military junta," which U.S. officials regarded as "the only cohesive force capable of prosecuting the war" (NYT, April 7, 1966). This view of the heart and soul of U.S. policy was strengthened by Ambassador Lodge's well-known statement in the same period urging the importance of preserving a strong military presence in the Saigon government. These insights did not prevent the press from subsequently passing on a series of incompatible claims about U.S. aims and the purpose of the elections in 1966 and 1967. A Hedrick Smith article (NYT, September 6, 1967) was headlined "U.S. Aides Foresee Saigon Peace Step As Result of Vote." Smith reported that the administration was disappointed at the lack of decisiveness of the vote for Thieu and Ky, on the ground that a big mandate "would put it [the military junta] in position to make peace moves." But maybe the smaller military vote would make the regime "more amenable to American pressures for economic and social reforms and for the inclusion of a broader spectrum of civilian politicians." If Frankel was right, and we believe that he was, then the "peace moves," civilian representation, and social reform were propaganda malarkey. But Hedrick Smith passed along these propaganda handouts without question, feeling no obligation to reject them as malarkey or to juxtapose them with other lines of thought that would show their real meaning.

Premise of Legitimacy. In the quality media there was a fair amount of pre-election news describing how the military junta pushed Minh and Thanh off the ballot, the junta's manipulation of the electoral process, its large built-in advantages based on incumbency, and making other points suggesting serious questions about the integrity of our client and the election.[54] Yet the mass media never called the election a fraud, nor did they ever spell out and discuss openly its true purpose—to legitimize the military junta and prepare the U.S. public for intensified warfare. The Frankel article cited earlier was written in connection with the Buddhist turmoil in April

1966, and its conclusions on the fundamentals of U.S. policy were not transferred to discussions of the elections. The election was treated as a serious enterprise, not as a staged legitimacy show with a fore-ordained outcome.

As in the other demonstration elections described in this book, the media allowed the government to use the familiar dramatic structure: (1) the election is good and important and from it will come a lot of good things like maybe peace moves and a peace settlement, civilian government, and increasing democratization; (2) "turnout" is the test of validation, measuring popular approval of the election, the managing junta, and the sponsor; and (3) left disruption and terror are pushed front and center to set off the drama, to vindicate the importance of "turnout," and to prove the virtue of the election. Let us examine each of these points, which constitute the government-media agenda.

The Government-Media Agenda

1. Elections are good, meaningful, and a step toward democracy and other good things. This impression is provided by simply taking the election at face value and relying heavily on the words of U.S. and Saigon government officials. Using these sources the media report on the election ins-and-outs, candidate foibles, weather conditions, the threat of VC terrorism, expected outcomes, turnout, and the hopes for the future. The focus is, first and foremost, on the touching event of democracy in action. In the 1966 election a moving article by Peter Arnett was titled "Peasants Grope Way Toward a New Liberty" (*Philadelphia Inquirer*, Sept. 12, 1966), where "quietly and purposefully, the people of the Mekong delta were exercising their right to vote." A *New York Times* editorial of Sept. 4, 1967 intoned that hundreds of thousands of villagers were "willing to risk participation in the elections held by the Saigon regime" in a heart-warming display of "popular support," etc.

Time magazine covered the 1967 election mainly through the eyes of Marshal Ky, General Thieu, and the "observers." It noted that there had been criticisms of the forthcoming election, which *Time* did not spell out. Instead, *Time* appropriately gave considerable space to that distinguished statesman Ky's indignant rejection of these criticisms (still unspecified), his huffy invitation to Johnson to send observers, his "disdaining" to answer charges (still unspecified), his asserted intention to curb corruption (no details or explanation), and Thieu's promise of a peace bid to Hanoi, etc. In short, there is zero substance, with the election placed in a setting of dignified rebuttal of unspecified criticisms by the dignified leaders of independent South Vietnam. In the postelection follow-up article (Sept. 8, 1967), the election was still treated with total superficiality and apologetics, with the Johnson observers serving to prove "fairness." The dignified Thieu was allowed to make his own reply to (unspecified) charges of election rigging: "If I were to win the election by foul means, it would be an insult to myself." The civilian candidates "had been crying foul," though the specifics of their claim must remain a mystery; but why not, as General Thieu has disposed of the issue. The presence of police, prisons, political prisoners, torture, and the exclusion of "neutralist" candidates from the ballot were never *mentioned* by *Time*. As in each demonstration election discussed in this book, *Time*'s treatment was unqualified propaganda.

Newsweek's coverage of the Vietnam election was most interesting in its regurgitation of official speculation on beneficent outcomes. Editors of a liberal magazine, perhaps restive in the face of the behavior of a client police state, escalating warfare against a defenceless peasantry, and an election that they knew (but could not admit) was fraudulent, wanted to believe that a liberal Democratic President was not just engaged in killing. He must have had good things in mind. Thus *Newsweek* quoted one official to the effect that a Thieu-Ky victory would allow them to dump the "slimier army officers" [implication: our agents Ky and Thieu are clean reformers, just needing more power to go at reform]; it quoted an Embassy official who was convinced that Thieu would appoint a civilian prime minister if he won the election [implication: we as well as Thieu were devoted to civilian rule]; and it quoted other officials on the chances of early peace negotiations, which these officials were dubious about no matter who won [implication: we are all for peace negotiations, but they are unaccountably elusive].In brief, *Newsweek* gave neither facts nor analysis, but served as a conduit for blatant and foolish propaganda.

The government line that we were deeply concerned with the restoration of civilian rule was pushed by other liberals, who struggled hard not to let facts interfere with their faith that their leaders had noble aims. Drew Pearson and Jack Anderson stated that Johnson traveled all the way to Guam "to make sure that U.S. military leaders are putting enough emphasis on the civilian and political rebuilding of South Vietnam."[55] Johnson had recognized from the Buddhist experience that "without equality of rule there could never be stability in South Vietnam." He had laid down the law to Ky at Honolulu on "equality of government." And at the forth-coming meeting at Guam, he would "make sure that progress toward full civilian-government continues." This nonsense was written while U.S. military forces were shattering the civil society of South Vietnam and while the administration was giving unconditional support to a military junta busily erecting a full-fledged police state.

The government's pretense that the election might yield "negotiations" also served, like the contemporaneous peace moves themselves, to add a warmer glow to the election and enhance the image of the generals. Thieu even offered to support a bombing pause after the election. The liberal media could attach themselves to this possibility in their search for ways to rationalize whatever their government does on the basis of principle. The *New York Times*, for example, editorialized on September 4, 1967 that the election, by legitimizing Thieu and Ky, "provides a viable basis for a peace settlement." This self-deceptive misreading of the point of the election helped to lend it sanctity.

2. Turnout. Turnout is central in a demonstration election. It is necessary, of course, to get turnout interpreted as a repudiation of any "outs" and a vindication of the election managers and sponsors. A subsidiary government ploy is that it is always worried that the turnout will be low because of leftwing "terrorism," and it is always gratified that the turnout is larger than it had anticipated. The media role is to repeat this malarkey, and never examine seriously the possibility that turnout may be a function of *state* terrorism.

At the moments of truth, September 11, 1966 and September 3, 1967, turnout reigned supreme in the U.S. media. On the day following the September 1966 election, the front page article by Charles Mohr (NYT, Sept. 12, 1966) was headed "Turnout is Heavy in South Vietnam Despite Vietcong." This is the same Mohr who explained on the back pages that turnout in South Vietnam was a reflection of control, not popularity, and that elections were now acceptable because an unfavorable result would produce a military coup! On September 4, 1967, the lead column in the *New York Times* read "Election is Held in South Vietnam: Turnout is Heavy," and the article featured prominently the fact that the turnout was "very heavy" in the provinces and that people were pressing to vote in Saigon. The same attention was given to turnout in other papers and on the TV networks. Turnout was uniformly identified with success, vindication of the military junta and the United States, a repudiation of the enemy.

3. The left disruption gambit. This dramatic foil of the election sponsors was used aggressively in the Vietnam elections in both 1966 and 1967. In a back-page article at the time of the 1966 election (NYT, Sept. 11, 1966), Charles Mohr noted that

> There has been a shameful amount of hoopla about these elections. American and South Vietnamese officials have outdone even the Vietcong in trying to spread the impression that the guerillas are determined to disrupt the voting—the better to argue later that the guerillas have been thwarted.

Yet Mohr's own election day article featuring "turnout" (quoted above) also stressed Vietcong disruption in headline and text. Mohr's article opens: "Despite attempts by the Vietcong to intimidate them, South Vietnamese voters turned out in large numbers..." This is in accordance with the dramatic formula, so that although recognizing it as "shameful hoopla," the obliging Mohr proceeds according to the rules of the stage.

Newsweek and *Time* magazine put "left disruption" at the very center of their dramas. For *Newsweek*, the VC effort to disrupt the election made the election much more important as a test of strength, obviously to be measured by turnout ("The Test of Time," Sept. 11, 1967). *Newsweek* gave no *evidence* that there was any attempt to disrupt, or any abnormal level of NLF activity, but we must not be too demanding. (William Corson states in his book *The Betrayal* that "During the election week there was Vietcong terrorism, but no more and no less than during any other week in the preceding six months."[56]) *Time* gave enemy disruption first-order attention. Its postelection article started on the theme that "the most convincing vote of confidence in the validity and significance of South Vietnam's elections was cast last week by the Viet Cong" (Sept. 8, 1967). In the case of the January 1947 Polish election, *Time* featured the presence of "170,000 Soviet-trained security police" and the coercive attempts to get people to vote; the disruption by the Polish underground was not a testimonial to the "validity and significance of the election" but, on the contrary, an excuse for government intimidation. But the Polish election was *their* demonstration election!

Off the Agenda

A demonstration election requires that the manipulative and "staging" aspects of the election be downplayed and that the historical and institutional context—that is, the conditions that make an election meaningful or devoid of meaning—be quietly bypassed. These are the items off the agenda.

1. Real purpose. The real purpose of the election was to give an aura of legitimacy to an armed minority and to prepare the ground for uncompromising war. This was occasionally disclosed, but almost never in the popular press, on TV, or in magazines like *Time*, *Newsweek*, *U.S. News and World Report*, or *Readers Digest*. The real intent was obscured under a welter of euphemisms (stability) and nominal aims that were proximate (order, legitimation of the government) or fraudulent (democracy, peace, a civilian government, or discovering the popular will). The reiterated claim that "U.S. Aides Foresee Saigon Peace Step As Result of Vote" (NYT, Sept. 6, 1967) integrated the two great PR instruments—the "peace move" and the "free election"—in a single fabric of deception. Just as there was no *real* "peace move" or intent to "negotiate," the role of the election was to diminish the pressure to settle short of victory.

2. Free speech, freedom of the press, and other basic parameters that are conditions of a free election. These were treated very sparingly by the U.S. media; they were never pushed aggressively or said to bear on the credibility and very possibility of a meaningful election. We show in chapter 5 that in Poland in 1947 the existence of 170,000 Soviet-trained security police was considered a background fact that in and of itself constrained electoral freedom. In the case of South Vietnam, a police establishment and military force of some one million, along with several hundred thousand U.S. troops, was considered of no electoral significance. Some newspapers mentioned that U.S. troops were ordered to be kept on their bases on election day, in order that their presence in the country could not be construed as involving any U.S. interference in the political affairs of another state. No doubt if the Soviets ordered their troops to stay in their barracks during an election held in Czechoslovakia, the U.S. media would take the position that the Soviet presence had ceased to be an electoral factor worthy of mention.

We have stressed that in Vietnam an entire body of citizens, perhaps 50% of the total, was barred from organizational activity and running a candidate, by law and threat of death. Candidates advocating not only Communism but a negotiated settlement ("neutralism") were also forbidden to run. It is not just that a large opposition party was badly harassed, as was the Peasant Party in Poland. In Vietnam the largest opposition party was totally excluded, and so was anybody that wanted to *compromise* with this opposition, the only mass-based political force in South Vietnam. The media took this all quite calmly as irrelevant to election quality. The assault on and arrest of Buddhist activists and the pacification of the student movement was interpreted by the U.S. media in terms set by the U.S. government: it contributed to "stability" and reduced "disorder." It was not seen as an attack on a pluralistic system, reducing its real democratic content and potential, and setting the stage for more fanatic military rule (as turned out to be the case).

In its editorial reflections on the election, the *New York Times* (Sept. 4, 1967) failed to mention the exclusion of the NLF, its mass base, and even "neutralists" from participation. Its view was that "Within the limitations created by the exclusion from the ballot of certain popular candidates and the abuses that marked the earlier stages of the campaign, most observers believe that on the whole the voting was fairly conducted."

If the Democratic Party were excluded from the ballot in a U.S. election, and anybody advocating a reduction in the arms budget was barred from running, along with a few independents with political clout, and the deck was further stacked "earlier in the campaign" by some legal technicalities, but the voters were not coerced as far as 22 non-English speaking observers could see from their limousines, no doubt the *Times* would call this a "fair election."

3. **The peace constituency and the "contradiction."** A CBS public opinion poll carried out in South Vietnam in early 1967 found that 81% of the 1,545 respondents wanted "peace" above all else; 4% listed victory over Communism as their primary aim.[57] This poll presumably didn't even include the "enemy" constituency, the peasants of the remoter rural areas. This presented a seeming contradiction: although "peace" was the primary value of the populace, the war faction supported by the United States won the "free election." This strongly suggests a phoney election and massive deception, but the mass media of the United States carefully avoided addressing this anomaly.

The Sequel

One of our main themes in this book is that the nominal ends of demonstration elections are regularly refuted by what happens after they are held. The mass media therefore complete their staging service by never engaging in major retrospectives. Let us conclude by looking briefly at the "free election" sequel.

1. **Democracy and civilian rule**. Democracy did not exist in any meaningful sense in Vietnam in 1967, but many of its vestiges were

weakened steadily thereafter under the regime of second-rate and ruthless mercenaries to whom the United States gave its full backing. A liberal U.S. study group visiting South Vietnam in 1969 found that 32 newspapers had been closed within the preceding year or so, censorship was more thoroughgoing than ever, and most of the political opposition had been driven underground. "Members of the Study Team met with leaders of five old-line political parties no longer permitted to function. . . . Their parties have been outlawed, their requests to publish a newspaper have gone unanswered and their voices have been muted."[58]

Despite what Drew Pearson and Jack Anderson described as the really deep commitment of President Johnson to civilian rule, no civilians governed from 1966 through the close of the tenure of the Saigon regime. The generals in Saigon were so greedy for total power and status, and Johnson's (and Nixon's) commitment to the generals was so complete, that they wouldn't even allow a *token* civilian in high office. Seymour Hersh has described how the Nixon-Kissinger team, in their eagerness to preserve Thieu in power in 1971, allowed or encouraged extensive CIA intervention in the 1971 election, "pouring millions of dollars into Thieu's private campaign treasury and helping him set up political support groups to give his candidacy the appearance of broad-based endorsement."[59] The CIA also helped Thieu push through a bill to get Marshal Ky removed from the presidential ballot by a legal technicality. It was thought that this would assure a victory over the unacceptable General Minh. The effect of this trickery was to induce General Minh to withdraw from the election, refusing to participate even when offered a $3 million bribe by the CIA.[60]

2. **The escalation of state terror.** With the essentially unconditional support of the United States, the Thieu regime gradually took on more and more of the trappings of a full-fledged totalitarian state. With U.S. technical "know-how" provided the police, the scope of torture and systematic police violence in the Thieu state bore comparison with anything Europe produced during the heyday of fascism.[61] The number of political prisoners rose steadily after the election of 1967, reaching an estimated total of some 200,000 by 1972. A great many of these prisoners were middle-of-the-road students, clergy, intellectuals, and labor leaders who had shown some interest in political affairs and therefore constituted a "threat" to the leaders of the budding South Vietnamese democracy. The vast repressive machinery of the regime was employed to a great extent against these center elements, in a determined effort to destroy any noncommunist

opposition to its rule. The degeneration of this state was so extreme, however, that a great many subjects of police terror were essentially "random" victims—brutalized as a matter of course once they had fallen into police hands.

3. Ending corruption and initiating reform. The military officers gradually brought to the fore by the United States were almost to a man mercenaries trained by the French colonial power.[62] Their propensity to steal was legendary. In a 1968 Senate report it was remarked that

> Corruption pervades all aspects of Vietnamese life, and it is brazenly practiced.... Government jobs are bought and paid for by people seeking a return on their investments. Police accept bribes. Officials and their wives run operations in the black market. AID funds and hospital supplies are diverted into private pockets.... In the field of refugee care and in many other fields the Government of South Vietnam has been engaged in the systematic looting of its own people.[63]

In the later phases of the Thieu regime it became an even more formidable corruption machine, with daily reports of officials pocketing the pay of "phantom troops" or the rice rations of live refugees, and stealing and smuggling medicine, scrap metals, and military supplies. Even new jet fighter planes were converted into ready money by Saigon officials: in 1974 a police raid uncovered the wings of at least 15 A-37 aircraft in an illegal scrap metal depot. Large numbers of these planes had been rushed to Saigon just prior to the cease fire, at a cost to the U.S. taxpayer of $500,000 per airplane. The most sensational scandal of 1974, however, was the siphoning off into speculative hoards of 150,000 tons of fertilizer, another gift of the U.S. taxpayer, by a group of importers and officials, including Thieu's brother-in-law, who sold it off later at high black-market prices.[64]

All through this period pledges were extracted from Ky and Thieu for reform and an attack on corruption. It was alleged that one beneficial effect of a strong electoral showing by Ky and Thieu might be their consequent ability to clean house. But Ky and Thieu were part of the problem, not means of its solution. So was the United States part of the problem; in fact, the main part. The usual formulation, that the United States lacked "leverage,"* misses the point, which is that its priorities put military victory first and thus required rulers who would do the same irrespective of the popular will or genuine national interest. Such rulers tend to be corrupt—it has always been hard to find honest Quislings.[65] The result was that corruption grew, and reform was always in abeyance or rendered ineffective by the constraints of power. Land reform, imposed from above as in El Salvador in the 1980s, was ineffective in scope and application, and was overwhelmed in its effect on the peasantry by the complementary program of pacification by firepower. The mass media never at any time gave much attention to or a satisfactory explanation of why corruption was so pervasive or why reform was hard to implement among these rulers we were helping preserve "freedom." The absence of any retrospectives on the unfulfilled claims and hopes of improvement followed a familiar pattern.

    4. Negotiations and the settlement of the war. Did the election victory of Thieu and Ky lead to a greater willingness to "negotiate" and settle the war by political means? The *Pentagon Papers* indicate that the election was seen by U.S. planners as providing the basis for an expanded war, in which "maximum military pressure must be maintained" on the enemy.[66] There was no mention at all of a negotiated political settlement as a probable outcome of the election in analyses and plans of U.S. officials. History also reveals that neither *Newsweek*, the *New York Times*, nor the other vehicles that had passed on the propaganda hints and analyses of peace moves and negotiations likely to emerge out of the election ever stopped to look back—to admit to their audience that they had misled them and to explain why.

    Seymour Hersh points out that by 1971 the North Vietnamese were ready to settle the war with a mutual withdrawal of forces, a prisoner exchange, and an Indochina-wide ceasefire, if the United States would allow a free election in South Vietnam. They felt that a *real* election held under conditions of U.S. neutrality would result in the victory of a non-Communist moderate like General Minh. They were prepared to live with a non-Communist but neutralist regime, which would not threaten them, would allow some NLF voice, and would give them a respite from the heavy costs of war. But Nixon and Kissinger refused to take a neutral stance in the 1971 election, investing large sums in support of Thieu and once again manipulating aggressively to assure the victory of a U.S. instrument.[67] This terminated negotiations and opened up a new and terrible further stage of warfare, which ended with a total defeat of the U.S. client. The irony, from the perspective of this book, is that the consistent refusal of the United States to allow a *real* free election in South Vietnam, from 1956 to 1971, resulted in the complete collapse of a regime without significant indigenous support but capable of regularly winning *staged* elections.

CHAPTER **4**

El Salvador

The failure of the United States to achieve a military victory in Vietnam served to inhibit U.S. intervention in Third World conflicts. Opposition to such military adventures, dubbed "the Vietnam Syndrome," extended to an important segment of the U.S. political elite, and was even translated into legislation restraining the war-making powers of the president. Thus in its first years in office the Carter administration was compelled to manage Third World conflicts according to the "Nixon doctrine," through surrogates like Iran, Israel, and Nicaragua. The Iranian revolution of 1978 and the hostage crisis the next year were key events in undermining the Vietnam Syndrome, however, and the U.S. involvement in El Salvador that followed bore a striking resemblance to the Vietnam War intervention of the early 1960s.[1]

Both economic and political interests were at work in the late 1970s to undermine the Carter administration's relatively liberal stance toward the Caribbean. In July 1979 the Nicaraguan revolution finally deposed the Somoza family. This was immediately followed by the "discovery" of a Soviet brigade in Cuba. Notwithstanding Soviet claims (supported by U.S. analysts) that the brigade had been in Cuba for 17 years and had no interventionary capability, the ensuing furor torpedoed Senate debate on the SALT II Treaty. A

Caribbean Joint Task Force headquartered in Key West was established in October 1979, and an attempt was begun to link the conservative governments of the region in a *cordon sanitaire* around Nicaragua. As the new military junta in El Salvador began to unravel, the Carter administration resumed military aid and also moved to reestablish military ties with Guatemala. Both countries had been previously ineligible for such aid under the Carter administration's "human rights" guidelines. The U.S. government even tolerated and tacitly supported the training in the United States of remnants of Somoza's hated National Guard, who were intent on overthrowing the Sandinista regime in Nicaragua.

When the growing conservative tide swept the Reagan administration into power in late 1980, Central America and the Caribbean became the first battleground chosen by the new regime to confront the alleged global challenge by the Soviet Union. By the beginning of 1982 the Reagan administration had stepped up pressure against Cuba, Nicaragua, and Grenada, and had become deeply involved with the daily administration of the Salvadoran government's war against the rebels. This government's "security forces" were killing civilians at such a rate, however, that even the overwhelmingly conservative Congress elected in 1980 was showing signs of reluctance to support the growing U.S. military commitment.

This was the situation that the March 1982 election in El Salvador was intended to alleviate. Its success is shown by the many times the election is now cited in justifying continued U.S. military assistance to El Salvador, and in the tenacity with which the United States has pushed El Salvador to have a second one. This chapter will examine the March 1982 election in its historical context, analyzing both its real purpose as a *demonstration* election and its complete failure to meet any of the fundamental conditions of a *democratic* election.

Roots of Revolution

The Reagan administration has shown little interest in the roots of El Salvador's civil war. Neither the long record of poverty and exploitation, nor the regular emergence and repression of popular movements in El Salvador are discussed in official U.S. analyses of the problems of the region. Indeed, one administration critic has pointed out that the "White Paper," issued in its first weeks by the Reagan regime and claiming that the guerillas were being armed and guided by the Soviet bloc, contained only one date prior to 1979.[2]

Despite the political convenience of such historical amnesia, however, the origin of El Salvador's civil war antedates both the Cuban and the Nicaraguan revolutions.

A fundamental fact of El Salvador's recent history is that a majority of its people have been desperately poor and continue to get poorer. Perhaps more than in any other Latin American country, wealth and poverty in El Salvador are tied to extreme inequalities in land ownership. In the course of the last century subsistence plots were taken over by large estates to grow commercial crops, at first cotton and more recently coffee. A growing proportion of this densely populated nation is landless: 11% of the rural population had no land in 1961, 40% in 1975, and over 60% in the early 1980s. Extreme pressure on the land was the major reason why some 300,000 Salvadorans had migrated to Honduras by the late 1960s. A study done in 1979 found that 0.85% of the land owners in El Salvador owned 77.8% of the land. Sixty percent of all Salvadorans earned an income inadequate to supply them with even a minimum diet. According to an USAID study done in 1977, 73% of the children suffered from malnutrition, while 50% of all deaths that year were of children under five.[3]

It would be astonishing if such wrenching poverty were accepted in silence. Indeed, more than a half century ago the stranglehold of the oligarchy—El Salvador's handful of major landowning families— on the land created widespread discontent. As coffee prices collapsed in the Great Depression, the burden of the crisis was borne primarily by the rural poor. A split in the oligarchy led to that country's first (and last) free election, in 1931, as a reform candidate built a popular alliance that swept him into office. Promises of reform polarized the nation, and, in response to growing demands from the peasantry for land reform, the army seized power.

Shortly after the military coup, Major A. R. Harris, U.S. attaché to Central America, visited El Salvador. "I imagine," he wrote, "the situation in El Salvador today is very much like France was before its revolution, Russia before its revolution and Mexico before its revolution. . . . A socialistic or communistic revolution in El Salvador may be delayed for several years, ten or even twenty, but when it comes it will be a bloody one."[4] Ten days later a mass insurrection began, led by the Communist party but in the main a spontaneous uprising. The rebellion itself was quickly crushed by the army. Then came the *matanza*—the massacre. Some 30,000 people, 2 percent of the population, were murdered, many after being tortured, by the government's security forces.

The *matanza* was a national trauma. For the next half century it loomed large in the thinking of both oppressor and oppressed n El Salvador. For the oligarchy it was the Red Nightmare, the uprising of the rabble who must never be given the opportunity for a second try. From the time of the *matanza* power was effectively—and willingly— shared with the army, which became, according to one Salvadoran historian, "the great elector...a type of political party permanently in arms."[5]

While the *matanza* haunted the memories of El Salvador's rulers, it also shaped the collective memory of the popular movement. "All of us were born half-dead in 1932," wrote Salvadoran poet Roque Dalton. "We survived but half-alive/Each one with an interest bearing account of 30,000/dead compounded daily."[6] As a popular movement reemerged in the 1960s and 1970s, however, it found once again that the channels of peaceful, legal reform were closed. To grasp more fully the hollowness of the call for "free elections" in 1982 it will be useful to trace briefly the forces which, in spite of the shadow of the *matanza*, drove a growing portion of the popular movement to abandon attempts to organize openly for political change and to join the growing guerilla movement in the countryside.

The Church. The traditional role of El Salvador's Catholic Church, as throughout Latin America, was symbolized by the union of the cross and the sword. The Church's departure from automatic support of the *status quo* in El Salvador awaited the influence of the Second Vatican Council (1962-65) and the Second Episcopal Conference in Medellín, Colombia (1968). Both meetings endorsed and legitimated the orientation of the Church and its priests towards the poor, and towards involvement in social change. In Latin America the process emerging out of Medellín became known as "liberation theology," and encouraged the Church and its religious workers to make a "preferential option for the poor." Priests supporting the new liberation theology were active in founding Christian Base Communities (CBCs), where in groups generally no larger than 20 or 30, members were encouraged to learn the new doctrines of the Church, read and interpret the Bible, and relate the messages of scripture and the Church to the conditions of their own lives. Because of the small number of priests in El Salvador, catechists (lay teachers) and "delegates of the Word" (lay preachers) were chosen from within the CBCs to carry on this work after initial instruction by a priest. Between 1970 and 1976 seven training centers for catechists and delegates were established in El Salvador; by 1980 they had trained 15,000 leaders.

In this way a popular, alternative social organization grew up alongside the formal institutions of the state.[7]

CBCs often provided the context for other, more clearly secular activity. The final statement of the Medellín Conference had maintained that while

> [The Christian] believes in the value of peace for the achievement of justice, he also believes that justice is a necessary condition for peace. And he is not unaware that in many places in Latin America there is a situation of injustice that must be recognized as institutionalized violence, because the existing structures violate people's basic rights: a situation which calls for farreaching, daring, urgent and profoundly innovating change.[8]

Priests were encouraged to *accompany* their people in their search for social justice. Initially this took the form of helping people achieve their basic needs, such as literacy or health. Often, too, CBCs became involved in activity to achieve higher wages or fairer rural class relations. Eight months after Father Rutilio Grande began his work in the town of Aguilares in 1972, for example, 1,600 workers at the La Cabana sugar mill struck for higher wages. These efforts were met by repression and violence, and religious workers were generally blamed by both government and employers for the activities of base community members. Church people were increasingly forced to choose how far they would accompany the poor in rising levels of confrontation. Some religious workers even began to study Marxism for its insights into the ideology and social system of capitalism, in line with liberation theology's critique of "structures of domination," and a few priests eventually joined the guerillas.

Worker and peasant organization. Even with the energizing and legitimizing role of the Church, autonomous organizations of the poor grew painfully slowly in the 1960s and early 1970s. By 1971, for example, there were only 40,000 labor union members out of a Salvadoran labor force of nearly one million. Union membership was splintered into some 100 small organizations, and agricultural trade unions were illegal. About half of the organized workers were in the 65 unions or guilds making up the General Confederation of Labor, which preached the harmony of interests of labor and capital.

Although agricultural unions were formally illegal, in 1965 church related organizations founded the Christian Peasants Federation (FECCAS), which was primarily concerned with issues of land distribution, wages, and working conditions. In 1968 the American

Institute for Free Labor Development (AIFLD) formed the Salvadoran Communal Union (UCS). Affiliated with the AFL-CIO, and with widely documented links to the CIA,[9] the AIFLD worked in collaboration with the Salvadoran government to sponsor coops and self-help projects in the countryside. Although the intention of the AIFLD was to channel peasant discontent into structures supportive of the government, it nevertheless aroused the ire of the oligarchy and was expelled from El Salvador in 1973.

Political parties. In the mid-1950s the first of a series of *official* political parties was established by the military and the oligarchy. Their goal was a multi-party state ruled by a succession of governments based on their own hegemonic party, modelled on the Institutional Revolutionary Party of Mexico. The Cuban Revolution of 1959 and the Kennedy administration's subsequent Alliance for Progress spurred the formation of *opposition* political parties. This development was not greeted with unqualified enthusiasm by the U.S. government, however. An illuminating story was told to a congressional investigating committee in 1976 by Dr. Fabio Castillo, a former President of the National University of El Salvador. When reformist military officers seized power in El Salvador in October 1960, Dr. Castillo was made a civilian member of the new junta. According to his account, among the primary goals of the junta was the "development of a free electoral and democratic process in which all existing political parties and those that were organizing themselves could take part." Shortly after the coup, according to Dr. Castillo, he was informed by the U.S. chargé d'affaires that "the Embassy did not agree with the holding of a free election and that he supposed we were not talking seriously. He added that the Embassy would agree on a 'free election' held with two candidates previously approved by them. Of course, I rejected that proposal." In late January 1961 the new junta was overthrown by a coup carried out by the traditional military forces. The ensuing conservative junta was quickly recognized by the Kennedy administration. Dr. Castillo testified that "the participation of U.S. diplomatic and military representatives [in the coup] was at that time evident and open."[10]

In response to the social and economic changes of the late 1950s and early 1960s, Christian Democratic parties were formed throughout Latin America. Christian Democracy promoted reforms, especially land reform, as an antidote to revolution, and thus posed a modest threat to the traditional elites. In El Salvador the Christian Democratic Party (PDC) was organized in response to the elections promised by the short-lived progressive junta of 1960-61. Their proclaimed intention was to base their party on the principles of social Christianity; and their leading political figure from the Party's founding, José Napoleón Duarte, made his mark as a populist mayor of San Salvador. Alone or in coalition with other parties, the Christian Democrats provided the main electoral opposition to the parties of the oligarchy and the military during the 1960s and 1970s.

The election of 1972. While every election after 1931 had been marked by fraud and corruption, the election of 1972 was particularly significant in foreclosing the electoral route to peaceful social change. In preparation for this election the three major reform parties—the Christian Democrats, the social democratic National Revolutionary Party (MNR), and the Communist Party's Nationalist Democratic Union (UDN)—formed the National Opposition Union (UNO, or "one" in Spanish). Despite the continuing hold of the military and the oligarchy on the official party (the PCN) and the machinery of state, the prospects for an UNO electoral victory were good. In the 1968 municipal elections the Christian Democrats had won the mayoralties of three major cities, including San Salvador, and 80 smaller towns. The Christian Democrats had also won 22 seats in the national legislature, while the MNR captured three more. The brief ("100 Hour") war with Honduras in 1969 had checked the momentum of El Salvador's economic growth, but by 1972 the nationalist euphoria briefly induced by the war had dissipated. In spite of some extraordinary efforts by the government's ballot box stuffers, it appeared momentarily that the UNO slate had won the February 22nd election when the Central Election Board in San Salvador issued a statement that UNO had prevailed by some 6,000 votes. The victory was short-lived, however, as a three-day news blackout was followed by a carefully revised set of figures giving victory once again to the PCN.

The particularly blatant fraud in the 1972 election precipitated an uprising by young military officers a month later. On the morning of March 25th, supporters of the coup seized the country's communications facilities and several military garrisons. According to the testimony of Dr. Castillo,

> [The coup] was supported by almost all the young officers because it at first sight promised a healthy and bloodless democratic change. The people's support was massive. Men and women of the smallest hamlets and those of the more elegant districts of the capital put on their Sunday's best.

People of various social strata stepped out in the streets to celebrate the triumph of a movement which, at least at the first sight, represented the overcoming of a repudiated and run down government.[11]

The U.S. Embassy immediately intervened, however, by calling in the armed forces of Guatemala and Nicaragua, and the uprising was quickly defeated. Unmarked planes bombed insurgent positions, while troops from "free" Nicaragua and Guatemala crossed El Salvador's borders. A U.S. Air Force jet whisked newly "elected" president, Colonel Arturo Molina, home from Taiwan where he had been travelling. According to Dr. Castillo,

A few days after the Constitutionalists' insurrection had been smashed, officers of that movement declared that they had been able to observe the participation of U.S. personnel using the U.S. Embassy's communications facilities for the purpose of coordinating the operations of the armies of Guatemala, Nicaragua and Honduras.... They further said that the planes had taken off from the Guatemalan bases and that they had failed on account of the foreign intervention. This opinion is accepted by the majority of the people in El Salvador.[12]

Killed immediately in the fighting were 200 civilians. Duarte, who belatedly supported the uprising and later sought asylum in the Venezuelan Embassy, was seized, tortured, and exiled to Guatemala. In July, two weeks after the inauguration of Colonel Molina, the National University was occupied by the armed forces. Eight hundred people were arrested, and 15 prominent educators, including Dr. Castillo, were chained together and flown into exile in Somoza's Nicaragua. The University remained closed for two years.[13]

The elections of 1972 marked a watershed in El Salvador's political history. By remaining neutral or actually supporting the March uprising, the United States would have permitted a constitutional restoration to take place, installing a reformist government led by the safely pro-American Christian Democratic Party and supported by the majority of El Salvador's people, including a significant segment of the armed forces. The parallel with the refusal to allow Bosch's return to the Dominican Republic in April 1965 is striking. By encouraging its rightist client states to intervene in order to preserve army-oligarchy control of El Salvador, the United States helped to eliminate the electoral path as a practical way to address the problems of poverty and inequality in El Salvador.

Civil War

In the decade following the fraudulent election of 1972, El Salvador became engulfed in a civil war. The ranks of the small guerilla bands formed in the early 1970s were swollen daily by new adherents: those fleeing the government-sponsored death squads, which murdered with impunity in the countryside; those incensed by the murder (frequently after torture) of a family member; and those convinced that their country could never be restored to political health by working within the discredited framework of the existing political institutions. The refusal of El Salvador's oligarchy, moreover, to consider meaningful measures of land reform condemned a growing proportion of the peasantry to starvation. Many believed they had little to lose by joining the struggle against the government.

At the beginning of the 1970s three small guerilla organizations were formed. The Popular Forces of Liberation (FPL) broke with the cautious electoral strategy of El Salvador's Communist Party in 1970. Consisting originally of teachers, students, and urban workers, in 1974 the FPL began to establish a base among the peasantry of Chalatenango province. In 1971 the urban student milieu gave birth to the People's Revolutionary Army (ERP), which stressed the importance of armed actions to incite popular rebellion. A schism within the ERP in 1975 led to the creation of the Armed Forces of National Resistance (FARN), which attempted to correct the perceived adventurism of the ERP and its inability to reach a mass base. The FARN reached toward the democratic center of El Salvador's political spectrum and gained adherents in the labor movement.

Each of the three guerilla organizations eventually established a structure consisting of an armed organization, an above-ground political party (except in the case of the FPL), and a mass organization comprised of a coalition of unions, popular organizations, and interest groups. Other mass organizations came into existence in the 1970s as escalating government slaughters of peasants, students, and other groups politically activated a long-submerged lower and middle class populace. As noted by Armstrong and Shenk, these organizations "channeled the cynicism generated by decades of electoral fraud into acts of civil disobedience, into massive rallies and protest demonstrations."[14] By 1980 the mass organizations were to become linked in the Democratic Revolutionary Front (FDR), while the guerilla groups were unified under the Farabundo Marti National Liberation Front (FMLN).

The election of 1977. The rise of the popular organizations paralleled a continuing elite refusal to allow a non-fraudulent election. In March 1974 UNO ran a full slate of candidates for the municipal and legislative elections, but this time the Central Election Board simply announced the victory of the official party, the PCN, without bothering to post the results. In 1976 the UNO coalition refused to participate in the local elections after some of their candidates were threatened by rightwing paramilitary groups, and after the electoral boards had disqualified more than two-thirds of their slates. Nevertheless, in the presidential elections of 1977 the UNO slate tried again. This election, however, turned out to be the most spectacular fraud of all. UNO officials intercepted military radio transmissions ordering ballot box stuffing, while UNO election officials were assaulted and evicted from polling areas. According to credible witnesses, in the 16 voting districts where a more or less honest count was made, the UNO slate won by a three-to-one margin. The Central Elections Council, however, announced that General Romero, the PCN candidate, was the winner by a three-to-one margin.[15]

Despite lame duck president Molina's warning that "any position supporting agitation or protest in response to the results of the Central Electoral Commission constitutes a flagrant violation of the sovereign will of the people freely expressed in the ballot box," a demonstration was called by UNO to protest this latest electoral fraud. More than 50,000 people came to San Salvador's Plaza Libertad. For several days peaceful demonstrations took place, while workers declared a general strike. Meanwhile, the security forces arrested more than 200 UNO officials, and on February 28 they opened fire on the demonstrators, killing nearly 100 of them. According to a U.S. government human rights report, "dozens of opposition party members, including the former vice presidential candidate, were allegedly forced to seek asylum or to go 'underground' for fear of their lives. Many are living as refugees at present; they are estimated to number in the dozens."[16]

The protests following the defeat of UNO unleashed a furious assault against all real and suspected opposition. Immediately after the election *La Cronica*, the only private newspaper not owned by a member of the oligarchy, was closed by the government. In May the presses of the Church's newspaper *Orientacion* were bombed, and the government threatened to close its radio station. Amnesty International (AI) reported that more than 70 peasant leaders disappeared or had been murdered between January and July, 1977. Perhaps the most dramatic focus of this repression was visited on the clergy, particularly the Jesuits. Between February 21 and May 14, 1977, two priests were assassinated, a dozen more were expelled from the country or refused reentry (charged by the government with subversion), and others were beaten and tortured. Following these actions by the government, a paramilitary organization called the White Warriors Union (UGB) issued "War Order No. 6," claiming that the Jesuits planned to "enslave" El Salvador to "International Communism," and gave them 30 days to leave the country.[17]

The White Warriors Union, led by Roberto D'Aubuisson, formerly head of intelligence of El Salvador's National Guard and now (late 1983) head of the rightwing ARENA party and president of the Constituent Assembly, was the creature of the powerful landowners association in eastern El Salvador.[18] It was but one of a half dozen clandestine "death squads," based largely in the security forces and the oligarchy. These repressive organizations fell into two general categories. Some, like the Anti-Communist Forces of Liberation (FALANGE), the Organization for the Liberation from Communism, the White Hand, and the Maximiliano Hernandez Brigade (after the General responsible for the *matanza* of 1932) were formed in the mid- and late-1970s. According to the congressional testimony of Captain Ricardo Alejandro Fiallos, formerly a doctor in a Salvadoran military hospital, the death squads "are made up of members of the security forces and acts of terrorism credited to these squads such as political assassinations, kidnappings, and indiscriminate murder are, in fact, planned by high-ranking military officers and carried out by members of the security forces."[19]

Quite different from the death squads, but no less terrifying or effective in crushing opposition, was ORDEN, a mass-based rural organization formed by the government in 1968 with the help of the CIA. It acted as an auxiliary to the security forces and as an unofficial arm of the government, sharing some of the characteristics of the mass fascist organizations of prewar Europe. Its primary function in the 1960s was to act as the government's eyes and ears in the countryside, while the security forces stayed garrisoned in the towns. After the 1972 elections, however, ORDEN undertook a more actively repressive role, and by the end of the 1970s it had some 10,000 men under arms, with a total membership of 50,000 to 100,000. Of course, membership in ORDEN might mean many things: a means of survival; a source of petty favors and privileges (schools, credit, preference in land reform decisions) in exchange for identifying subversives; or the power to dominate one's neighbors and settle personal scores by violence without the danger of arrest and prosecution. Whatever the motives of its members, the growth of ORDEN made it more difficult for even mildly reformist organizations to survive in rural areas.

Though ORDEN was supposedly dissolved in 1979, it was never disarmed, and was apparently reorganized as the National Democratic Front, a constituent of D'Aubuisson's rightwing coalition, the National Broad Front.[20]

In brief, the 1977 presidential election and its immediate aftermath marked a bloody ending to El Salvador's 15-year experiment in electoral democracy. Though this experiment facilitated the growth of popular organizations, at no time were either the security forces or the oligarchy willing to abide by even the most elementary rules of bourgeois democracy. After the 1977 fiasco only the most naive or uninformed observers could expect that the desperately needed social changes in El Salvador could come about through the ballot box. Thus, when Ambassador Kirkpatrick or Secretary of State Shultz pontificate on the flagrant injustice of "armed minorities" attempting to "shoot their way into political power," they are accurately describing not the guerillas, but those who governed El Salvador for 50 years in violation of all democratic norms, and whose heirs, now in power, are supported by the United States government.

The October Coup

On October 15, 1979 the regime of General Carlos Humberto Romero was overthrown by members of the armed forces. The leaders of the coup were primarily younger officers, who announced as their aims, first, to "lay the bases and create the appropriate environment for a true and dynamic democracy; and second, conduct free elections which will reflect the will of all Salvadorans."[21] Beyond this simple statement, however, the coup leaders displayed little in the way of a political program. Nor were they willing to challenge the command structure of the army itself, believing that a united army could enforce the will of a majority caught between the violence of the extreme right and the extreme left.

On the surface, the Revolutionary Junta seemed to promise satisfaction for many of the grievances of El Salvador's opposition. Civilian members outnumbered those from the military; the cabinet represented a broad spectrum of the political center; and the junta promised a land reform program and free elections. Yet while one hand of the junta reached out in friendship toward the popular movements, the other became a fist of repression. According to one of the young officers participating in the coup, the U.S. Embassy strongly urged them to bring Colonels José Guillermo Garcia and Jaime Abdul Gutiérrez into the government. Gutiérrez was in fact selected as the second military member of the junta, representing the unreconstructed old guard military—and the United States. (Colonel Majano, the other military member of the junta, was one of the reformist officers.) Gutiérrez immediately appointed Garcia Minister of Defense. Without consulting the civilian members of the junta, Garcia and Gutiérrez then installed other hard-line officers as heads of the National Guard and the National Police, immediately tipping the balance of military power away from those supporting reforms. Moreover, the members of the High Command—the leaders of the various branches of the security forces—rejected the junta's claims that the armed forces should be controlled by civilians. The composition of the young officers organization, the Permanent Council of the Armed Forces, also shifted in favor of Garcia. One young officer told a reporter that "80% of its membership changed, all of them loyal to Garcia."[22]

Thus, virtually simultaneously with the formation of the new junta, a countercoup took place that assured hard-line military control of the security forces. While it was not apparent at the time, the "progressive coup" was immediately aborted. This was manifested in the flight abroad of five of the progressive officers within a few months of the coup. It was more brutally displayed in the fact that the civilian death toll in the first two weeks after the coup exceeded that of the first nine months of the deposed Romero dictatorship. In fact, on the day after the coup, the security forces attacked factories that had been occupied for weeks by members of the People's Revolutionary Bloc. Eighteen were killed, and others were arrested and tortured. A suburb of San Salvador held by the People's Revolutionary Army was attacked the next day with tanks and helicopters, killing 24. According to AI, the "security forces acted with the same brutality as those under Romero.... Within a week, the new government was held responsible for more than 100 killings of demonstrators and striking workers who had been occupying farms and factories."[23]

The events of its first week in power anticipated the entire history of the Revolutionary Junta. In the government's front office sat the alleged "center," a shifting collection of politicians that supposedly marked the accession to power of a progressive, civilian coalition, attempting to steer a course between the terrorists of the right and the left. But in reality power lay behind the scenes, with the security forces, their paramilitary auxiliaries, and increasingly the United States. As AI pointed out at the end of February, 1980: "Since December 1979, summary executions, arrests and disappearances in the countryside have been carried out on a large scale by uniformed security forces—the National Guard, Hacienda Guard and local Army detachments—working closely and openly with local personnel of the paramilitary organization ORDEN.... "[24] In mid-December, for example, 35 people were killed when the security forces used tanks and helicopters to break a strike. At the end of December, the security forces and ORDEN launched a wave of attacks in the coffee-growing areas of Chalatenango, San Salvador, and Morazan provinces where FECCAS and the Union of Rural Workers (UTC) were strong. And on January 22—the 48th anniversary of the *matanza*—a march of more than 80,000 people celebrating the formation of the Revolutionary Coordinating Council of the Masses (CRM) was fired on by security forces, killing 67 and leaving 250 wounded. In a March 1980 report, AI noted that it had under investigation 102 cases of people detained and killed in rural areas in January, 248 cases for February, and 130 cases for the first week of March alone, as well as many cases from the towns and cities.[25] The wide-ranging character and great scope of the terror carried out by the security forces in the early months of the rule of the "progressive" Junta is dramatically illustrated in Table 4-1, put out by the Legal Aid Office of the Archdiocese of El Salvador in October 1980. In this breakdown by type of action and target, 1,186 "repressive actions" are attributed to the security forces through the first seven months of 1980.

The slaughter quickly alienated civilian members of the Revolutionary Junta, but their protests were rebuffed by the High Command. The first defections from the government came at the end of December. A week later two of the three civilian members of the junta resigned, along with nine cabinet ministers and 37 other government officials. Their place in the front office was taken by leaders of the PDC, which hoped its support would allow the implementation of their program of land reform and bank nationalization. But soon the Christian Democrats were also swept up in the slaughter. In February D'Aubuisson went on television—obviously with government approval—and read a list of the names of politicians, priests, and professionals whom he described as "subversives." One of those he named was a Christian Democrat government official, who was assassinated in his home within days. The PDC then split over continued participation in the junta, with the Popular Faction, comprising 20% of its membership, leaving the Party. The illusion of civilian hegemony and the continuing presence of a democratic center was preserved, however, by José Napoleón Duarte's entry into the

Table 4-1: Repressive Actions[1] and Targets[2] by National Army, Military Security Corps, and Paramilitary Groups by Month: January through July 1980

Actions/Targets	Jan	Feb	Mar	Ap/May	Jun	Jul	Total
Army/Military Corps invasions of peasant areas	81	59	74	60	85	78	**437**
Army/Military Corps operations in urban shanty towns	17	13	25	31	23	11	**120**
Army searches/raids of union or student sites, democratic institutions, Church/Archdiocesan offices	5	6	29	15	21	14	**90**
Machine-gun/dynamite attacks on union/student sites, democratic institutions, Church/Archdiocesan offices	23	34	19	29	17	11	**133**
Army raids which destroy/burn peasant houses	35	21	17	45	140	148	**406**
Totals	**161**	**133**	**164**	**180**	**286**	**262**	**1186**

1. Repressive actions constitute invasions, operations, searches, raids, dynamiting, machine-gunning, acts of sabotage, destruction and burning of houses or other property.

2. Targets are peasant communities; union buildings; educational institutions; Church and Archdiocesan buildings; democratic, private or official institutions.

Source: Legal Aid Office, Archdiocese of San Salvador, El Salvador, Central America, October 1, 1980.

junta on behalf of the PDC majority. No other party would participate in the new junta.

The centerpiece of the junta's reform program was its U.S.-designed land reform program. Its architect was Roy Prosterman, a professor at Washington University who had designed a similar program in Vietnam during the Indochina War. Prosterman's program included three different phases of land reform. Phase I, which was to be implemented immediately, would turn over (after compensation) all estates of 1,235 acres or more to peasant cooperative associations, which would manage them under the supervision of the government's Agrarian Reform Institute (ISTA). This phase was partially crippled by the landowners, who removed an estimated 25-40% of the nation's farm machinery, slaughtered 30% of the cattle, and used political pressure and bribery to limit implementation of the reforms. Phase II was to expropriate all the medium-sized estates. As this would have particularly affected the powerful coffee-growing interests, it was never implemented. Phase III, the "land-to-the-tiller" program, was supposed to give peasants title to the small plots they rented each year. In fact, the program was designed hastily and entirely by North Americans who had little knowledge of conditions in El Salvador. According to an AID memo, "it is widely believed that 'land-to-the-tiller' is a political move on the part of the US Embassy and the State Department. Many believe it is a 'symbolic' and 'cosmetic' measure. . . . " Perhaps not surprisingly, the program, if implemented, would have had its greatest impact in areas where the guerillas were strongest. Phase III was also subject to endless complications and delays; although possession was supposed to be automatic, few titles had been transferred by the summer of 1983, and many beneficiaries have had land forcibly repossessed by their landlords. The program offered no benefits to the more than 60% of the rural population that was completely landless.[26]

In Vietnam, Prosterman's land reform program had been implemented at the same time as Operation Phoenix, the police terrorist program in which more than 40,000 civilians living mainly in rural areas were killed between 1968 and 1972. In El Salvador the land reform program was once again accompanied by extreme repression. Jorge Villacorta, an official at the Ministry of Agriculture, resigned two weeks after the commencement of the program. In his letter of resignation he stated: "In reality, from the first moment that the implementation of agrarian reform began, what we saw was a sharp increase in official violence against the very peasants who were the supposed 'beneficiaries' of the process."[27] The land reform program was accompanied by a legal state of siege, supposedly to allow the security forces to aid the land reform program, presumably by countering any landlord resistance. In fact, according to an AI report submitted to the Organization of American States just two weeks after the beginning of the land reform program:

> Initial eye-witness reports since the 9 March decree instituting an agrarian reform, and establishing a state of siege, affirm that troop movements by Army and National Guard units that were announced as measures for the implementation of the land reform have in fact involved the disappear-

ance and killings of hundreds of *campesinos* in villages supporting opposition labor organizations in Morazan, Cuscatlan, Chalatenango and San Salvador departments. Reports say that Army, National Guard and ORDEN forces virtually wiped out several hamlets in Cuscatlan on 13 March, killing four persons outright, and detaining and causing to "disappear" 30 others. By 16 March reports obtained from the estimated 600 *campesinos* that have fled Cuscatlan to seek refuge in San Salvador say that at least 80 *campesinos* have been detained and killed in Cuscatlan since the land reform was decreed, including 28 children.... There appears to be no doubt whatsoever that members of the major *campesino* groupings, all of them affiliates of oppositionist political coalitions, are being systematically persecuted in areas to be affected by the agrarian reform....[28]

According to the Catholic Church's Legal Aid Office, the reign of terror escalated further after the officer corps voted to give Gutiérrez sole command of the country's armed forces on May 10. Gutiérrez had previously shared this command with Colonel Majano, the more progressive of the military members of the Revolutionary Junta. Observers connected Majano's demotion with his arrest of Roberto D'Aubuisson (in early May), when troops loyal to Majano caught D'Aubuisson with documents linking him to plans for a coup. Eight of the 14 garrisons in El Salvador demanded D'Aubuisson's release, and Majano was forced to back down. After Majano's subsequent demotion, the Church Legal Aid Office recorded 2,500 killings in the next 50 days:

In qualitative terms, the reign of terror would appear to be the most distinctive characteristic of this period. The cruelty of the tortures practised against the victims of the repression had no precedent in the previous stages. The corpses appeared scalped, beheaded, with throats cut and dismembered. The heads of the decapitated began to appear hung from trees or impaled on fences. In addition to the paramilitary-based repression, large-scale military operations were mounted in the north and central-east regions of the country. Massacres included that of women and children fleeing from the country to seek refuge in Honduras. In the towns members of the teaching profession and students, health employees and the Church were the victims of repression without mercy at the hands of the armed forces. Educational centers were constantly searched; the two principal universities were victim to repeated armed intervention; convents, Catholic schools and health centres were constantly checked. In the month of May alone, twenty-one teachers were assassinated.[29]

Insofar as any peasants benefitted from the land reform, they often did so at the expense of disfavored sectors of the peasantry, whose lands were seized and transferred to others. AI noted in its report for 1980 that "villages supporting opposition peasant unions, such as the Christian Federation of Salvadorean Peasants [FECCAS] and the Union of Rural Workers [UTC] were attacked by troops, and the land seized was handed over to members of government organizations, including the Salvadorean Communal Union [UCS] and ORDEN." But even active collaboration with the government did not ensure one's safety in the countryside. Testifying before a subcommittee of the U.S. House of Representatives, AIFLD head William Doherty presented a chart showing the "responsibility for 184 violent deaths of agrarian reform beneficiaries and personnel on 23 farms" between March and October, 1980. Not one of these murders of people nominally under the protection of the AIFLD's UCS was at the hands of a guerilla or a member of the popular organizations.[30]

The repression associated with peasant-landlord conflict under Phase I escalated during the first year of the Reagan administration. In a report issued on December 10, 1981 by the Salvadoran Communal Union and addressed to President Duarte, it was declared that the "failure of the agrarian reform process is an immediate and imminent danger." The report said that:

—"at least 90 officials" and a "large number of beneficiaries" of the reform "have died during 1981 at the hands of the ex-landlords and their allies, who are often members of the local security forces";

—more than 25,000 sharecroppers or tenants had been forcibly evicted from their farms, "in the majority of cases with the assistance of members of the military forces";

—15,000 families eligible for individual ownership had gotten provisional title to land, but none had received permanent ownership; and

—of more than 300 peasant cooperatives formed on large estates, only two had received title to the land.[31]

While land reform was the vehicle by which the junta (and United States) tried to shift the balance of power in the countryside away from the popular organizations, no such carrot was offered in the cities. Only the stick—the state of siege—was applied to residents of towns and cities. Once again repression was targeted on the popular organizations and other centers of resistance like the universities. The Church's Legal Aid Office noted that "the vast majority of the workers assassinated were either trade union leaders or trade union members."[32] Between January and October, 1980, for example, at least 90 teachers were killed, almost all of them active in ANDES, the teacher's union, which was an important force within the popular organizations. At least 19 primary and secondary schools were raided by security forces; and on July 26, 1980 the army carried out a military occupation of the National University, in which 22 students were killed. "As a result of this persecution," noted AI in a report issued in late October, "numerous teachers have gone into exile and 85 percent of schools in the [east] of the country (departments of La Union, San Miguel and Usulutan) have reportedly been closed." In all, AI estimated that more than 8,000 people, including 3,300 peasants, died in political violence in 1980, almost all at the hands of the security forces, ORDEN, or the death squads. Other estimates ran to 13,000 deaths for 1980. In his Sunday homily of January 3, 1982, Salvadoran Apostolic Administrator Arturo Rivera y Damas estimated that 30,000 civilians had been killed and 600,000 made refugees—13% of the population of El Salvador.[33]

The immediate consequence of this repression was to greatly lessen the possibility that some moderate center might gain power in El Salvador. The process was in fact the reverse: independent organizations were increasingly unable to operate openly. The University was occupied by the security forces; opposition peasant associations, trade unions, and other organizations found their headquarters destroyed and their cadre attacked and frequently killed; and demonstrations and other public political activity became a high-risk business. During the latter part of 1980 the labor movement was severely weakened by a wave of arrests. In November, six leaders of the FDR were kidnapped, tortured, and killed, their mutilated bodies found later. Even Archbishop Romero, whose sermons, articles, and radio broadcasts had done much to inform and protect the popular organizations, was assassinated on March 24, 1980 while saying Mass. Documents found on D'Aubuisson at the time of his arrest in April strongly implicated him and his organization in the killing.[34] The repression unleashed by the security forces and the death squads following the coup of 1979 shifted the balance of power in the opposition from the popular movements to the guerilla forces. The opposition began to withdraw from the cities and towns into the protection of liberated zones in the remoter countryside. The ground was being cleared for a "free election."

The U.S. Takeover of the War

The October 1979 coup erected a facade of civilian rule, but effective power was retained by the military. The ability of the security forces to rule El Salvador soon became linked with their ability to obtain military and economic aid from the United States. Conversely, while the influence of the United States in El Salvador grew behind the onrush of dollars, soon only the security forces had sufficient power to enforce the wishes of the U.S. government. Military aid built up the power of the security forces, while diminishing that of the civilians in the junta. Thus the United States and the Salvadoran Army became dependent on one another to maintain their respective positions on the scene; and U.S. criticism of the junta became increasingly muted throughout 1980 and virtually disappeared under Reagan.

There is today a tendency to read back into the transition from the Carter to the Reagan eras a sharp change in U.S. policy towards El Salvador. In reality, the U.S.-sponsored counterinsurgency program so apparent under the Reagan regime was initiated within days of the coup by the Carter administration. And a goal of both administrations has been to enlist the repressive military forces of the other Central American dictatorships to prop up the falling domino of El Salvador. The October 1979 coup had presented the Carter administration with an opportunity to resume an active role toward El Salvador without the embarrassment of the Romero regime. The United States initially endorsed the coup, but by pressing the claims of Garcia and Gutiérrez, as noted earlier, it helped shift the balance of power within the junta and bureaucracy toward army rule. It also gave little encouragement to the reforms announced by the junta. In fact, the only aid sent to El Salvador in the wake of the coup was $205,000 worth of riot equipment and a six-man training team to advise the army on its use. A special training course for Salvadoran troops called "The Human Rights Aspects of Internal Defense and Development" was established at the U.S. School of the Americas in the Canal Zone. The bias toward military rule and interventionary solutions by violence was thus modified only by an exceptional input of hypocrisy.[35]

The goal of the Carter administration was "clean counterinsurgency." According to Hector Dada, a founder of the Christian Democratic Party in El Salvador and briefly a member of the junta, in early February 1980 James Cheek, the interim U.S. Ambassador, arrived to outline the plan of the Carter administration. Civilian representation in the junta must be maintained: the military officers and the right, said Cheek, were not to stage a coup. He proposed instead that El Salvador accept 36 U.S. military advisers and carry out a program of reforms. "Not," according to Dada, "as a part of a program of socio-economic development, . . . but rather, reforms like those carried out in Vietnam, according to a plan used by the military to control the population. And to do this, we had to accept all this: a war directed by North Americans."[36] In spite of Dada's opposition, the "clean counterinsurgency" program was put into operation. It produced, as described in the previous section, a land reform program and the slaughter which accompanied it. On March 3, as the program was about to begin, the State Department forwarded to Congress a proposal for $5.7 million in so-called "nonlethal" aid to help implement it, including cargo trucks, jeeps, communications and riot control equipment, and night vision devices and image intensifiers for locating the enemy. Pentagon officials told Congress the equipment "would help strengthen the Army's key role in reforms," and give the U.S. government "leverage"* to demand reforms and an end to "human rights abuses." As Congress considered the request, the reign of terror in El Salvador mounted; and in the days following Archbishop Romero's assassination, a supine Congress voted to support the administration's request for military aid.

The military buildup in the final days of the Carter administration helped to provide a graceful transition to the apparently more aggressive strategies of the Reagan administration. Many other elements of the Reagan policies toward El Salvador also had been anticipated under Carter: the revival of the domino theory; the projected illusion of a "democratic center" caught between two violent extremes; the myth that counterinsurgency would ever be "clean"; and an essentially military perspective on the requirements for acceptable solutions. One thing that changed with the advent of the Reagan team was the jettisoning of the encumbering concern about human rights violations, to be replaced, as Secretary of State Alexander Haig announced at his first press conference, by a focus on "international terrorism" directed from the Soviet Union.

Another change from Carter was the warmer relations of the

Reagan team and its supporters in the U.S. political elite with the "death-squad" right in El Salvador. In April 1980, for example, D'Aubuisson visited the United States on a trip hosted by the American Security Council and the American Legion. In June, *after* his latest coup conspiracy had been foiled by forces loyal to Colonel Majano, and *after* his complicity in the murder of Archbishop Romero was known by Ambassador White and forwarded to the State Department, D'Aubuisson again visited the United States, where a press conference was held by the American Security Council and meetings were arranged with conservative members of Congress. Keeping in mind the fact that his coup attempt had been intended to displace a savagely repressive army rule with one even more brutal, it is noteworthy that a list of people who were expected to be sympathetic to the coup, which was taken from him when he was arrested, included the names of Senators Strom Thurmond, Richard Stone, Harry Byrd, and S. I. Hayakawa.[37]

The greater acceptability of the extreme right in El Salvador to the Reagan team flowed, in part, from ideological sympathy, but it also rested on the administration's lesser need for a "reformist" and "center" moral crutch on which to ground its policies. The liberal administration of Carter had difficulty in openly supporting the army and death squads, and had to pretend—maybe really believe—that Duarte was the nucleus of a center that could be rehabilitated with real power. What made this especially pathetic was that the Carter administration's de facto support of the military faction and counter-insurgency, and its identification of "reform" with a land redistribution imposed from above by the army, quickly polarized the situation, helped escalate the violence, and ended definitively the role of any Salvadoran center. The Reagan team recognized that Duarte was a figurehead and that it could ignore the mythical center. During the presidential election campaign some of Reagan's advisers wrote that "the center in El Salvador has disappeared, and the current junta is supported more by the U.S. Embassy than by anyone else."[38] Nevertheless, the Reagan administration also preferred a Duarte in office as a continuing symbol of "reformism" and the "center," largely for domestic and international demonstration purposes. Venezuela and the European Christian Democratic parties continued their support for Duarte's allegedly "Christian Democratic" regime in El Salvador, and their backing was useful to the administration.

A special characteristic of the Reagan administration was its intensive PR campaign alleging decisive Nicaraguan, Cuban, and Soviet roles in El Salvador's civil war. This was possibly a cynical ploy to help carry through a large "commitment" to defend "freedom," just as Johnson's decision to bomb North Vietnam required invoking the Chinese conspiracy operating through the "proxy" of North Vietnam (in turn operating through the proxy NLF). Large resource outlays require large threats. Shortly after the inauguration Secretary of State Alexander Haig told a group of NATO ministers that "we consider what is happening [in El Salvador] is part of the global Communist campaign coordinated by Havana and Moscow to support the Marxist insurgency."[39] In support of these claims, and to gain domestic and international support for their stepped-up military aid to El Salvador's Junta, the Reagan administration concocted a "White Paper" allegedly showing Soviet aid and direction to El Salvador's guerillas. These public relations efforts had little success in Europe, but the White Paper was useful at home and was initially accepted by all the major media as true. When the fabrications and distortions in the White Paper became evident in early June, the State Department was forced to fall back to the position that the claims of Soviet influence were actually based on further, still-secret sources.

By the beginning of 1982 the direction of the antiguerilla struggle in El Salvador had become a major preoccupation of the Reagan administration, which had passed through the stage of "assisting" and was now directing, arming, and financing the war for the government of El Salvador. U.S. political, economic, and military policies and supplies bore a heavy responsibility for the mounting civilian death toll; and all the evidence contradicted the claim that the U.S. role had any moderating effect on the human rights abuses of the security forces and the death squads. According to Church sources the civilian death toll in El Salvador at the end of 1981 was about 1,000 murders a month. Far from being extraneous abuses, these murders were the direct result of the U.S. strategy and weaponry. And just as the land reform program and other PR gambits were essentially window dressing for counterinsurgency, so was the demonstration election of March 1982.

The March 1982 Election

The escalating slaughter in El Salvador quickly aroused opposition within the United States. After the murders of the four Catholic women in December 1980, the Roman Catholic Church became particularly active in opposing and publicizing the U.S. role in El Salvador. Many others joined in demonstrating against the war, and congressional mail ran 20 to one against U.S. involvement in El

Salvador. The Vietnam syndrome was far from dead; and by February 1982 a *Newsweek* Gallup poll reported that 89% of those surveyed opposed the use of U.S. troops in El Salvador, while a Roper poll in the same month showed a majority against even increased economic aid.[40]

Responding to the rising public concern about the situation in El Salvador, as well as the apparent willingness of the Reagan administration to send troops to El Salvador and/or involve the United States in a regional war, Congress attempted to restrict the U.S. role in the region. Language was attached to the foreign aid legislation for fiscal year 1982 requiring that the administration certify that El Salvador was taking adequate steps to end human rights abuses and promote reforms as a condition for receiving U.S. economic and military aid.

To head off the threat that Congress, responding to public opinion, would curtail military aid to El Salvador, the Reagan administration organized a PR campaign to assure Congress and the public that our course in El Salvador was both prudent and necessary. The White Paper and other efforts to frame the region's conflicts within the New Cold War were energetically pursued. But the most important PR device to keep the aid pipeline flowing was the promise of a "free election." As in Vietnam and the Dominican Republic, an election would reassure the American people that the killing in El Salvador was on behalf of a greater good, and show also that opponents of the government were opponents of "democracy." The guerillas could be counted on to refuse to participate in the election under the conditions proposed by the United States and its client. The mass media would surely provide intensive coverage of the spectacle and present it in the dramatic format fixed by the government to maximize its propaganda value.

The 1982 Salvadoran election differed in some details from those held in the Dominican Republic and Vietnam. First, there was no "opposition" contesting the election. In contrast with the Dominican election, where Bosch was able to run, in El Salvador only the prowar parties could field candidates. The FDR was excluded by law, threat of death, and the intention of the election sponsors. The Salvadoran election was closer to that in Vietnam, where the NLF and all major peace candidates (Minh and Thanh) were off the ballot. Yet even in Vietnam there were ten civilian candidates who, although unable to win in that staged election, at least offered a slightly wider range of options than were available in El Salvador. A second feature of the Salvadoran election was that there was no official candidate or single U.S.-sponsored instrument, roles filled by Balaguer in the

Dominican Republic and by the Thieu-Ky ticket in Vietnam. True, many commentators thought that it was the U.S. interest and hope that Duarte and the Christian Democrats would win; and in late 1981 it was generally assumed in the United States that he had the best chance, in part because he was a familiar figure in the U.S. media. But the National Conciliation Party, or PCN, had long been the traditional governing party of El Salvador; and its close ties to both the Army and ORDEN, and thus to U.S. interests, made it an important and acceptable contender. Most clearly identified with a strategy of violence was the ARENA party, formed for the purposes of the election in late 1981. Its leader was Roberto D'Aubuisson, whose reputation as a torturer when serving as chief of security for the National Guard had given him the nickname "Blowtorch Bob." D'Aubuisson's involvement in many of the death-squad murders, including that of Archbishop Romero, had led former ambassador Robert White to describe him as a "pathological killer"; and even the Reagan administration viewed him as unreliable, and something of a loose cannon, although not beyond the pale of acceptability. D'Aubuisson may have been a fanatic and a killer, but by 1982 he represented a substantial fraction of the oligarchy. The elite members represented by D'Aubuisson were referred to by Ambassador Deane Hinton as a "Mafia of gorillas," and they constituted the core of the forces that had fought democracy in El Salvador for many decades. But democracy was not a real aim of the United States in El Salvador. Thus, each of the major parties contesting the March 1982 election was prepared to advance the U.S. military strategy in El Salvador, with differences in emphasis on secondary matters. The United States did not *need* an official candidate because there was no one running in this free election with goals seriously disturbing to the election sponsor.

The Salvadoran election of 1982 is a case study in the transformation of an instrument of democratic self-rule into its opposite. Elections were placed on the agenda by the leaders of the October 1979 coup, but the good intentions of the junior officers had been rapidly swept away as real power was seized by the senior military officers behind a facade of civilian rule. In March 1981, the same month in which the armed forces published a list of "traitors" responsible for the country's woes—essentially a death list—the junta announced its intention to hold elections in March 1982. There ensued an increase in violence under a state of siege, with many thousands of civilian murders and the emergence of a society whose most revealing feature was the daily search for and removal of mutilated bodies. This "background" was the basis for the refusal by the Salvadoran Bar Association to participate in the planning for the election, citing, among other grounds, "the state of siege and martial law [that] continue in effect," and "the generalized climate of violence that dominates El Salvador."[41] The legal framework for the elections was clearly intended to exclude the left from participation, though it may have been hoped that "moderate" political forces could be enticed away from their alliance with the opposition. The clearest exclusionary tactic was the Provisional Law for the Formation and Registration of Political Parties, which required a new party to submit the names and addresses of at least 3,000 of its members—in the context, a convenient death list. Four parties—the PCN, the PDC, the MNR, and the UDN—were exempted from this requirement, and were automatically registered. Both the MNR and the UDN were members of the FDR; they viewed their inclusion in the list as an attempt to split the FDR, and rejected recognition and thus participation in the election.

The left's rejection of the offer to participate in the March 1982 election framed a debate and a propaganda instrument which continues to be useful to the U.S. government to this day. The Reagan administration has successfully demobilized congressional liberals and other critics of its El Salvador policy by pointing not only to a "freely elected" government in El Salvador, but also to the fact that the guerillas refused to participate in the election. Even a superficial reading of the Salvadoran left's position, however, shows that the guerillas have not rejected free elections, but rather reject the proposition that elections carried out under the army's reign of terror can be called free. In an FMLN-FDR statement presented to the United Nations on October 7, 1981, the Salvadoran opposition outlined their proposals for negotiations and the role of elections in this process. They stated that "elections will be an important element as a mechanism of popular participation and representation," and that they "consider elections a valid and necessary instrument of expression of the people's will whenever conditions and atmosphere exist that allow the people to freely express their will." In rejecting the junta's invitation to participate in the March elections, the FMLN-FDR stated that "in El Salvador today we do not have such conditions to carry out the electoral process, inasmuch as the regime's repressive apparatus, which assassinates political and labor leaders and activists, remains untouched...."[42] Thus the FMLN-FDR conceived of elections in the context of broader negotiations, while the Reagan administration and its clients viewed elections as an *alterna-*

tive to negotiations, and would agree to negotiate only about the time, place, and manner by which the FMLN-FDR would be included in the election process. Broader negotiations were rejected out of hand as "allowing the guerillas to shoot their way into power" (Secretary of State George Shultz), or as "power sharing," allowing them to "gain at the bargaining table what they haven't been able to win on the battlefield."

These two Reagan versions are contradictory but revealing. "Power sharing" based on political strength without regard to military force is what democracy is supposed to be all about. Rejecting it because the guerillas haven't been able to win power on the battlefield is an appeal to the right of military force. But if the guerillas use force, they are trying to "shoot their way into power"! As we saw earlier, the Salvadoran elite never allowed "power sharing" by democratic rule, but shot large numbers of people to *maintain* power. The United States never questioned this; in fact, it supported the elite at critical junctures, as we have shown. Having watched and encouraged a process that drove the population into revolt, we chide it for trying to "shoot its way into power." Now, having pacified the population for several years, and helped erect a system of terror without equal in Latin America, we are ready for "free elections."

Basic Electoral Conditions in March 1982

What are we to make of a "free election" in which the Central Election Commission invited the FDR to participate, while conceding that it would have to campaign from outside the country, by radio and television?[43] As in the Dominican Republic and Vietnam, the basic conditions in El Salvador that determine the viability of an election *beforehand* had been so affected by the army, death squads, and the U.S.-supported reign of terror that the election was meaningless as an exercise in self-government or self-determination. The focus of both the mass media and many critics of the Salvadoran election on the issue of the "fairness" of the election's mechanics— balloting, counting, etc.—missed the point. The most important influence on the quality of the election was the effect of pacification on the institutional arrangements, laws, and practice that defined basic electoral conditions. While we have discussed many elements in this argument already, let us review and, where possible, quantify them.

1. **Erosion of the rule of law.** Following the October 1979 coup, political life in El Salvador was conducted within a steadily narrowing circle of permitted activity. Decree No. 114 on February 8, 1980

subordinated the Constitution to proclamations of the Armed Forces. Decree No. 115, dated March 6, 1980, declared the country under a state of siege. This suspended the guaranteed freedoms of movement, residence, thought, and assembly for 30 days, and gave military courts jurisdiction over a wide range of political offenses. The state of siege was renewed monthly with two exceptions. It was lifted in early 1982 solely for the six parties contesting the election, an act for which there was no provision in the Constitution; and it was lifted entirely on March 20, 1982, though unfortunately the citizens of El Salvador were not informed that their freedoms had been restored until after the election, at which time the state of siege was reimposed. Thus the rights of speech and assembly have been allowed in El Salvador only briefly, and then only for the conservative and rightwing parties who supported the war against the guerillas. Finally, Decree No. 507 of December 3, 1980 essentially destroyed the judicial system, permitting the military forces to hold citizens without charges for 180 days, and effectively eliminated standards of evidence.[44]

   2. Freedom of the press. Genuinely free elections are not possible if political organizations cannot communicate their programs to the citizenry. This condition was not met in El Salvador. According to the Legal Aid Office, "between January 1980 and September 1981 17 news offices and radio stations were bombed or machine-gunned, 12 journalists killed outside of combat situations, and three journalists 'disappeared'."[45] In the period between the coup of October 1979 and the March 1982 election, 26 journalists were murdered in El Salvador.

   The only two Salvadoran newspapers critical of the government, *La Cronica del Pueblo* and *El Independiente*, were closed in July 1980 and January 1981 respectively. Under the legal dictatorship noted above, all remaining newspapers were subject to censorship, even though all were progovernment in orientation to begin with. The Committee to Protect Journalists, a private group based in New York, has documented 179 "incidents of threats against, attacks on, censorship and murders of Salvadoran and foreign media and reporters between January 1980 and March 1982."[46] On March 10, 1982— two weeks before the election—a death list of 35 Salvadoran and foreign journalists appeared signed by the General Maximiliano Hernandez Martinez Brigade. It read: "This is the first list of pseudo-journalists at the service of the international press who have been condemned to death by the patriots of our organization. We are investigating others who come and go to find out to whom they are of service." According to the Committee to Protect Journalists, the goals of these attacks on the media were "to inhibit news coverage and to punish journalists for what they write, photograph or broadcast. Those responsible appear to operate without fear of government arrest or sanction." Despite protests by journalists, the Salvadoran government has completed no known investigation of any "facts of terrorism against the press." In addition to this effective domination of the nation's print media, the Salvadoran government also controlled all radio transmissions. The National Telecommunications Administration (ANTEL), which has authority over Salvadoran radio stations and telephone lines, was placed under military control in August 1980.[47]

3. The decline of independent organizational activity. Both the legal right of assembly and the ability to organize a trade union or any other association in El Salvador were quickly eliminated after the October 1979 coup. Decree 507 prohibits collective bargaining or the right to strike, and between August 1980 and the March 1982 election not a single strike occurred in El Salvador. In December 1981 the Salvadoran Communal Union reported that 83 of its "promoters" and members had been murdered by the security forces and death squads in 1980 and 1981. Shortly after the beginning of the land reform program and the proclamation of the state of siege in March 1980, AI declared that "there appears to be no doubt whatsoever that members of the major *campesino* groupings, all of them affiliates of oppositionist political coalitions, are being systematically persecuted in areas to be affected by the agrarian reform." Urban trade unions also suffered heavily. On June 24, 1980, Decree 296 called for the firing of anyone who organized a strike; and in response to an August strike at the Rio Lempa power station, the government arrested 15 union leaders and militarized most of the vital public works of the country, including power, communications, hydroelectric, aqueduct, and sewage facilities, automatically enlisting all the employees in the armed forces.[48]

In addition to peasant organizations and trade unions, leaders of other strategic groups have been subjected to violent repression. Teachers have suffered particularly heavy attacks from the security forces and death squads. Some 186 were killed or "disappeared" under the regime of General Molina (1972-77), and 96 were killed during the tenure of General Romero (1977-79). Between October 15, 1979 and July 31, 1980, 181 school teachers were killed. AI noted that between January and mid-March, 1981, 156 more teachers were killed. According to the National Association of Salvadoran Educators, all rural schools were closed by May 1981, as well as more than 500 other public and private educational institutions.[49]

We have seen that Catholic clergy and lay workers contributed significantly to the awakening of political consciousness in El Salvador, and had borne much of the repression in the mid-1970s. Documentation by the Church's Legal Aid Office for the period October 11, 1979 to February 17, 1981 showed that the repression continued after the coup, including: "11 assassinations; 5 bombings; 40 threats; 25 detentions; 2 machine-gunnings; 15 robberies; 19 searches;" and several military occupations of religious facilities. This included the assassination of Archbishop Romero in March, 1980. Killings and other military attacks on the Church continued throughout 1981. As shown in Table 4-2 below at least 25 religious leaders were murdered in El Salvador between the "progressive" coup of October 1979 and the 1982 election. According to a senior Church official in El Salvador, these attacks have been particularly successful in greatly reducing the ability of priests and other religious workers to support the peasantry against the government.[50]

The universities in El Salvador have played an important role in the development of political opposition. Historically, and constitutionally, the National University of El Salvador had been a place exempt from government control, and off-limits to police and military authorities. It was there that the formation of the FDR was proclaimed in 1980. Following a two-day national strike in June 1980, the army and National Guard attacked the National University, killing at least 22 students and causing an estimated $8 million in damage. The University was closed and has remained so; at a meeting in February 1981 to plan the originally scheduled reopening of the University, 21 senior university officials including eight deans were arrested. There has been no more talk of reopening the University. Table 4-2 records the murder of minimum of 224 teachers between October 1979 and March 1982.

4. Political party casualties. We saw earlier that the entire six-person top leadership of the FDR was seized by the security forces in 1980, and tortured, murdered, and mutilated. Any left political leader or organizer who surfaced in El Salvador in the years 1980-83 could have been murdered, and many were. To the extent that there was even the smallest amount of organized political opposition to the military dictatorship allowed in El Salvador in the pre-election period, it was found in the Christian Democratic Party. Though the army chose to rule behind the facade of "civilian rule," represented by the presence of Duarte and Morales Ehrlich in the Revolutionary Junta, in fact the PDC was little more than window dressing and represented only a small fraction of the popular base it once had.

**Table 4-2: Clearing the Ground for a Free Election:
Political Murders by the Security Forces in El Salvador,
October 1979-March 1982**

Class of Victim	Number of Murders	U.S.-Equivalent Murders*
Political Leaders[1]		
a. Christian Democratic Party officials	20+	900+
b. FDR officials	6+	270+
Labor Leaders[2]		
a. Salvadoran Communal Union Officials	83-92	3,735-4,140
b. ISTA employees	40	1,800
c. Trade Union leaders	Not Available	Not Available
Human Rights Workers[3]		
a. Oxfam staff	17	765
b. El Salvador Commission on Human Rights	3	135
Clergy and Religious Workers[4]	25	1,125
Students[5]	1,090	49,050
Teachers[6]	224	10,080
Journalists[7]	26	1,170
Peasants, Workers, and, "Others"[8]	21,453-30,000 (minus the total of the above)	965,385-1,350,000 (minus the total of the above)

*We use a multiplier of 45 as the population of the United States in 1982 was approximately 45 times that of El Salvador.

Sources:

1. **Christian Democratic officials**: The Pell Report (March 1982) quoted Duarte to say that 20 PDC mayors had been killed since the 1979 coup. (Cited in Americas Watch and ACLU, *Report on Human Rights in El Salvador, July 20, 1982, Supplement*, p. 75; **FDR leaders**: Six were killed on November 27, 1980. *Report on Human Rights in El Salvador*, p. 56. These numbers are gross underestimates of the appropriate totals, which are generally unavailable.

2. **Salvadoran Communal Union officials**: The December 1981 report by the Salvador Communal Union, cited in *Report on Human Rights in El Salvador*, pp. 56-57; **ISTA employees**: 40 were killed between March 1980 and September 15, 1981. *New York Times*, September 15, 1981. Hard data on the deaths of union officials in other industries and sectors are unavailable.

3. **Oxfam staff**: Seventeen were killed in the first four months of 1981. *Report on Human Rights in El Salvador*, p. 61. **El Salvador Commission on Human Rights**: *Report on Human Rights in El Salvador*, p. 60; and *July 20, 1982 Supplement*, p. 59.

4. **Clergy and Religious Workers**: Legal Aid Office, see Appendix Table 1 for 1980; for 1981 see *July 20, 1982 Supplement*, p. 48.

5. **Students**: Legal Aid Office, see Appendix Tables 1 and 2.

6. **Teachers**: Members of the teachers' union ANDES killed in 1980 and 1981, according to "Education and Human Rights in El Salvador," prepared by Faculty for Human Rights in El Salvador and Central America, and published in Senate Foreign Relations Committee, *Presidential Certification on Progress in El Salvador*, (98th Congress, First Session), February 2, 1983, p. 108.

7. **Journalists**: The Committee to Protect Journalists, cited in *Report on Human Rights in El Salvador, July 20, 1982 Supplement*, p. 80.

8. **Peasants, Workers, and "Others"**: See Jenny Pearce, *Under the Eagle*, p. 274; *July 20, 1982 Supplement*, p. 13.

Nevertheless, the fact that it also served as a target for attacks by the security forces and death squads indicates some measure of non-cooperation, if only at the local level, with the goals of the army and the oligarchy. It also suggests the level of social pathology that El Salvador had reached as it was being readied for a "free election." Although we have no comprehensive figures on Christian Democrat casualties, a *Washington Post* report of April 9, 1981 said that the Christian Democrats held government security forces responsible for the murders of 40 PDC mayors and "scores of party leaders and workers." A full-page advertisement by the PDC two months after the election claimed that more than 600 party activists had been murdered by the security forces.[51]

5. **The assault on the peasantry and growth in refugee numbers**. We have indicated earlier the scale of the onslaught on the peasantry that accompanied the land reform program in the spring of 1980 and thereafter. In 1982 the UN High Commissioner for Refugees estimated that there were between 220,000 and 272,000 Salvadoran refugees in other countries in Central America. It is commonly held that there were some 500,000 Salvadoran refugees in the United States in 1982. Thus the external refugee total would appear to be on the order of three-quarters of a million. About the time of the election, the International Committee of the Red Cross (ICRC) estimated that there were some 300,000 Salvadorans displaced *within* El Salvador. According to a report by Americas Watch, more than half of this latter group were families and collaborators of the military and paramilitary groups, who were evacuated from conflict areas before military sweeps. Those peasants not so connected to the security forces who remained were presumably more readily treated as an enemy population. In July 1982 the ICRC was aiding 40,000 internal refugees, while the Archdiocese of San Salvador supported ten camps for refugees, many from Christian base communities. This vast internal flow of humanity represents not only a great number of individual tragedies, but also the complete disruption of family, kin, and village ties through which the lifeblood of political self-government must flow.[52]

6. **State terror and the mass murder of civilians**. Under the military rulers supported by Carter and Reagan, El Salvador became a charnel house. Between October 1979 and March 28, 1982, killings of ordinary citizens, frequently accompanied by rape and mutilation, occurred at the average rate of *over 800 per month* on the conservative estimate of the Legal Aid Office of the Archdiocese of El Salvador. Monthly numbers with a distribution by occupation are presented in Appendix Tables I and II.

In Table 4-2 we have put together a very conservative overall summary of estimates of state-sponsored civilian murders in El Salvador for the pre-election period, with a conversion to U.S. numbers, based on the difference in population size. The conversion to U.S.-equivalents gives a little more feel for the implications of the numbers murdered in El Salvador and the compatibility of that violence with a positive electoral environment. It allows us to imagine an election in the United States preceded by the murder of a thousand-odd officials of the Democratic Party; 5,000 labor leaders; 1,200 journalists; and a million ordinary citizens. Internal and external refugee numbers in El Salvador (not on the table) would correspond to a U.S.equivalent of over 30 million refugees.

None of the killings described above ever involved any kind of due process, with charges stated, evidence presented, and the like. These were citizens "in the way" during a sweep of urban squatters areas or peasant communities in parts of the country deemed unfriendly. We consider these numbers, and this process, to be background facts of some significance in appraising the election environment, possibly suggesting to the ordinary citizen the advisability of being part of the "turnout" for "democracy" and "reform."

It is also worthy of mention that those declared noncombatants who attempted to aid (or at least record the numbers of) the victims of the military dictatorship were not immune from the slaughter. The Legal Aid Office was attacked by the security forces on July 3, 1980, and many papers were taken, including lists of people who had been aided. Some of these people were later found murdered. In December the office was temporarily closed after it had been raided 17 times in one week. The Commission on Human Rights was also attacked by the security forces; a January 1981 communique from the Armed Forces Press Committee accused its members of being "traitors." The attacks on both organizations continued up to the election, and several members of each organization were abducted and killed.[53] Table 4-2 shows that 20 different officers or employees of human rights organizations were murdered in El Salvador in the 29 months between the 1979 coup and the 1982 election.

7. Conclusion on basic conditions. The categories we just examined describe some very fundamental parameters that determine beforehand whether an election can be meaningful. It would be an understatement to say that the basic conditions of a free election had been seriously impaired by the slaughter and organizational breakdown which preceded the March 1982 election. The immediate consequence was to eliminate any *public* political opposition; all potential opposition leadership had the alternatives of either joining the guerillas in zones they controlled, going abroad, or remaining silent. As James Petras noted in the aftermath of the election:

The political divisions which existed in the 1960s and 1970s, following class lines in the cities and countryside, have been temporarily blurred: the mass organizations of teachers, workers, peasants, professionals, university students and others cannot operate in the areas occupied by the military. Under the threat of immediate death, opposition in these areas has a very low profile. In most cases, the opposition has either gone into exile or joined the guerillas. Hence, the concentration of opposition forces in the military guerila struggle has left the less politicized populace without any organized structure. Paradoxically, while guerillas have gained in political and military strength,... the opposition has only limited influence over the cities and among the otherwise intimidated population who voted in the election.[54]

In sum, by March 1982 pacification by terror had proceeded to a point where an election could be held. The drama could be staged, "turnout" was assured, and the exclusion of any nonwar option would allow a good turnout to be equated with a vote for the military junta and escalation. All that was required were "observers" and a compliant press.

The Mechanics of the Election

Although the political conditions in El Salvador in March 1982 assured a victory for the war party (there were no others on the ballot), the election managers engaged in important forms of chicanery and fraud. The reason for this was the importance of turnout. The PR strategy was to get the media to interpret turnout as a triumph for democracy, the security forces, us and our intervention strategies, and a repudiation of the rebels. Thus the frauds consisted of those devices designed to obtain a large vote and the appearance of a massive turnout. We will confine ourselves to three issues relevant to these deceptions: (1) least important, the obtaining of long lines of waiting and enthusiastic voters; (2) the question of compulsion and pressure to vote; and (3) the issue of the inflated vote count.

1. **The secret of long lines.** The most potent media image used to evoke feelings of the positive meaning and significance of the election was the long lines of people waiting to vote. Photographs and

television clips of voters standing in long lines were an effective means of conveying the appearance of voter enthusiasm and a massive turnout. In reality, however, these long lines were the product of the small number of polling places established by the authorities. In San Salvador, the largest city, there were only 13 polling places for a potential voting-age population of 500,000, as compared with 20-25 used in past elections. Santa Ana, the second largest city, was given nine polling places; while San Miguel, the third largest, had four. Thus in San Salvador, the source of most of the visual images of the high voter turnout, an 80% participation rate would require more than 30,000 voters to pass through each polling place. We suspect that the small number of polling places in the larger cities and towns was deliberately designed to produce long lines of voters, rather than to reduce the workload of the security forces guarding polling places against projected election day violence, as in the official view. Whatever the rationale, however, with so few polling places, even a turnout of 10% would have produced long lines of voters.[55]

2. The legal obligation and other inducements to vote. Was voting a genuinely free act in El Salvador? A high voter turnout would mean little if Salvadoran citizens believed they were endangering themselves by *not* voting. There is solid evidence, essentially suppressed by the U.S. media, that this was in fact the case.

It was not made clear to the U.S. audience, for example, that voting was a legal requirement. The junta's Electoral Law stated that "voting is a right and a duty of all citizens and its exercise is nontransferable and compulsory." Moreover, "eight days before the election the municipal mayors of the entire country will remind the electorate of their obligation to vote, under the penalty to incur the sanctions imposed by law." Finally, during the ten days after the election, "the authorities shall demand evidence from the people that they voted and report anyone without such evidence to the town mayor." If the nonvoter did not have a reasonable excuse, he or she was subject to a fine of 80 centavos.[56]

The legal requirement to vote was backed up by both informal pressures and real threats to jobs and to life itself. Testifying before the House of Representatives, for example, AIFLD's William Doherty claimed that the U.S.-backed Popular Democratic Unity organization "was responsible for putting about 500,000 campesinos and workers at the polls," advising everybody "to vote their conscience, to vote, and to vote for the party of their choice, and to vote for those candidates who they thought were in favor of reforms." The worker and peasant organizations controlled by AIFLD had a clear stake in a Duarte victory, and they used their organizational net-works and the rewards and punishments at their disposal through control of millions of dollars of AID money to turn out the vote. FDR leader Ruben Zamora charged that paychecks were withheld from public workers until the Monday following the election, when they had to prove that they had voted before being paid. Another source claimed that the same practice was followed by banks and some other private sector employers.[57]

More important than these localized pressures were the voting procedures adopted by the junta, which established a clear record of who voted and who did not. Claiming that the disruptive effects of the civil war had made the electoral roster out of date, the junta decided to stamp the voter's *cedula*, or national identity card, to prevent multiple voting. A *cedula* is necessary for survival in El Salvador; without it, many business transactions are impossible, and identity checks by security forces would be extremely risky. According to pre-election information prepared by the Central Election Commission and published in two newspapers in El Salvador, the *cedula* would be marked when the voter cast his or her ballot; in actuality, election officials gave each voter a receipt instead, claiming that the guerillas would victimize those having *cedulas* with a voting stamp. This was not publicized before the election, however, nor was it universally adopted, and voters went to the polls believing that they would be fined and perhaps otherwise punished if they did not have their *cedulas* stamped on election day.[58]

Also in the alleged interest of preventing multiple voting, the Central Election Commission adopted the procedure of marking the finger of each voter with an ink visible only under ultraviolet light. Thus before voting one's finger was checked for any trace of ink from a previous visit to the polls. Invisible ink allegedly was used to prevent harassment of voters by the guerillas, but this marking process obviously provided a means whereby the security forces could check on citizen loyalty and contribution to "turnout."

Thus, a failure to vote on March 1982 would have been illegal, and the nonvoter would have been identifiable as such. Two weeks before the election, Defense Minister General José Guillermo Garcia asserted in the San Salvador press (but unmentioned in the U.S. media) that anyone who failed to vote was committing "an act of treason."[59] With some 22,000-30,000 deaths credited to the security forces in 28 months of pacification, and nonvoting a mark of treason, the presumption must be that if large numbers of poor people in the countryside and urban slums went to vote, they did so out of fear of reprisal. The mass media and official observers, however, were advised by official sources that the only threat of reprisal came from leftwing objectors to the election. Furthermore, no voter standing in a line told a reporter or an observer that he or she feared violence from the nearby soldier. This is how the official mythology plus "facts" yielded conclusions about coercion.

Some 12% of the ballots cast were blank or were in some way defaced. Election officials contended that these ballots should be considered protest votes, indicating support for the guerillas. While the FMLN-FDR did not attempt to organize a campaign to encourage voters to cast blank ballots or deface them, it might be asked why more voters did not do this? To put it another way, did the election results show that 88% of participating voters were satisfied with the spectrum of political parties presented to them?

To interpret the voting this way is to ignore not only the pressure to vote, but the pressure to vote in a certain direction. This was applied in two ways. First, the ballot boxes used in the election were made of clear, transparent lucite. The ballot consisted of a thin piece of paper with the symbols of the six parties on it. To cast one's vote the voter put an X through the party symbol, folded the paper, and dropped it into the transparent box. According to the election law, the ballot box must be "placed near and within view of the precinct board members." Thus voting was hardly secret. Nor was this procedure concocted for this election, but was the standard practice in Salvadoran elections. Historian Alastair White, for example, wrote in 1973:

> As the ballot papers are thin and the voter marks the party symbol with a thick black cross, another person can stand on the opposite side of the box from the voter, watch his ballot paper come down through the slit into the transparent box, and see through the thin, once-folded paper which party he has voted for.[60]

There was a second factor that compromised the privacy of the El Salvador ballot. The election law stated that "based on the data of the ID card [the government] should be able to elaborate a list of all voting decisions which should contain: the first and second names of the voter, their personal and identification card number, and the rest of the data that the respective format will indicate."[61] In the March election each voter was given a numbered ballot. After casting his or her ballot, the voter would sign a register, along with the identification number of the ballot. While a U.S. official observer said that the

Central Election Commission's guidelines allowed voters to remove the number from the ballot if they wished, the ARENA party women's organization published a full-page ad on the morning of the election claiming that it was illegal to remove the number. It is likely, therefore, that a great many voters did not remove the number from their ballot, and would thus believe that someone could determine how she or he voted. In sum, a voter going to the polls in El Salvador in March 1982 could reasonably expect that his or her choice would be known to election officials. Under these circumstances, casting a blank ballot would involve a potentially grave risk. The security forces of El Salvador had proven their mettle in dealing with unarmed subversives.

3. **The inflated vote count.** The long lines of voters freely exercising their franchise were apparently not enough to satisfy the March 1982 election managers, who wanted not only the image of a high turnout but the votes to go with it. Here they overreached themselves, however, for as the vote totals kept rising in the days following the election, the turnout rapidly reached and then exceeded the 100% mark for pre-election eligible voter limits. On election day, for example, the *New York Times* quoted unnamed U.S. officials as hoping for a turnout of at least 500,000 of the estimated 1.3 million eligible voters. The final returns, however, claimed that more than 1.5 million Salvadorans voted, causing one unnamed diplomat to tell a reporter that "it's impossible. Only in a Communist country is there voting like this."[62] Admittedly, estimating the number of eligible voters was a tricky business: there was no register of voters; no census had been conducted since 1971; and estimates of the number of internal and external refugees varied greatly. Yet a later (conservative) estimate by the Central American University could produce a figure no higher than 1.8 million eligible voters, indicating a turnout greater than 80%. While there was perhaps a sufficient level of coercion and fear among the populace to turn out such a vote, there is also strong circumstantial evidence that the "official turnout" was officially exaggerated for PR purposes.

The most persuasive evidence that the vote total was inflated by the election managers was produced by two studies from the José Simeon Cañas University of Central America in June 1982. The first effort, published in *Central American Studies*, concluded that it was not possible for more than 777,000 ballots to be cast, about half of the final official total certified by the Central Elections Commission. The second study, by the Center for Documentation and Information, concluded that the maximum possible number of votes that could have been cast was 1,281,600. Each study arrived at its conclusions by considering three factors: the number of voting tables in use; the number of hours the tables were in use; and the length of time it took to vote. The more conservative of the two studies took the number of tables to be 3,781, the figure given in the Central Elections Council's final report, and calculated that the average table was available for ten hours. Thus there were 37,810 "table hours" for voting. The key—and hotly contested—variable was the length of time it took to vote. This process was in fact quite cumbersome because of the steps allegedly taken to prevent fraud. Although there were apparently slight local variations, the standard voting procedure was as follows:

> When a voter reached the table, the name, number and date on the voter's identification card were checked, first by one of the Government officials and then by representatives of the political parties [there were six parties]. The voter's hand was also examined by a machine designed to react to an indelible mark showing that a person had voted. Then the voter received a ballot, walked a few feet to the voting booth, marked the ballot, folded it and stuffed [it] into the slot in the ballot box. After voting, the voter returned to the voting table, where the name and identification number were written by hand in a ledger and an identification card was stamped.[63]

The argument thus became how fast people voted. Assuming 37,810 "table hours" and no interruptions between voters, for example, the total potential vote would be as follows:

Time	Total potential vote
one minute	2,268,600
two minute	1,134,300
three minute	756,200

Holding to our assumptions, the "final official total" of 1,551,687 votes works out to 41 votes per hour per table, or just under one and a half minutes per voter. While this issue does not seem resolvable, it is significant that no reporters or unofficial observers were quoted in the U.S. press as saying that voting went this quickly. Rather, estimates ranged upward of two minutes per voter, supporting conclusions that the maximum possible vote was around a million. To our knowledge only Dr. Jorge Bustamente, the President of the Central Elections Council, and U.S. official observer Howard Penniman maintained that 41 votes per table per hour was even possible.

The studies presented by the University of Central America show that the "final official returns" strain credulity, exceeding what was a plausible technical maximum. There is other evidence, however, that also points to fraud. For example, the Central Elections Commission had three million ballots printed, justifying this by concern that the guerillas would attack polling places and destroy ballots, and claiming not to know where people would actually vote, given the high level of population displacement within El Salvador. Yet the excess printing was great and arouses a suspicion that the loyalists of the different parties were encouraged to "vote early and vote often." To vote more than once someone would also need to present an unstamped *cedula*, or identity card, to the election officials. (But where receipts were given rather than *cedulas* stamped, this alleged safeguard was not present). Prior to the election a spokesperson for the ARENA party complained that *cedulas* were for sale in San Salvador. In his postelection testimony before the Senate Foreign Relations Committee, Robert Leiken asked: "And why were 250,000 *cedulas* issued in San Salvador in the weeks before the elections? How could so many people have been without their identity cards when not to have one meant certain death? (Only guerillas have no identity cards, it is assumed at police and army barricades.)"[64]

Was it also possible that the ballot boxes were stuffed—or the vote artificially inflated—after the hours of polling were over? There is strong circumstantial evidence that somewhere between the polling places and the Central Election Headquarters this was what happened. For some reason the results from each voting table—not just each polling place, which included up to 60 tables—was the subject of a separate telegram to the Central Election Headquarters.[65] Each telegram thus passed through the hands of ANTEL, the nation's telecommunications network, which is and has been traditionally controlled by the army.[66] The reporting and tabulating of the votes was significantly delayed, and was not finally completed until a week after the election. During this time, the estimates of the numbers of votes cast simply kept growing. The results reported in the *New York Times*, for example, looked like this:

Date	Estimated Registered Voters	Comments
March 28	500,000/ 1.3 million	"officials hope at least..."
March 29	----	"...official results to be announced Monday"
March 30	900,000/ 1.3 million	428,924 counted; "euphoria" among U.S. officials
March 31	est. "more than a million"	a final tally not till tomorrow
April 1	"almost 1.2 million"	"subject to confirmation"
April 2	----	tabulation "final but unofficial"
April 3	1.2 million/ 1.4 million	
April 4	1,491,255 votes	final "unofficial" returns
April 5	1,555,687 votes	Central Election Council official returns

Bustamente blamed the delays on the communications system and the computer program. Yet at one point in the count he announced that 881,883 ballots had been received, representing 80% of the total. Then there occurred a three-hour delay, followed by the discovery of nearly 700,000 additional ballots. If 80% of the vote had indeed been counted at this point, the final turnout would have been a little over 1,100,000, within the estimates of the University of Central America studies.[67]

Thus there is a basis for suspicion that the vote totals were somehow inflated. *How* this was done, however, remains a mystery; but the revelation that the CIA was active in election preparations, and the more recent discovery that a super-secret operations unit within the Pentagon was on the spot during the election certainly raises the possibility that ANTEL's computer operations could have been reprogrammed at a critical point during the election count to produce the extremely high final vote count.[68]

Interpreting the Election Drama

The Salvadorans had performed their parts well. They had gone to the polls in large numbers, waited patiently in long lines, and cast their ballots. But in a demonstration election the key actors are not the voters but the *interpreters*, those members of the cast who advance to the front of the stage, lean over the footlights, and explain the significance of the activity going on behind them. Without their interpretive skills the audience is literally in the dark.

1. The media. The most important of these interpretive roles is played by the mass media. More than 700 journalists flocked to El Salvador to cover the election, and their presence in such large numbers became itself a major news story, prime evidence that something very *significant* was happening. The amount of time the U.S. television network news programs devoted to the events in El Salvador was unprecedented in their attention to a foreign election. The reporting of the mass media, and particularly the questions it did *not* ask, was the main vehicle through which the desired meaning of the election was conveyed to the public. We will reserve for the next chapter a detailed examination of the role of the media in shaping the lessons of the election.

2. The observers. A secondary but significant interpretative role is played by the observers. In El Salvador the observers arrived after the campaigning had ended, and were whirled and herded through photo opportunities on election day, both seeing and being seen. The role of the observers in the spectacle is much larger than their brief appearance would indicate, however. Their *intention* to appear, their *imminent arrival*, helps to publicize and validate the drama even before the observers are whisked to their first polling place. And though they have seen little and, as we argued in chapter 1, are in no position to really observe anything, their *pro forma* postelection report that indeed all was well is useful in reassuring the audience about the quality of the performance they have just witnessed.

The U.S. managers of El Salvador's election began planning the role of the observers early in the campaign. In mid-September 1981 President Duarte issued a public invitation for international observers to witness the March elections. Two weeks later a State Department delegation under the direction of Everett E. Briggs, himself later a member of the official U.S. observer delegation, arrived to begin laying the groundwork of the election mechanics, including the role of observers.[69] The following month the State Department sent William Kimberling, the Deputy Director of the National Clearing-house on Election Administration, to El Salvador to discuss election procedures. In early November, Kimberling provided the State Department with a report, "Notes on the Upcoming Election in El Salvador," and in mid-December he produced another report for the State Department, "A General Plan for Providing International Observers to the March 82 Election in El Salvador." According to a study by the General Accounting Office (GAO), on December 21, 1981 the "Department of State sent a message to the American Embassy-San Salvador commenting on the mechanics of the election process, the administrative and logistic support necessary, *and the problems of international observation and credibility"* (our emphasis). In short, the available evidence indicates that from the start the State Department realized that the presence and cooperation of international observers was a key factor in producing the desired effect.[70]

In December the Government of El Salvador invited 60 countries to send official delegations to its election spectacular. But who would pay for these junkets? In early 1982 AID was persuaded to contribute $220,000 for the expenses of the observer delegations, but the money could only be used for travel, housing, and expenses. According to the GAO Report, the Government of El Salvador itself would be obliged to come up with at least $120,000 to cover "publicity, printing, and binding; receptions; entertainment of any kind; and support of news media personnel." In an extraordinary example of the generosity of private philanthropy, Elliott Abrams, the State Department's Assistant Secretary for Human Rights and Humanitarian Affairs, proposed that $150,000 be raised for these purposes from private foundations, and four foundations associated with the support of rightwing causes—the Scaife Foundation, the Olin Foundation, the Smith Richardson Foundation, and the Grace Foundation—quickly contributed the necessary funds, which were then passed on to the government of El Salvador.[71]

In spite of intensive lobbying by the State Department, few of the nations invited to send an observer delegation seemed inclined to do so. A month before the election only Great Britain, Colombia, Costa Rica, Egypt, and Uruguay had made public commitments; while Salvadoran officials reported that they had received private assurances from the governments of Argentina, Chile, Ecuador, Haiti, Honduras, and Panama. The generally rightwing and non-democratic character of the countries accepting El Salvador's invitation indicated the skepticism with which the election was viewed worldwide. According to a pre-election assessment in the *New York Times*, "the issue of observers reflects a growing division of opinion in Washington as well as in foreign capitals over whether there should be negotiations before the election." For many European countries, in fact, the request to send observers to the election served to crystallize a domestic debate on the U.S. alliance. The Prime Minister of Denmark, for example, publicly charged that the United States was hypocritical in supporting the military regime in El Salvador while attacking a similar regime in Poland. The Mitterand government in France openly favored negotiations, while the governing coalition in West Germany found the U.S. policy in El Salvador undercutting its ability to retain support within its own ranks for installing new U.S. missiles in Europe. Many Europeans were also acutely aware of the parallels between the Vietnam war and the emerging war in Central America. Eventually some 100-200 official and unofficial observers attended the election, with the largest delegation coming from Guatemala; but 40 nations that had been invited to send official delegations, including Japan, Canada, and all West European nations except Great Britain, declined to do so.[72]

The most important international observers were of course those from the United States. On March 1 the State Department announced that the U.S. delegation would be headed by Senator Nancy L. Kassebaum (R.-Kansas), and would include Congressman Bob Livingston (R-Louisiana); Everett E. Briggs, Deputy Assistant Secretary for Inter-American Affairs; the Rev. Theodore Hesburgh, President of Notre Dame University; Clark Kerr, President Emeritus of the University of California at Berkeley; and Richard Scammon and Howard Penniman, professional election experts connected with the conservative American Enterprise Institute. It was frequently noted in the press that these two experts had monitored some 45 prior elections, including that in South Vietnam in 1967. Their political affiliations and biases were rarely mentioned. What of the qualifications of the other observers? None of them, for example, had any expertise in the region. At least half of the delegation had official or personal ties that seriously compromised their potential objectivity. Everett Briggs was an official of the Reagan administration; Clark Kerr had participated in a "study mission" to El Salvador in December which had vigorously supported the forthcoming elections; and Rev. Theodore Hesburgh had been close to Duarte since he had been the latter's teacher at Notre Dame in 1945.[73]

The observers arrived on Friday, March 26, two days after campaigning had officially ended. They spent Saturday receiving official briefings, and on Sunday fanned out to observe the balloting. What did they—indeed, what could they—see? Let us follow the path of observer Hesburgh, who later described his experience at length. Hesburgh reported helicoptering to six or more spots in four departments in the eastern and northern parts of El Salvador. In one village in Morazan province, for example, he spent an hour being briefed on the war in the region by 45 election commissioners. He reported the following dialogue with those waiting to vote (presumably taking place in the presence of 45 commissioners—i.e., officials of the Christian Democratic and rightwing parties):

The campesinos told us that there were more than 500 guerrillas a kilometer or two from where we stood. These peasant farmers had walked through the lines and had been told, "Vote this morning, and you die this afternoon." "Are you afraid?"—silly question—I asked. "Well," they all said, "they can't kill us all, and we are all voting." "What are you voting for?" I asked. "Against violence and for peace," they said. "Who is going to win?" Their answer was simple and eloquent: "The People—El Pueblo."[74]

After this illuminating exchange—which could as easily have been scripted in South Bend, Indiana on the basis of State Department press handouts—Hesburgh helicoptered to a few more villages before returning to the capital. Apparently neither the observers nor the voters (in the presence of the commissioners) had touched on the government slaughters in Morazan a few months earlier, in which hundreds of refugees had been killed attempting to flee a sweep by U.S.-trained forces. Once back in the capital Hesburgh and other observers "checked on the counting of the ballots—again an almost foolproof system that is better than ours." Hesburgh is not moved even to the slightest degree of skepticism in noting that "the monumental vote. . . was at least three times greater than the most optimistic previous guess." Nor did he have any critical comments to make about the use of transparent ballot boxes, which an AP photo (reproduced on the following page) accompanying an article entitled "US Observers Find Election Untainted," shows him "observing" on the day of the election.[75]

Hesburgh's cooperative attitude toward the election drama is illustrative of the role played by the entire official observer delegation. In its formal statement submitted to the State Department, the observers claimed that "over and over again we heard the people say 'we are voting for peace and an end to violence.'" "This is amazing," said Clark Kerr on the day of the voting. "I've never seen people so eager to vote. This one lady we stopped and talked with said they were voting for peace." Rep. Bob Livingston called the election the "most inspiring thing I've ever seen"; and Senator Nancy Kassebaum called the show "an exceptionally fair election." Howard Penniman claimed that the large turnout "was in the face of enormous opposition from the guerilla forces and certainly not out of any form of pressure from the government." Penniman, an alleged expert, never found out that it was legally obligatory to vote. His "certainty" of an absence of government pressure could certainly not have been a result of observation—it had to reflect sheer personal bias. Indeed,

The Rev. Theodore Hesburgh, "observing" the Salvadoran election, but not "seeing" the transparent voting box.

Penniman's colleague Richard Scammon had observed before the election that "we have no way of knowing whether force has been exerted or threats made. And we can't see collusion like when six parties get together and decide they're going to divy up the ballots." These of course were several of the controversial issues in the post-election assessment: was the vote total inflated by direct fraud, and was the turnout significantly influenced by coercion? As Scammon said, the observers had "no way of knowing"; but to our knowledge no congressional or media sources pressed the observers on the validity of their conclusions on the unknowable.[76]

In addition to the official U.S. and international observer delegations, several U.S. organizations sent unofficial observer teams or acted to help legitimate the election for the home audience. Freedom House and the AFL-CIO, for example, sent unofficial observer delegations to El Salvador, which had predictably enthusiastic responses to the election. Freedom House said that the election "clearly demonstrated the electorate's broad desire for peace to be achieved through peaceful—not violent—means."[77] This statement contains a small mountain of premises and conclusions about the motives of the populace, the election managers, and the political parties, that the Freedom House team could not possibly have "observed" (see Appendix 1). But with the western media passing on their unobserved observations without question, this and other unofficial delegations helped to legitimate the election.

The Outcome

Though Freedom House, Hesburgh, and the observers in general found the populace eager for "peace," the real election outcome shifted the political spectrum somewhat further to the right, suggesting a public "choice" for intensified warfare. The observers, analysts, and media never addressed this oddity except in the form of elliptical inanities such as *New York Times* reporter Warren Hoge's statement that "at the center of the diplomats' frustration is the conviction that while Sunday's outpouring was above all a plea for peace, the consequences could well end up being increased dissidence and violence."[78] To press any more deeply would call attention to the absence of any candidate who proposed resolving the conflict by means other than further violence. As this was a given for all the parties, in a clear and obvious sense there was no peace option. The voters seeking peace could have voted for the "reformer" Duarte, who had presided over the killing of some 30,000 civilians and had plunged El Salvador into an inferno of institutionalized state terror. Of course, Duarte was not in *control* of these events, as he himself admitted just prior to the election, but he allowed himself to be used as the symbol of civilian control and reformism while the army and death squads did their work.[79] The trade-off that he exacted for presiding over the escalation of terror was confined to the disastrous land reform, which was integrally tied to pacification by violence. All other social conditions and liberal values eroded during the Duarte tenure. To vote for Duarte, therefore, would be to vote approval of the U.S.-sponsored pacification of 1980-82. Alternatively, one could have voted for the death squads; which is to say that the options were (1) warfare and state terrorism along the lines of the recent past, and (2) the "let's get it over with" or "final solution" route.

While ignoring the limits of these choices, once the euphoria over "turnout" and the vindication of democracy had been exhausted, there were occasional expressions of concern over the drift to the right and its possible impact on human rights and reform. Duarte, who had hoped to capture a majority of the votes, won only a plurality, with over 50% of the vote divided among rightwing parties. There was thus an excellent chance that the reformist facade would collapse. The *New York Times* warned on the first of April that if the election put D'Aubuisson and the ARENA party in power, it could lead to a ruthless war against both the guerillas and the land reform. As a stopgap measure the observers were once again quickly rushed on stage to deflect the crisis, as the administration hastily arranged a press conference where, according to the *Washington Post*, they might submit their report directly to the President and "play up the high voter turnout in the face of guerilla attempts to disrupt the elections." But the drama had to give way momentarily, as "the observers' attempts to describe their impressions of the balloting were turned aside as reporters shouted demands for the administration to clarify whether it will continue U.S. military and economic support to El Salvador if the new government is controlled by rightist forces such as the extremist political leader Roberto D'Aubuisson."[80] As the *Boston Globe* editorialized on April 8th: "Now that the meaning of the results is becoming clear, jubilation about voter turnout has faded to foreboding."

Did it really matter to the Reagan administration that Duarte failed to win? The evidence is unclear. True, Duarte's media image was useful in maintaining congressional support for continuing military aid. It was, after all, liberals like former Ambassador Robert White who had seen the elections as an opportunity to give greater legitimacy to Duarte, who would then have the power to dismantle the death squads, bring to trial the killers of the several U.S. citizens, and reconstruct the fabled "center" of Salvadoran politics. Prior to the election the Reagan administration appeared to share this preference, at least for public consumption; but there was ample evidence that the administration was not really too uncomfortable at the thought of a D'Aubuisson government. One month before the election the U.S. Embassy in El Salvador described ARENA's program as "ultra-rightist, anti-Communist, pro-free enterprise"—not unlike that of the administration itself. The main dilemma D'Aubuisson posed was one of saleability. The election actually helped here, serving as a legitimizing instrument by which the administration could back D'Aubuisson in the name of supporting the outcome of the democratic process. Appearing on NBC's "Meet the Press" on election day, for example, Secretary of State Haig stressed that the United States was not wedded to a particular candidate, but to a set of policies. If the voters elected a Constituent Assembly dominated by rightwing forces, "that's their business." At hearings held by the Senate Foreign Relations Committee a few days after the election, Everett E. Briggs, one of the official observers and a deputy to Enders, indicated which way the wind was blowing by criticizing the use of the "rightwing" label in regard to ARENA. According to Briggs, ARENA included "some very liberal and some very moderate people." What about D'Aubuisson himself? Immediately after the election Washington declared that his *persona non grata* status would be lifted, and "in the future" he would be allowed to come to the United States to meet with policy makers. As it became apparent that D'Aubuisson would head the Assembly, Ambassador Hinton told reporters: "He denied the rough stuff. He should be judged by his actions and performance and not on his past. Anyone who believes in the democratic system should give him the benefit of the doubt until he demonstrates in his new role that he doesn't deserve it." (One can easily imagine Germany's President Paul von Hindenburg making the same statement about the leader of the Nazi party following its strong election showing in November 1932.) Thus the Reagan administration conceives of the electoral process as a kind of moral sheep dip, from which any candidate, even "Blowtorch Bob," emerges ready for a fresh start in life.[81]

Washington and the media were nonetheless taken aback in April when the ARENA party succeeded in electing D'Aubuisson president of the Constitutent Assembly. Despite ARENA's clearly stated intention to exclude the Christian Democrats from power, both the press and the administration spokesmen had made soothing noises that reason would prevail and some kind of bargain would be struck, if only to keep the aid pipeline flowing. On April 8th an eight member congressional delegation met with El Salvador's leading politicians, warning them that a rightwing government would not be acceptable to Congress. Two weeks later, however, D'Aubuisson was installed as President of the Assembly, and the Christian Democrats were excluded from all positions in the Assembly's directorate. Ambassador Hinton called D'Aubuisson's selection "an example of democracy at work."

In spite of their devotion to the workings of democracy, the Reagan administration now began an all-out effort to prevent ARENA from similarly forcing its choice for a Provisional President through the Assembly. Now the Embassy energetically used its power with the army, and persuaded a substantial majority of the PCN to go along with a "moderate," rather than face the possibility of a U.S.-backed coup by the army. The Assembly's ensuing choice for President was Alvaro Magaña, one of three candidates put forward as acceptable by the military. Magaña was the head of the country's largest mortgage bank, with close personal ties to the military leaders. A Salvadoran political leader described the process as "something like a coup within a democracy." Though Magaña was indistinguishable from those members of El Salvador's elite who had served under the regime of General Romero prior to the October 1979 coup, the U.S. media cooperated in presenting him as a "moderate," i.e., a continuation of the phantom centrist tradition formerly personified by Duarte.[82]

The Sequel

What were the real world consequences of the "free election" in El Salvador? In our view, the real goal was to pacify the U.S. population with a symbolic act in order to clear the ground for intensified warfare. Supporters of the election process maintained, however, that it would have beneficial effects in El Salvador itself. According to this view, the election would help to establish a government perceived to be legitimate by broad sectors of Salvadoran society, and the new Constituent Assembly would provide an arena for the nonviolent resolution of many of the country's conflicts. A regime legitimized through elections would also be able to carry forward the land reform program and other measures necessary to ameliorate the desperate poverty of El Salvador's majority, and thus rally to the government those who would otherwise find the guerillas their only hope for survival. Finally, a legitimately elected government was seen as the only means to strengthen civilian sectors of the elite in relation to the armed forces, and to force them to conduct the war with a greater regard for human rights.

The election, in fact, contributed to a *deterioration* in all of these sectors of concern. The land reform process was halted and reversed; terror against the peasantry by the death squads and the security forces was vigorously renewed; and the army's military operations were now supported by troops newly trained in the United States, who proved to be even more efficient killers of unarmed civilians. However, as developments in El Salvador were the outcome of a "free election," liberal forces in the United States who had given at least lip service to the March 1982 charade now found themselves saddled with the results.

Land Reform. The ARENA party had campaigned forthrightly against the junta's land reform program. Shortly after the election, however, D'Aubuisson pledged that "from the moment the new government starts we will carry out agrarian reform"; and ARENA assumed the Ministry of Agriculture in the new government. The first substantive acts of the Assembly, however, essentially halted the land reform program. One decree foreclosed the important Phase II of the land reform program, which had not yet begun. A second decree exempted almost all land potentially available for Phase III—the "land-to-the-tiller" program—from further transfer from owner to renter. According to a report in the *Washington Post* at the end of May, "the rightists were sending out orders through [the Agriculture Minister] that virtually shut the whole program down." The *Post* noted that "the agency responsible for handing out titles to eligible peasants was told to stop giving them even the receipts that acknowledge their applications."[83]

The electoral victory of the right had other negative effects on the land reform program. Taking the right's victory as a signal that land reform was dead, former landlords moved to evict the new occupiers of their land. According to José Antonio Morales Ehrlich, the former head of the Institute of Agrarian Transformation, more than 5,000 peasant families were evicted from their land in the two months following the election. He contrasted this with 2,000 evictions in the 22 months between the time that the law was passed and the election. The Popular Democratic Unity coalition put the number of evictions at nearly 12,000; while a report by an official of the government's National Financial Institute for Agrarian Lands (FINATA) noted that in the western province of Ahuachapan, where there was almost no guerilla activity, 1,043 peasant families were evicted in the two months following the election. According to this official, 95% of those evicted had acquired provisional title to their lands. Evictions were frequently accompanied by the use of military force. At the end of May 1982, for example, an employee of the Salvadoran Communal Union in Sonsonate province estimated that of some 200 recent evictions, about half had involved the use of local military forces. The president of a large peasant organization called ACOPAI estimated that 3,600 peasants had been killed because they tried to exercise their rights under land-to-the-tiller. "Dirt is stuffed in their mouths as a symbol," he said. "Filling out an application is sometimes like painting a red cross of death across your chest."[84]

The hearings conducted by the House of Representatives to review President Reagan's certification of "continued progress" in El Salvador's land reform in late July showed that these trends were continuing. Perhaps the most damaging indictment of the Reagan

Administration's position was the testimony of Roy Prosterman, the architect of the "land-to-the-tiller" program. Although he continued to defend the beneficial results of land reform during the first two years of its life, Prosterman maintained that the election marked a turning point in the program. "Both in its administration and at the hands of the ARENA-PCN coalition in the Constituent Assembly, the land reform has suffered severely," he maintained. "Indeed, in relation to what the voters were led to expect what has happened is a betrayal—even a virtual coup d'etat." Prosterman also noted that the number of peasants applying for titles had dropped off sharply, "the most obvious sign of their declining faith in the reality of the program." During the four months preceding the election, for example, the number of applications had averaged 1,143 a month. In the two months after the election, there was an average of 653 applications a month; and in the following month there were only 105. The number of evictions also continued to grow. Prosterman cited UCS figures claiming some 9,600 new evictions among provisional title holders, while noting that "an even larger number of beneficiaries have probably been evicted among the 75 to 80 percent who have not yet received provisional titles."[85]

Murder, Inc. Did the organized slaughter in El Salvador recede after the election? In certifying to Congress in July 1982 that El Salvador was meeting the necessary conditions to continue receiving U.S. aid, the Reagan administration stated that "the development of a firm democratic order in El Salvador is likely to be, over the long term, the best guarantee of human rights improvement in other areas." Whatever the "long term" might bring, the immediate consequence of the election was an escalation of violence by the security forces against the civilian population. A month after the election Raymond Bonner reported from San Salvador that the available evidence appeared "to have borne out the fears of many Salvadorans that assassinations by Government security forces and rightist death squads would increase as the result of the success of rightist parties in the elections." Bonner quoted a member of the Human Rights Commission who told him that before the election they would find some 20 to 25 bodies a week around the perimeter of the capital, while after the election the number had risen to about 35 a week.[86]

This impressionistic evidence was apparently belied by the statistics presented by the Reagan administration in its second certification report in late July 1982. While acknowledging that human rights abuses remained high, the Reagan administration's figures apparently showed a relative decline, whether measured by the

Embassy's method of counting reports in the government-controlled press, or based on the reports of the Human Rights Commission, the Church's Legal Aid Office, or the Central American University. As presented in the government's certification report, the figures for the first six months of 1982 were as shown in Table 4-3.

Table 4-3: Deaths Attributable to Political Violence in El Salvador During the First Six Months of 1982				
Month	Press Reports	Legal Aid Office	CDHES[1]	UCA[2]
January	279	466	626	539
February	361	532	405	387
March	438	526	905	483
April	194	805	235	353
May	301	375	269	334
Total:	1,573	2,704	2,440	2,096
June	189	355	N/A	N/A[3]

1. The Human Rights Commission of El Salvador (CDHES).
2. The University of Central America (UCA).
3. Not yet released.

Source: *Certification Hearings*, 1982, Vol. II, p. 487.

The administration's claims of "progress" are dubious on several grounds. One is the heavy reliance it places on the evidence of those alleged to be committing atrocities. Consider the following exchange between Thomas Enders and Congressman Don Bonker:

Mr. Bonker: In April, the *New York Times* and other international press reported that 48 members of an extended family in Barrios, El Salvador were killed by army soldiers. All eye-witnesses agreed that it was the army who was responsible. 25 of the 48 victims were children under 12 years old. Has there been any investigation into this incident? Have any army officers or soldiers been charged, detained, dismissed, or punished?

Mr. Enders: There is no conclusive evidence that this event took place. The international press did find what they thought to be a mass grave and reportedly filmed blood and bodily parts in the area. No one, however, informed the Embassy that they saw bodies. Salvadoran Armed Forces officials reported that they had no information on the alleged massacre. A review of written military action reports failed to produce any evidence that the Salvadoran Armed Forces were in the village on the day in question.[87]

The faith in testimony of the Salvadoran armed forces and reliance on the absence of the evidence of their unprovoked murders in their own written reports reflects a close and protective relationship, of parent and unruly children. If people failed to tell the Embassy, perhaps this is because people felt that telling the Embassy was virtually the same thing as telling the army. If the Embassy was interested, why didn't it go out itself using U.S. personnel to examine the sites specified by the international press?

A second reason to doubt the administration's claims of "progress" is that by starting from such an extraordinarily high base of murders per month, "progress" is achieved by reducing the level of killings from "wholesale slaughter" to "moderate slaughter." In fact, the relevant phrase in the certification legislation calls not for "progress," but for the Government of El Salvador to make "a concerted and significant effort to comply with internationally recognized human rights." On the face of it it would not seem that a reduction to even 100 murders a week—equivalent to nearly 5,000 murders a week in the more populous United States—reflects any effort other than a murderous one. For as the Church's Legal Aid Office remarked in a report released in July 1982, "the executions are the result, almost in their totality, of the action committed by government agents, the army, [the national] guard, national police and treasury police." Finally, reports at the end of the summer by both the Embassy and the Legal Aid Office showed a resurgence of civilian deaths during the first two weeks of August, while the Central American University reported 316 killings for July and 681 for August.[88]

More importantly, there is reason to believe that the statistical methods used by the administration, and indeed by the human rights groups themselves, were of poor and diminishing utility. The U.S. Embassy has measured killings on the basis of reports in the pro-government newspapers in El Salvador, which makes its data hopelessly biased to begin with. In its comments on the Reagan administration's certification statement in July, the ACLU-Americas Watch report listed six reasons to believe that the downward trend represented by the several indices are increasingly unable to record Salvadoran reality:

1. political violence has shifted increasingly to the countryside;
2. a larger portion of El Salvador has become a "war zone;"
3. attacks on journalists and human rights monitors further confine them to the vicinity of San Salvador;
4. security forces and death squads, who used to leave victims of political violence in plain view, apparently to intimidate others, increasingly dispose of corpses in secret mass graves;
5. it is unclear whether to count civilians bombed by the increasingly well-equipped Salvadoran Air Force as victims of conventional combat tactics or of deliberate terrorism;
6. the most important independent organization monitoring human rights abuses, the Legal Aid Office, was recently reorganized with a small and less-experienced staff. "For these reasons," stated the Americas Watch and the ACLU, "there is simply no basis for concluding that the actual numbers of political murders in El Salvador has declined."[89]

By the time of the election there were few active political organizations that remained potential candidates for targeted repression. Organizations sympathetic to the program of the FDR had long since been dissolved, decimated, or gone underground. The Christian Democratic Party suffered heavy attacks from the right in the postelection period. In late May the PDC issued a statement accusing the right and the security forces of responsibility for the murders of more than 600 members of their party over the previous two years. The PDC's immediate grievance was the murder of some dozen party officials in mid-May, including three mayors and seven election-day poll watchers.

Other candidates for the postelection wave of terrorism at the hands of the death squads and security forces were those non-combatant relief organizations that were trying to ameliorate the effects of the civil war. AI, for example, reported to Congress in August 1982 that since May they had "documentation that at least ten persons working in the human rights area in El Salvador have disappeared." They also reported the arrest of Patricia Cuellar, a U.S. citizen and former secretary in the Church's Legal Aid Office, and the disappearance of her father, on the very day that the Reagan administration sent its certification statement to Congress.[90] Perhaps the most dramatic example of the postelection repression against humanitarian workers was the arrest and torture of a volunteer for the Salvadoran Green Cross. Many of the 1,700 volunteers for the Green Cross had been the object of repression by security forces, and at the end of May Juan Francisco Zamora, the head of the Green Cross, was kidnapped by police and charged with possessing illegal literature and helping "subversives" get medical equipment.[91] The case of torture that came to light at the end of July was particularly embarrassing for the administration because the volunteer was known to an Embassy official, and his story became public on the eve of the government's certification statement. According to the torture victim, he was strapped to a rotating wheel similar to a medieval rack; forced to inhale lime; and in a third operation, called "the Carter," he "was strung up by ropes tied to his hands and feet while severe pressure was applied to his testicles by means of a wire." The torture was carried out over several days in a secret, sound-proofed room on the third floor of the National Police headquarters, whose commander was Col. Reynaldo Lopez Nuila. Queried by a *Washington Post* reporter about the alleged torture, Undersecretary of State for Human Rights and Humanitarian Affairs Elliott Abrams said that Col. Lopez Nuila had "a strong commitment to human rights," that was not matched by some of the heads of other security agencies.[92]

Controlling the Armed Forces. Both the U.S. and the Salvadoran leadership have regarded the human rights abuses by the military as primarily a public relations problem. For example, in his instructions to the Armed Forces on March 9, 1982, cited by the Reagan administration as an indication that El Salvador was "achieving substantial control over all elements of its own armed forces, so as to bring to an end the indiscriminate torture and murder of Salvadoran citizens," General Garcia said: "Actions outside of legal procedures or in violation of citizens' rights must not be repeated and must be avoided at all costs. Only by this conduct can we contribute to [the goal that] friendly countries continue offering us their support."[93] And after the election, in his "confidential" telegram to the U.S. Embassy in El Salvador, Secretary of State Haig proposed "casting our human rights program in military improvement terms, [which] will hopefully avoid provoking the opposition of the political parties of the right."[94] The election, in strengthening the right in El Salvador, diminished the power of the United States to pursue *anything other* than a counterinsurgency program in that country.

A second matter addressed in Haig's cable also illustrates the way in which the administration's attitude toward its client's atrocities was governed solely by PR considerations. Haig told the Embassy that "we need to demonstrate immediately an improvement in both the handling and disposition of insurgents who are captured in the field and political opponents who have been arrested by the government. A specific order to take and protect prisoners issued and publicized by the Ministry of Defense should be highly desireable." The reason for Haig's sudden concern about the "no prisoners" policy of the Salvadoran military was that the International Red Cross "has made it clear that it is prepared to pull out of El Salvador if its concerns are not met." Red Cross departure, according to Haig, "would be a severe blow to our efforts to maintain Congressional support." According to a spokesman for the International Red Cross delegation in El Salvador, there had never been more than a few prisoners captured on the battlefield during the 18-month civil war.[95] Perhaps in line with the Reagan administration's policies encouraging private enterprise, Haig proposed to solve the PR problem by the "installation of a material incentive system to ensure that prisoners are not killed and good treatment of captured guerillas and suspected guerilla collaborators. Army intelligence could pay a nominal sum to civilian military units or civil defense personnel who turn in prisoners or suspects later proven to be guerillas or collaborators." In Vietnam, this system of material incentives had led to widespread abuses, as personal enemies were denounced for money. Contrary to the promise that "free elections" would gain greater control over the military by the newly legitimized civilian government, the United States was now proposing to bribe the military and security forces to prevent the Red Cross from causing an international scandal.

In yet another way the election seems to have increased the level of violence in the countryside. The victory of ARENA and the PCN was reflected in the renewed power of the local paramilitary forces, or "military escorts," which dated back to the 1932 massacre and were later loosely incorporated into ORDEN. When the Christian Democrats entered the Revolutionary Junta in January 1980, one of the means by which they attempted to restore their battered political base was to appoint their party members as mayors in most of the country's 261 municipalities. After the March election these Christian Democratic appointees were "lame ducks," no longer with any power in the central government, and prime candidates for assassination by the local paramilitary forces. According to PDC chief Duarte, this was the process of revenge—"revanchismo." One of the most publicized of these episodes was in the town of San Francisco Chinameca, which had cast 903 votes for D'Aubuisson and 294 for the Christian Democrats. The paramilitary forces had killed the founder of the local Christian Democratic Party in January 1980, just three weeks after the national party had joined the junta. The first mayor of San Francisco Chinameca appointed by the party in San Salvador refused to sleep in his new domain, but commuted each day by bus. Six weeks after the election armed men wearing hoods dragged him off the bus and murdered him in front of the other passengers. The Christian Democrats then named Evangelina Garca as interim mayor, but she was killed two weeks after her predecessor, three days before her term was to begin, along with her 18-year old daughter. According to her brother, her family had never entered politics before.[96]

The March election sharpened these longstanding local conflicts. For Salvadorans the level of violence and terror in their daily lives was further increased. For the Reagan administration it was an important step in the development of a viable pacification strategy. This was illustrated in a *Washington Post* profile of Lt. Col. Sigifredo Ochoa some three months after the election. Ochoa later gained fame as the military commander who went on strike in 1983, an act which eventually led to the ouster of General Garcia, for which Ochoa was rewarded with "exile" to a post in the United States. In June 1982, however, Ochoa was known as one of the few commanders who had successfully adopted an aggressive counterinsurgency strategy. He had undoubtedly learned much from his training in Taiwan and from Israeli instructors in El Salvador; but according to the *Post* "a major element in his formula for success . . . is the most notorious adjunct of the Army, the collection of local paramilitary informers and militias called the Civil Defense." Ochoa maintained contact with "scores" of armed paramilitary groups: "All of these send us information," Ochoa said; and as a result he claimed to know where the guerillas camped, where they moved, "and other intelligence necessary to exterminate insurgents."[97]

Washington was eager to organize and modernize El Salvador's pacification program against the guerillas, and it attempted to reorganize the Salvadoran army into an efficient counterrevolutionary force. To do this it began to arm and train the entire Salvadoran armed forces, which greatly intensified the level of violence they could inflict on the enemies of the government. In justifying the unprecedented training of an entire battalion—the Ramon Belloso Quick Reaction Battalion—in the United States, the Reagan administration stated in February 1982 that they believed such training "will produce not only officers and soldiers well-schooled in military skills, but also men with a well-defined sense of the need to maintain the support of the populace through respect for basic human rights and the promotion of a close working relationship with the people."⁹⁸ Though large-scale training of Salvadoran troops began in January 1982, these troops did not return home and see action until late May. In the climate of violence engendered by El Salvador's first "free election" and its aftermath, the Belloso Battalion was rushed into combat in Chalatenango province, along the Honduran border. Attempting to catch the guerillas in a pincer operation, with Honduran troops preventing the guerillas from crossing the border, the two-phase sweep was described by the *Washington Post* as "in part a test of the counterinsurgency tactics advocated by the United States."⁹⁹

The military operation itself was a failure, as the guerillas slipped away. What about the battalion's "close working relationship with the people?" According to interviews conducted in Honduran refugee camps by Janice Hill of the National Council of Churches, at the end of May, two days after the offensive began, some 2,000 fleeing refugees were attacked by the Army at the Sumpul River, near the border of Honduras and El Salvador. According to one refugee account: "Then we had to go right past the Army. They shot at us with mortars and they threw grenades at us from all directions. . . . We were all trying to escape with our children. Lots of children were lost." Another refugee, a women in her twenties, said: "Then we reached the Sumpul River and there lots and lots of people died. Children, women who gave birth to their children right in the Sumpul river. . . . On the other side of the Sumpul River, they captured people and killed them. They killed a lot of people." Some 600 people were killed in the attack.¹⁰⁰

According to Lt. Col. Domingo Monterrosa, Commander of the U.S.-trained Atlacatl Battalion which also participated in the operation, these civilian deaths were inevitable. "It is natural," he said, "that in these subversive redoubts the armed men are not there alone. That is to say, they need their 'masses'—people, women, old people, or children, including the children who are messengers, or the wives, and they are all mixed up with the subversives themselves, with the armed ones. So in the clashes. . .it's natural that there were a series of people killed, some without weapons, including some women, and I understand some children."¹⁰¹ This bizarre justification for civilian slaughter was not some Latin American deficiency. In supporting continued security assistance to El Salvador in July 1982, the Reagan administration's certification statement also blamed the guerillas for the civilian casualties inflicted by the army: "Human rights problems concerning the military," it maintained, "have been exacerbated by guerilla tactics which have resulted in the deaths of noncombatants. The guerillas routinely travel with civilians who provide logistical support for their units. When the guerillas are attacked by government forces, the ensuing hostilities often produce civilian casualties."[102] The client had learned the master's lesson well. In making war against an entire population, everyone is the enemy.

CHAPTER 5

Role of the Mass Media in a Demonstration Election

A demonstration election is a *media event* above all else. Its success requires massive publicity at home, carefully focused on the right questions, and avoiding the wrong ones. The media, moreover, must not follow up this reporting to see whether "peace" and "reconciliation" result from the election, or whether it merely consolidates the power of the war party and allows intensified violence. "Good questions" are those about election day weather and prospective turnout, candidate foibles, and the likelihood of "leftist disruption;" bad questions concern security force murders, the rise and operations of ORDEN, the legal requirement to vote, and the bearing of all these on the "turnout." Many of the bad questions fall under the general heading of "conditions essential to a genuinely free election." It is taken as a patriotic *premise* that an election sponsored by the home government is democratic in intent and carried out in good faith.

Hard questions about the election's real purpose, its possible manipulative function, or the feasibility of conducting a meaningful election under conditions of warfare, military occupation, and terror are rarely raised and never pressed. Similarly, the election is never condemned and ridiculed beforehand as a staged fraud and a deliberate attempt to mislead the public, even when this is patently obvious. This would be a grossly unpatriotic insistence on consistency, truth, and adherence to basic democratic values, and the mass media are not unpatriotic.

Information Sources: Governments versus Refugees

Closely paralleling the fixing of premises and asking only the right questions is reliance on proper sources of information. Giving dominant place to U.S. and Salvadoran government press releases, and addressing questions only to officials of these governments, allows the agenda to be set by the holocaust managers. If the media were to talk mainly with rebels, peasants, ordinary intellectuals and professionals, members of the Salvadoran Church Legal Aid Office, or refugees, a different set of facts and a different agenda would force themselves into media cognition and prominence. The U.S. mass media almost never derive information from peasants,[1] who constitute the majority of the population of El Salvador, or from refugees, whose numbers run into the hundreds of thousands and who are very accessible in refugee camps in Mexico, Honduras, and Costa Rica, as well as in El Salvador and the United States itself. Amnesty International (AI) and various other human rights groups interview these refugees frequently, finding them strangely negative concerning the incipient El Salvadoran democracy. It is easy to catalog from refugee sources eyewitness reports of massive arbitrary and sadistic violence. Edouard Bailby, a special correspondent for *Le Monde Diplomatique*, reported that

> Search and destroy operations have taken on such proportions, that eyewitnesses can be found by the dozens. Contrary to what one could imagine the soldiers committing these crimes against the civilian population are neither drunk nor drugged. "They kill coldly, methodically" say some witnesses, "accusing their victims of being dirty communists." In most cases, they hit with machetes, to save ammunition. Those trying to escape are machine-gunned . . . . Other witnesses from the village of Puente-DeSumpul, in

the Department of Chalatenango, recall the murders of "los dos viejitos". Warned by their neighbors of the National Guard's arrival, they chose to stay home, believing they would be spared because of their great age. The soldiers arrived, decapitated them, and hung their heads by the hair to the top of their house. When some courageous men came back to the village, at night, to find some food for their families hidden in the mountains, they saw the horrible spectacle.[2]

To focus on the testimony of refugees would quickly suggest that SS-type mass murder and unlimited terror is the *modus operandi* of the Salvadoran government. This will clearly not do.

The U.S. mass media do use refugees as a major information source in the case of *enemy* states, such as Cambodia, Vietnam, Cuba, and Afghanistan,[3] where the focus on anticivilian terror is consistent with the agenda of the national leadership. Refugees have not been given any substantial publicity, however, in reporting on East Timor (Indonesia being the invader), Uruguay, Chile, Turkey, or present day Lebanon. This is again consistent with the fact that U.S. leaders look with favor on the regimes committing the violence.

Certainly the media will be even more careful in "sourcing" for El Salvador, where the U.S. leadership is actively supporting the government. In the exceptional cases where reporters seek out the victims of U.S. government sponsored pacification—peasants, refugees, or rebels—they are subjected to abuse and hostility as "aiding the enemy."[4] Those journalists, on the other hand, who serve strictly as propaganda conduits of their government are free from flak. Thus, not only are U.S. officials like Enders and Hinton centers of media attention, but Roberto D'Aubuisson has a media access and exposure greater than that of the entire mass of El Salvador's peasants and refugees.

The Dramatic Framework

In his *Symbolic Uses of Politics*, Murray Edelman shows how easy it was for the Truman administration immediately after World War II, even with the stench of the Nazi death camps hardly dissipated, to transform the symbol of "Germany" from ultimate evil to an ally in the struggle against Communism:

Germany became an ally against Russia; and if former Nazis in high military and political posts could help cope with the new dangers, they were welcomed and their past actions rewritten or ignored. It thus turns out that very intense mass concerns about denazification were not generators of public policy, but rather highly vulnerable victims of a changed perceptual world.[5]

The "perceptual world" was changed by concurrent shifts in policy and the manipulation of symbols, by stress on newly selected facts, and by mass media accommodation in implementing this shift in policy.

A recent illustration of the shifting of media attention and indignation in accord with state propaganda needs is the changing role of the Cambodian leader Pol Pot. During the period 1975-80, when the U.S. elite was attempting to overcome the "Vietnam syndrome" and produce a more conservative public world view, the violence of Pol Pot and the Khmer Rouge was dwelt upon by the media with great intensity and passionate indignation, as an object lesson in the evils of Communism.[6] After Pol Pot's ouster by the Vietnamese in 1980, however, his regime in exile was quietly rehabilitated as a U.S. ally against the Vietnamese. Reagan administration spokesman John Holdridge explained to a congressional committee in 1982 that we continue to recognize and support the Cambodian exile group, of which Pol Pot's is the dominant faction, because this group represents a "continuity" with the past (i.e., to the ousted Pol Pot regime).[7] This statement was not mentioned in the U.S. press, and the new U.S. alliance with Pol Pot is kept carefully under the rug. No questions are raised about the propriety of giving support to a leader so recently castigated as in a class with Hitler, nor is there any mention of the hypocrisy in the media's shift from wild indignation to placid acceptance.

A demonstration election uses a similarly shifted perceptual framework to accomplish its PR objectives. The media portray the election—following in detail the lead of their government—as a dramatic confrontation between the forces of good and evil. The election and the forms of democracy are used as the symbols of good; and objections to the election, threatened boycotts, and disruptions are the symbols of evil. An aggressive pressing of this symbolism by the government and mass media makes it possible to transmute evil into something benign, even heart-warming, and to sell it to the public. Security forces which murdered and mutilated women and children yesterday become the (perhaps reluctant) cooperators in groping for democracy today. We may juxtapose the two pictures of the security forces in action. First:

> On January 10, 1981, troops took 22 teen-agers from Meji-
> canos; all were later found dead, with marks showing that
> they had been tortured. An army spokesman said that they
> died of bullet wounds in a confrontation with troops; but a
> doctor who examined 17 of the bodies said that they had all
> been shot after dying. Five of the young women were uni-
> dentifiable because their faces had been erased.[8]

Twenty-two bodies divided into 30,000-odd civilian murders gives us
1,364. Multiply the above episode by 1,364 to get the picture of what
the "security forces" mean to the people of El Salvador. Or consider
the statement of a parish priest in a working class district of San
Salvador, reported by former Senator Dick Clark, that fully 90% of
the families in his parish had suffered at least one kidnapping or
murder by the security forces.[9]

But then read what *New York Times* reporter Warren Hoge has
to say, in his summary of the election "issues," concerning the security forces and their relationship to the election:

> Is the military playing any role in the elections? [Answer:]
> Members of the military are not allowed to vote, and the
> armed forces has pledged to protect voters from violence
> and to respect the outcome of the contest.[10]

This is the only context in Hoge's summary of the issues in the
election where the security forces of El Salvador have any place. They
are a protector of the public against "violence," helping move the
country toward democracy.

If the Nazis and Pol Pot can be quickly rehabilitated by a shift in
political demands and a parallel shuffling of the *dramatis personae*,
why not Major Bob D'Aubuisson and the death squads of El
Salvador as "fighters for freedom"?

Government Staging: Manipulating the Personae and Organizing the Props

Demonstration elections are staged in what we may call a
"legitimacy show." The show is held in a Third World country, but
the idea, the implementing plans, and the resources originate in the
United States. This is reasonable, given the fact that the point of the
show is to manipulate the U.S. audience. In the three cases discussed
in earlier chapters—the Dominican Republic, Vietnam, and El
Salvador—Washington had a PR problem. It was the function of the

"free election" to alleviate that problem.

Demonstration elections also reflect the readiness with which successive U.S. administrations take over and manage the internal affairs of their allegedly independent clients. "Independence" is used by imperial powers in a completely opportunistic fashion—they are always protecting it from some distant foreign power, while violating it brazenly in their own manipulations of the client. By definition the United States (or the Soviet Union in its own sphere of influence) never threatens a country's independence. If the puppet is doing something awful, the parent regrets this but couldn't possibly intervene in the affairs of this proudly independent country! We also lack "leverage."* Thus one manipulates and controls, but assumes the posture of benevolent Godfather trying to move things toward "reform," sadly limited in capacity to influence by respect for sacred sovereignty. The mass media generally swallow this routine, which allows incessant and sometimes ruthless intervention, while providing a moral cover for consequences that are usually acceptable or even planned by the parent.

Former CIA officer Joseph B. Smith, for example, has recounted in detail how the United States in the 1950s organized in the Philippines a vast array of committees supporting free elections, bought and blackmailed politicians, and managed the campaign of its chosen vehicle Ramon Magsaysay.[11] In Brazil in the early 1960's, the CIA provided substantial funding to hundreds of politicians, in a scandal whose investigation was only terminated by the U.S.-sponsored coup of 1964.[12] In Vietnam, we have seen that the United States imported its chosen leader, financed and advised him, organized and trained his police and military forces, colluded in his overthrow and murder, and chose and defined the limits of behavior of his successors. One of Diem's early replacements told newsmen that he found out that he was going to be the next head of state of Vietnam only when his U.S. adviser "told me that a coup d'état was planned in Saigon and that I was to become President...."[13] It is interesting to contrast the disavowals by U.S. officials of any "arrogant" attempts to influence client governments with their matter-of-fact assumption that *they* determine who rules in these client states, as disclosed later in released government documents. In an internal briefing of November 27, 1964, for example, General Maxwell Taylor speaks about our "establishing some reasonably satisfactory government" in South Vietnam; and that if we are not satisfied with the way things are going, "we could try again with another civilian government.... Another alternative would be to *invite back* a military dictatorship on the model of that headed of late by General Khanh."[14] Taylor, in fact, also expressed his contempt for his Vietnamese puppets quite openly. In his book *From Swords to Plowshares*, he describes Diem's "unexpected resistance" to the American demand for direct participation in civil administration, and adds: "On the chance that Diem might continue to be intransigent, the old search for a possible replacement for him was resumed in State." Later he speaks of "the impetuosity of Diem's American critics and our opposition to ousting him without a replacement in sight." When General Khanh began to lose his shaky political base, "the question was: If not Khanh, who? This time there was again the possibility that 'Big' Minh might do. He had been behaving quite well..."[15]

The mass media of the United States never pointed out (or questioned the fact) that their leaders had arrogated to themselves the right to determine the rulers of South Vietnam. The government of that province shifted after 1963 into the hands of corrupt and violent military men who made Diem look like a paragon of virtue, but whose aims were compatible with those of Washington. For the media, this deterioration of leadership was an inexplicable exogenous happening that the United States sometimes regretted, being devoted to "reform," but was unable to control. As we noted earlier, even Ky was made a reformer. But for unknown reasons reform never took place.

Putting together a demonstration election is expensive. The total outlays made by the Reagan administration in staging the El Salvador election of March 1982 are not on the public record, but $6-8 million has already been directly allocated for its successor.[16] The unacknowledged and indirect outlays must be larger still. The expenses of the CIA, for example, which was acknowledged as an active participant in the 1982 El Salvador election,[17] will appear under other financial entries. A newspaper report allegedly based on intelligence sources claimed that the Reagan administration "considered" covert funding of the Duarte and Christian Democratic election campaign in 1982, but "it could not be determined whether such aid was actually approved."[18] This would have helped Duarte offset the $200,000 fund available to Roberto D'Aubuisson from private sources, along with the advertising services provided to D'Aubuisson "at cost" by the U.S. agency McCann-Erickson (as "our duty to the political system of El Salvador," in the words of an agency officer).[19]

A large chunk of U.S. aid to the 1982 election was dispensed to the Electoral Commission and elsewhere under the guise of promoting voter registration. It was recently disclosed that AID spent $220,000 in a "get-out-the-vote" campaign in 1982.[20] The Salvadoran junta is already reportedly going to spend $600,000 in the next election under a "contract with a media consulting firm of unspecified nationality that will publicize the elections to induce people to go to the polls." With the left kept off the ballot, and "turnout" equated with support of the status quo and repudiation of the rebels, making the case for voting provides a seemingly apolitical and virtuous way of propagandizing for army rule.[21] To make sure that the turnout is properly appreciated, AID is currently requesting $780,000 for observer expenses for the next election.[22]

The various satellite organizations of the evolving totalitarian state were mobilized and subsidized in 1982 to help with the campaign of encouraging the "civic virtues." The rightwing propagandist Daniel James explained to a congressional committee that a leaflet touting the election was circulated among Salvadoran workers and peasants by two trade union and peasant groups, the Popular Democratic Unity (UPD) and the AIFLD-sponsored Salvadoran Communal Union (UCS). James mentions that leaders of both of these organizations traveled to Washington, D.C. before the election of March 1982. The content of the civic action leaflet stresses the citizen's responsibility for voting, and also the fact that the vote is an expression of the public's desire for "peace."[23]

A major effort was made by the Reagan team to get credible sources to say that the election was a great idea. The Salvadoran churches were pressed to approve the election and urge voters to go to the polls. Several of them did this, although usually reluctantly and with qualifications that the election "might be" a first step in a peace process that would have to involve a negotiated settlement with the left. The Reagan administration seized upon these statements as propaganda wedges, using them to further condemn and isolate the rebels and other objectors. It ignored the qualifications and stress on compromise, and of course never mentioned the fact that the churches and church personnel were themselves subject to a steady diet of bombings and murders by the security forces. The churches generally insist that dialogue and negotiations are central to achieving peace. It was theoretically possible that an election might have strengthened the hand of governmental elements that would support dialogue. After the fact, it is clear that it strengthened the hand of the war party, and we believe that this was its clear intent. Thus the churches' tentative sanctioning of the election, partially coerced, partially based on a naive faith in elections and the stated goals of the Reagan team, was quickly perverted to the PR needs of the war party.

In the early months of 1982 the administration also sponsored the Central American Democratic Community, comprising Honduras, Costa Rica, and El Salvador. Its goal was to generate support for the election by tying in the satellite getting a PR massage (El Salvador) with two other local satellites that could lay claim to being "authentic democracies."* Under the auspices of the Reagan administration the two authentic democracies were rapidly being militarized, and their already flimsy democratic facade was eroding at top speed.[24] Nevertheless the plan was to provide some kind of "democracy by association" to the El Salvadoran junta, as if it wasn't already enough proof of its democratic credentials that Reagan and Kirkpatrick were lined up solidly in its corner.

The Government-Media Demonstration Election Agenda

The accommodation of the mass media to the dramatic staging requirements of the government was just about all the government could ask in El Salvador in March 1982, as it had been in the earlier elections in the Dominican Republic and Vietnam. The government was allowed complete domination of the flow of information and opinion, defining an agenda and context for the election. The press was unable or unwilling to generate counterfacts, a counteragenda, or an alternative framework from which to examine alleged facts. The murder of four Dutch journalists 11 days before the election, and the death list of 35 journalists put out at the same time, were helpful reminders to the huge press assemblage that it would be wise to stay in town, avoid the rebels and refugees, and accept the guidance of the security forces and U.S. Embassy. Media pliability was helped by the patriotism of many journalists, who accepted the premises of their government and were willing, even eager to serve it.

The net result was that the government carried the media along, a pseudo-event was made real, hype took over the "news," and even the honest and objective members of the press were compelled to take the pseudo-event at face value. The patriotic current and the hype made it impossible to question directly and forcefully either the *aims* or the *cynicism* of an election held by a "state-of-siege" government freely killing civilians under a legal system "out of control" (Enders). It would have been physically hazardous to raise such questions while reporting from El Salvador, and it was also hazardous to job security and status at home, as the *New York Times* demonstrated to Raymond Bonner, who was transferred from reporting on Central America to the financial pages.[25]

Mass media accommodation to the government agenda may be read from three sets of facts. First, the government wanted the media to feature the El Salvador election as Big News. The media came through with flying colors. The number of journalists and networks present in El Salvador on March 28, 1982, was staggering: at least 700 media representatives attended the election, along with 200-odd observers. Media attention levels were very high, surpassing that of any other recent foreign election. Election day and day-after coverage on the major TV networks averaged over eight minutes, and there had also been extensive prior network coverage. Three top U.S. newspapers provided 34 front page stories over a seven day span, and the three biggest news weeklies each gave the election four to seven columns of coverage.[26]

A second indicator of media accommodation to the PR strategy was its reliance on the government as a source of information. Between February 1, 1982, and April 10, 1982, the *New York Times*, which we believe was better than the mass media average in diversity of election news sources, had 51 news items on the El Salvador election. Thirty of these, or 59% of the total, were based primarily or exclusively on statements by U.S. or Salvadoran officials. Of 18 front page items during this period, 12, or 67%, relied primarily or exclusively on government sources. Thus basing stories on government sources increased front page access. The *Times* reporter relying least on government handouts, Raymond Bonner, reached the front page in only two of 11 articles; Warren Hoge, who served as a virtual government press officer, hit the front page on six of 15 articles. Interestingly, Bonner's stories were only put on the front page when they were compatible with the official interpretation of the election: one was based on an extended interview with Duarte; the other was a postelection item that stressed the severity of the defeat suffered by the insurgents as a consequence of the election.

The third set of facts indicating media accommodation to government PR needs in a demonstration election are those showing that the media ask the right questions, avoid the wrong ones, and start out on suitable patriotic premises. We will describe briefly and illustrate the three main categories of items that meet the government's requirements for "pulling off" a demonstration election. While these do not exhaust the list, they are of prime importance. We then address the main items that are "off" the agenda.

On-the-Agenda Items

1. U.S. government assertions of the purpose, importance, and beneficence of the election. The government strives first and foremost to convey the impression that the election is a *very important thing*, with creditable aims and desirable consequences. The first aim is to initiate "a first step" (Abrams) or a "step in the beginning" (Enders) of the institutionalization of democracy. Sometimes the matter is put a little differently, as in President Reagan's contrasting Nicaragua's corrupted revolution with "El Salvador's revolution [which] is one that is building democracy" (NYT, July 19, 1983). A second objective is to encourage "reform." In the words of Alexander Haig, "we have supported the current regime based on the reforms the regime had initiated—land reform, improved pluralization, democratic reform, efforts to improve the human rights situation, economic reforms" (NYT, March 29, 1982). Or, as expressed by Thomas Enders: "We want to help the Salvadorans prevent the insurgents from disrupting the political and social transformations that are now under way" (NYT, Feb. 9, 1982). A third aim is peace, and "it is equally important that the United States continue to be the foremost protector of peace" (Reagan, NYT, July 27, 1983). Assertions of this character dominated the flow of media news in a direct conduiting that was carried out on a massive scale, objectively.

Besides direct transmission, however, the indirect conduiting of government opinion is very important. Consider Warren Hoge's statement that "making El Salvador ready for democracy is the stated purpose of the expanded United States interest" (NYT, April 3, 1982). Hoge never asks whether the stated purpose is the same as the real purpose. In another article Hoge says that "El Salvador is trying to accomplish the feat of peaceably trying to change governments through the ballot box..." (NYT, February 27, 1982). This packs a lot of apologetics into one sentence—personification; the implication that the election is organized by Salvadorans in a democratic way and with democratic intent; the implication that the aim is change rather than ratification of the status quo; and the implication that change is possible through the March 1982 election. In another *Times* article, the heading reads "For First Time Since 32 Crackdown, Democracy Is Trying for a Comeback" (March 29, 1982). The article goes on to say that "today Salvadorans are casting ballots and hoping that a democratically-elected government will be able to settle a civil war that many say has its roots in the events of 1932." Note here again the positive assertions about Salvadorans (in general) and their purposes and hopes, the implication that "democracy" is really functioning in the March 1982 elections and that Salvadorans are voting, not because of a legal obligation and coercion, but with a general expectation of influencing the course of events. This goes beyond the objectivity of transmitting government propaganda by quotation; these are assertions of alleged fact about a personified Salvadoran populace and democracy in El Salvador which correspond to the government propaganda line but are based on no evidence and are largely untrue.

Sometimes ends other than furthering democracy and reform (or protecting these against "totalitarians") are acknowledged, such as legitimizing the government and delegitimizing the rebels. Occa- sionally the government and media acknowledge the possibility that the election will not lead to a quick settlement of the conflict. But these admissions are kept in the background. The media feel no obligation to weigh, to analyse carefully, or to consider the internal consistency of the propaganda line.

2. Left disruption. In the demonstration election drama it is extremely important to have forces of evil *challenge* the forces of freedom. This was very well expressed by Warren Hoge in the *New York Times*:

> The elections have taken on a significance beyond their outcome because leftist guerillas mounted a campaign to disrupt them and discourage voters from going to the polls. Simply conducting the balloting in the midst of violence and political uncertainty that grips much of El Salvador had become a challenge in itself for the junta and its principle [sic] international backer, the United States. (March 29, 1982)

The guerilla challenge allows the army and other components of the system of state terror to be transformed into good guys, trying to protect an "extraordinarily courageous and unflinching people" who, "in spite of massive violence at the polling places and threats of retaliation by guerilla forces against voters,...voted in unprece- dented numbers" (Kirkpatrick).[27]

Left disruption was a central and essentially unopposed theme in the mass media presentation of the March 1982 election in El Salvador. Hilary Brown of ABC-TV explained on election day that "the guerillas tactic today was to so terrify the people that they would stay away from the polls."[28] Richard Meislin of the *New York Times* never deviated from the line that the rebels "threatened to kill those who cast ballots." Neither did the *Times'* Warren Hoge, who repeated this claim in virtually every one of his articles. In the certification hearings of February 1, 1982, the administration and its supporters pushed this line aggressively. According to Thomas Enders, the FMLN-FDR has "sworn to destroy them [the elections] physically and the people involved in them."[29] Apologists for administration policy William Doherty of the AIFLD and Max Singer of the Hudson Institute made the same claim. When asked to give evidence for this assertion, neither of them were able to do so either in the hearings or in later submissions for the record.[30]

This disruption line was based on a lie, disseminated as a matter of propaganda necessity—left disruption was required for the drama and a myth would suffice. The rebels had been put in a strategically awkward position by the election, and they made a number of disparate statements, but *there is not one yet quoted by anybody* that indicated an intent to hurt people trying to vote or even to disrupt the election per se. What is more, the most authoritative rebel statements— one by Guillermo Ungo, the head of the FDR, and a March 23 statement on Radio Venceremos—advised the public not to worry about the elections in one way or another. The media, however, insofar as they bothered with evidence, dredged up an earlier statement by Ferman Cienfuegos of the Armed Forces of the National Resistance (one of the guerilla organizations) that the election would be terminated by a general uprising that he forecast would sweep the country before election day. Even this statement the media misrepresented—it was not an election disruption statement, but an erroneous forecast that the war would be over by election day. It is notable that the several authorized statements by the rebels that contradicted the disruption strategy myth were, with minor exceptions, ignored by the media.

The media also inflated the importance of the modest military activity that took place during the election period. In an analysis of the media's treatment of the Salvadoran election, Jack Spence notes that "every media outlet, particularly the networks, cast the election day story in a framework of voting in the midst of extensive guerilla violence at polling places."[31] He shows that there is no evidence of any voters being attacked or killed, that the level of violence on election day was below average, and that guerilla behavior was consistent with the view that their strategy was to ignore the election. In short, the facts were not consistent with a guerilla strategy of disruption, which was a uniformly accepted centerpiece of mass media coverage of the election.

Time magazine, while adhering to this central theme, added its own unique touch of deception to the disruption ploy ("Missing The Story In El Salvador," April 12, 1982). According to its version, the "media-wise" rebels attempted to disrupt the election in order to attract attention to themselves! Most of the media were fooled by the rebels, but not the deep thinkers at *Time*, who could penetrate through the mists and see that the really important thing happening was the *magnificent turnout* reflecting the Salvadoran people's yearning for a free election! In fact, both the government and general run of less perceptive media put their chips on "turnout," but most added on the disruption gambit as the dramatic counterpoise. *Time*, pathetically trying to differentiate its "news" product without departing from the standard propaganda line, does so by understating the general focus on turnout and by its own original add-on lie about the media-wise rebels.

It is interesting to note that in the *New York Times* there was divided opinion among the reporters on the "disruption" theme. Alan Riding had an article on the subject that focused (excessively) on the Cienfuegos blustering statement about military victory (March 2, 1982). Riding was careful to point out, however, that even Cienfuegos didn't threaten the voters or the election per se, although Riding failed to give adequate weight to other rebels' statements that completely contradicted a disruption intent. Raymond Bonner was the only *New York Times* reporter who carefully noted the Ungo statement and the absence of any authenticated rebel claims of intent to kill voters, etc. Bonner even noted that the rebel disclaimers had been published in San Salvador newspapers. As we pointed out earlier, Richard Meislin and Warren Hoge consistently put forward the government propaganda myth that the rebels *vowed* to kill voters and/or disrupt the election. It is noteworthy that neither Meislin nor Hoge ever provided a single piece of evidence for this important and repeated claim. As these reporters must surely have read Bonner and Riding, if nothing else on the subject, some interesting questions arise. First, if Bonner is correct—and we believe he is—Meislin and Hoge were consistently presenting government propaganda lies, and felt no obligation to obtain corroborating evidence. Second, as Hoge and Meislin were given much more space and prominence than Bonner, and Bonner was giving independent and verifiable evidence whereas Meislin-Hoge were transmitting a government claim unsupported by any evidence, it follows that the *New York Times* was making a choice for a government-sponsored lie. Third, as Bonner was subsequently transferred whereas Meislin and Hoge remained as Central America correspondents, the *Times* in effect rewarded reliance on propaganda fabrications and penalized journalistic integrity.

3. Turnout. In the demonstration election drama the struggle is for "turnout." People turning out are bravely defying rebel terror in their eagerness to express approval of military juntas we are supporting and whatever policies we and the juntas choose to pursue. This game was played with increasing intensity and success from the Dominican Republic to Vietnam to El Salvador. At the conclusion of election day in El Salvador, Dan Rather exclaimed: "A triumph! A million people to the polls." But Rather was too quick. A few days later it was discovered that 500,000 more people had gone to the polls. While the exact number of phantoms in the voting figures are unknown, as we discussed in the previous chapter, the manipulation of numbers is absolutely clear. But the mass media, so enthralled with the triumphant "turnout" on March 28, were quite uninterested in the sequel of revelations that the vote was inflated.

The turnout-in-the-face-of-disruption gambit deflects attention from the substantive issues that are off the agenda—most notably, is it possible that there was coercion *to* vote, by law and by the ministrations of the security forces prior to their democratic service on March 28?

Off-the-Agenda Items

1. The background and context of the election. In 1972 there was an election in El Salvador apparently won by a civilian coalition headed by Duarte, but overturned by the Central Election Commission—a tool of the oligarchy—with the support of the army. There was another election characterized by massive fraud in 1977. Why did the United States fail to exercise the slightest pressure toward democratic outcomes in those elections, or at least maintain a neutral stance toward the subsequent attempted coup in 1972 by constitutionalist forces rather than actively oppose it? Why did the United States organize an election only very belatedly, under conditions of extreme violence, and in de facto support of exactly the same military elements that had overturned real elections only a short time previously? Why does the United States play the election game only in El Salvador, not in Turkey or Guatemala or Chile? On rare occasion the media will mention the democratic failures of the past in El Salvador, perhaps to show that Duarte, who was the victim of the

1972 election fraud, is therefore a true spokesman of Salvadoran democracy. As rare as dodo birds would be questions like: "Where was the United States back in 1972 or 1977?" Or, "Is it not odd that the United States is now supporting through free elections the same army and oligarchy that had prevented or upset all prior elections?"

2. The real purpose of the elections. It is our view that the Salvadoran election of 1982 (like that in Vietnam in 1967) was arranged in a militarized and terrorized state precisely because "getting out the vote," and confining it to rightwing parties, would be easy. The purpose was to use this coerced vote, with appropriate hype, to mislead the U.S. public into believing that the people of El Salvador wanted us, that they approved our policies and the political choices given them, and that we favored democracy in some meaningful and operational sense. The further and more basic end in both Vietnam and El Salvador was to allow an escalation of the war, deeper U.S. involvement, and a further pursuit of military victory.

The media were important props for this staged PR drama, but they could hardly admit this. Thus, while the mass media provided assorted details on U.S. interest in the election, a close examination of the exact intent and purposes of the sponsor was off-the-agenda. That the U.S. government *imposed* the election from afar and managed it in detail was muted at best. The media preferred elliptical references to the Salvadoran people trying out the democratic route.

3. Free speech. A first condition of free elections is that people be able to speak, exchange views, and get uncensored information, all without fear of violence. We have pointed out in chapters 1 and 4 that El Salvador had no freedom of speech in 1982.

It is a notable fact that even Duarte, the figleaf head of state, was practically a prisoner during the campaign, confined almost exclusively to making TV broadcasts from San Salvador. Only Major Bob D'Aubuisson could campaign throughout the country, enjoying as he did the support of the hardline military and the death squads. Robert White, former Ambassador to El Salvador, stated in 1982 that

> It is abᶜolutely certain that any candidate who campaigned on a platform of conciliation for the Salvadoran family [sic: meaning all Salvadorans] and peaceful elections would be shot by the military. There is no question about that.[32]

The U.S. mass media almost never discussed freedom of speech—never in depth or with any strong inferences as to compatibility with a free election.

4. Freedom of the press. After a siege of totalitarian violence that had destroyed most of its independent private elements and left the remainder cowed by state-sponsored terror, the press of El Salvador in March 1982 was largely government controlled. Nearly a year before the election, on May 6, 1981, exiled Salvadoran publisher Jorge Pinto wrote in the *New York Times*:

> The regime presents itself as a supporter of free elections. Elections, of course, require a dialogue, which in turn requires freedom of expression. This is what I was attempting to carry out with my newspaper. But how can a dialogue be sustained if those participating in it are assassinated? If a newspaper like *El Independiente* is assassinated?

Pinto's question was never considered by the *Times* or any other member of the U.S. mass media; a serious focus on this core aspect of freedom, and inferences as to the viability of elections without free speech or a free press, are off the media agenda.

5. Independent organizations: survival and destruction. In democratic theory, intermediate organizations like unions, social and political clubs, and professional bodies are important components of a pluralistic system. They stand between the unprotected individual and state power. We have pointed out in earlier chapters that all such bodies have been attacked in El Salvador, thousands of their leaders have been killed, and many of the organizations have been destroyed or pushed underground. Two observers of El Salvador's medical community point out that

> Patients have been taken out of hospital beds or operating rooms to be executed. Doctors, nurses and medical students have been abducted while attending patients, then tortured and murdered. A National Committee for the Defense of Patients, Workers and Health Institutions was formed to protect the neutrality of medical practice, but most of its founding members were later killed, "disappeared" or were forced into exile.[33]

This case is merely illustrative of a general phenomenon. Robert White himself has testified that

> The guerilla groups, the revolutionary groups, almost without exception began as associations of teachers, associations of labor unions, campesino unions, or parish organizations [that had limited and local improvement aims, but found that] first they were warned and then they were persecuted and tortured and shot.[34]

Organizations not destroyed or pushed underground in totalitarian societies must seek the protection of the state. In El Salvador, it is also possible for an organization to survive above ground if it is under the protection of the United States, or one of its service arms. Thus the AIFLD, an AFL-CIO and U.S. government supported enterprise of long standing, entered the El Salvador picture in 1979 as the sponsor of the Union Communal Salvadorenz (UCS). The Salvadoran scene is so out of control, however, that over 100 UCS officials and cadres have been murdered by the army and death squads, while the head of the land reform program and two AIFLD officials have also been killed. The AIFLD has not even been able to protect its own officials and indigenous collaborators.

Although apologists for the status quo regularly stress the importance of private bodies as a protection against the threatening omnipotent state, in El Salvador, where the state is clearly prone to violence, and where its attacks on private organizations have been extensive and deadly, the U.S. mass media are silent. In Warren Hoge's list of "the issues" in the March 1982 election this question of the preservation of a pluralism of independent private bodies does not come up. It was off-the-agenda elsewhere in the U.S. mass media as well.

6. Political casualties. Media bias is displayed in full potency in the playing down of the systematic murder of entire *generations* of centrist and dissident politicians in Central America. If Lech Walesa is arrested in Poland, media indignation is high. For Guatemala, on the other hand, the *murder* of 76 officials of the Christian Democratic Party in 1980-81 was treated very matter-of-factly if at all. Indignation was entirely absent. The *New York Times* subsequently editorialized that the refurbishing of democracy in Guatemala would take a bit of time because an entire new set of leaders and officials would have to be produced to replace those murdered. "Too quick an election would deny Guatemala's centrist parties—the Christian Democrats and Social Democrats—the time they need to rebuild their smashed organizations and to replace their assassinated leaders."[35] Note that this is said casually and without indignation. There is no suggestion that the system that had resulted in mass murder was illegitimate and would have to be replaced before anything useful could be done; or that the United States, whose interventions in 1954, 1966 and at other times had put the system in place and built up the "security forces" now in power, has perhaps disqualified itself as an arbiter of Guatemalan affairs. Imagine the Polish regime massacring all the officials of Solidarity, and *Pravda* then intoning solemnly about the need to "rebuild" trade union cadres under martial law and Soviet sponsorship in order to rehabilitate working class leadership! In this case the chutzpah and hypocrisy would be clear.

In El Salvador, we have seen that the Christian Democrats as well as the parties of the left have been decimated by political murder. The genius of the Free Press is to make such facts boring background details. Administration leaders can even speak passionately about the refusal of the rebels to "abandon violence" or to come out into the open and "compete" in the "free election" the security forces and the United States have waiting for them. The media never point out that many of the leaders can't compete because they have already been murdered (see Table 4-2)—and that the rest are on official death lists.

7. **Exclusion of parties and candidates**. The Reagan administration's position is that the left refuses to field candidates because they don't have popular support. The mass media swallowed this government line, mainly by transmitting it without question and by failing to state as a central election truth that the left could not run and was not intended to run. Sometimes the media would present an assertion by the left that they could not safely run, but this was usually offset by U.S. government claims that the left was unwilling to put their popularity to the test of a free election. The supposed "balance" constituted a deception.

8. **The structure of state terror**. It is off the mass media's agenda to enumerate in detail the structure of the security forces—their numbers, training, weaponry, funding, and relations with other power elements at home and abroad, and to examine fully their *modus operandi*. Almost never do the media mention prisons, the number of prisoners, the bases on which people are arrested, or their treatment. We have noted that ORDEN, long an adjunct of the "security forces," is an important institution in El Salvador and a classic totalitarian outcropping, serving to spy and carry out violence in the countryside. The security forces and ORDEN are background factors of enormous relevance affecting the climate within which elections can take place. ORDEN, "death squads," and their relation to fear and coercion of the electorate in El Salvador were almost never mentioned in the numerous articles in the mass media preceding and following the 1982 election. They do not show up anywhere in Warren Hoge's enumeration of election issues in the *New York Times*.

9. **Legal obligation to vote**. If turnout is to be equated with uncoerced public support of the security forces and the U.S. agenda for El Salvador, it is essential that the mass media downplay all forms

of state coercion. The final touch in propaganda service, the media masterpiece in the El Salvador election of March 1982, was their blithe disregard of the fact that *voting was required by law*. This fact was only peripherally and very occasionally mentioned by the best reporters. Nowhere was it put up front that people *had* to vote. No major mass media enterprise, to our knowledge, quoted General Garcia's statement, which was printed prominently in the Salvadoran newspapers, that a failure to vote would be considered not only illegal but an act of treason. (Warren Hoge did quote Garcia on election day, but to the effect that the vote proved the Salvadoran people's rejection of "the subversives.") This legal obligation to vote was reinforced by the indelible stamp made on the hand and the stamping of voters' identification cards at the polls. Nonvoters could suffer retaliation by employers and by the security forces. Dr. Charles Clements, a U.S. citizen serving as a medic in El Salvador, was assured by the Legal Aid Office of the Archdiocese of San Salvador "that many civilians have been killed for such reasons."[36] But for the mass media of the United States the role of the security forces was to protect the threatened right of the campesino to vote!

10. Real options? Real power? To be meaningful an election must provide options to the voting public that relate to their real interests and that do not confine their choices to insignificant variants of the status quo. As we discussed earlier, polls and independent observers found that *peace* was far and away the prime concern of the majority of voters in both El Salvador and Vietnam. But neither election offered a peace option.[37] In both cases there was a *real* government, centered in the army and backed decisively by the United States, that was pursuing military victory and which could not have been beaten in the staged election. Nevertheless, the propaganda disseminated by the Electoral Commission and other U.S.-sponsored conduits in El Salvador (UCS, etc.) stressed heavily that *voting was a step toward peace*. This was precisely the line taken by the Ky government in Vietnam in 1967 and the Smith government in Zimbabwe Rhodesia in 1979. Serious observers in these countries noted that all the candidates relied on vacuous clichés, charisma, and manipulative PR strategies. There were no serious issues or agenda addressed, though all were for "peace" and "reform."

In short, there was a fabulous hoax perpetrated in all of these demonstration elections. In El Salvador the hoax may be summarized as follows: the *real* government was unchallenged, as no voting outcome held forth the possibility of dislodging the army-security force-U.S. government triumvirate from power. All the parties favored a military solution and opposed negotiations, but proclaimed the election, and they themselves, to represent the peace sought by the public. For the U.S. mass media the issue of a contradiction between an election-for-peace and all-candidates-for-war never *arose*.

11. Ignoring the sequel. U.S.-sponsored demonstration elections are put forward with a nominal purpose seriously at odds with its real purpose. It is therefore essential that once the election is over and the high turnout is recorded the subject be quickly dropped. In the Dominican Republic, the official and media claim was that the election was designed for peace and reconciliation. In fact, the election was followed by intensified repression that resulted in perhaps a thousand political murders during the succeeding five years. In Vietnam, the nominal aim was muddy but the real aim was to clear the ground for escalation. The media failed to identify the real aims or note after-the-fact that the elections had been PR complements to intensified violence.

In El Salvador, a unique initial follow-up item was the admission by the Electoral Commission chief, Bustamente, that the vote had been inflated by 10%. This raises a host of questions. If the vote total and "turnout" was admittedly misrepresented, why should we believe the election managers at all? On our hypothesis that the mass media served as a propaganda arm of the government, helping it to put over the election, the revelation of a manipulated vote total would be disregarded. It was. The *New York Times* allowed Raymond Bonner a few inches of back page space, but no serious investigation was initiated and no inferences were drawn. The curtain had been drawn by the stage manager, and the service of the props had ended.

The voters in El Salvador were said by the U.S. government and the media to have been motivated to go to the polls by a deep interest in peace, democracy, and greater control over their destiny. Did the election move El Salvador toward peace? Did democratic conditions ensue? Did the Salvadoran people assume greater control over their destiny? Or did the United States and the Salvadoran war party consolidate its hold? These are questions off the mass media agenda.

A Soviet-Sponsored Demonstration Election: Poland 1947

The Soviet Union sponsored an election in Poland in 1947. It is illuminating to see how the mass media of the United States switched the dramatic context and moved strongly toward a focus on the fundamental issues that are off-the-agenda for U.S.-sponsored elections.

The Yalta and Potsdam Agreements provided that regimes in Eastern Europe would be broadly representative and that elections would be arranged at the earliest possible date. The Soviet Union had occupied these countries in the wake of the retreating Nazi armies and was determined that they not be ruled by groups hostile to Soviet "security interests." Ultimately this was incompatible with free elections. Initially, however, the Soviet Union was willing to tolerate a certain amount of freedom of choice; and in a relatively free election in Hungary in 1945 the non-Communist and pro-Western Small-holders Party achieved an absolute majority of the vote. In countries where anti-Soviet hostility was more profound, the Soviet Union was less tolerant, and the intensifying Cold War made it still less so.[38]

From liberation to January 1947 the Polish government was dominated by Communist leaders who had been active in the underground. They had formed a Government of National Liberation that ultimately received Soviet sponsorship. A rival socialist party had a minority status in the postwar coalition. The most important opposition came from the Peasant Party, a mass-based party headed by Stanislaw Mikolyczyk, who had been the leader of a government-in-exile located in London and was supported by the West. Its tradition had been conservative and strongly anti-Soviet; but Mikolyczyk returned to Poland in 1945 hoping that his popular support, willingness to get along with the Soviet Union, and western backing would eventually enable him to rule. He joined the government as a Minister of Agriculture, accepting this minor position pending an election that he hoped would bring him to power.

The election was finally held on January 17, 1947. The turnout was superb, and the government in power won a crushing victory. The Peasant Party and Mikolyczyk received only 10.5% of the vote and 27 of 444 seats in Parliament. The election was not a free election, however; fraud was massive and the result was therefore meaningful only as an expression of government control of electoral conditions and the electorate. It is conceivable that the Communist government would have done well in a free election without massive fraud, and that fraud made what might have been a modest victory an overwhelming one. The economic recovery under Communist auspices had been impressive, and Mikolyczyk's position had been weakened by U.S. support of German territorial claims in its dispute with Poland. One Polish Communist leader claimed that "had we known before the January election by what a large margin we would win, we would not have engaged in those pressures and minor dishonesties which did take place in many localities."[39] This is very probably PR gloss and apologetics; the dishonesties were not minor, and a majority of believable observers were of the opinion that the Peasant Party would have won a really free election. One historian claims that in the 35 polling stations where the Peasant Party was allowed a presence at the vote count, the Peasant Party had a 62-38 margin of victory over the government bloc.[40] Whatever the truth about the probable outcome, there is little question that the actual one was fraudulent and that it marked the death of the Peasant Party and the onset of an intensified Stalinist period in Poland.   ·

The Polish election was marked by some exceptional crudities. In addition to polling place intimidation there was an absence of external control over government manipulation of the vote count. In 97% of the polling places the Peasant Party poll watchers were denied admission. The government made strenuous efforts to get people to the polls and to openly declare for the government by displaying their ballot. (This latter tactic worked better in the countryside than in the larger cities; Sidney Gruson of the *New York Times* observed that Warsaw voters disregarded these attempts to force a declaration.) There were also thousands of instances of arbitrary voter disqualification and arrests in Peasant Party areas of strength. Only 428 of 862 Peasant Party candidates were allowed to run, which pushed the Party off the ballot in 10 of Poland's 52 electoral districts. There was also a good deal of pre-election harassment, arrests, and occasional beatings of Peasant Party officials, cadres, and supporters. Mikolyczyk was allowed to make two major pre-election radio addresses, which Sidney Gruson says "got over a powerful appeal," even though they were censored. Media access of the Peasant Party was poor; it had its own papers that functioned through the election period, but they were censored and their circulation arbitrarily limited.

Without for an instant claiming that the Polish election was anything but a brazen fraud, we believe that it was certainly no more of a fraud than the U.S.-sponsored demonstration elections recorded in this book. It differed from them in its greater crudity of election day manipulation, although these were more observable in Poland than in Vietnam and El Salvador because of the greater freedom of movement of foreign correspondents.[41] On the other hand, Polish election abuse involved far fewer killings of enemy officials and cadres than in Vietnam and El Salvador. In Poland, furthermore, the enemy party was able to run candidates; in Vietnam and El Salvador they were off the ballot altogether. In Table 5-1 we offer our own comparative estimate[42] of the extent to which the various conditions of freedom of elections were met in Poland, the Dominican Republic, Vietnam, and El Salvador. In our view, none of the four elections met the conditions of a free election. The Dominican election emerges as the "best," with fewest conditions unmet. In Vietnam, El Salvador and Poland none of the conditions of a valid free election were present.

Table 5-1: Conditions Necessary for a Valid Free Election and Ratings for Four Demonstration Elections

Demonstration Elections Held In:

Conditions To Be Met	Dominican Republic	South Vietnam	El Salvador	Poland
Free speech	4**	4	5	4
Freedom of the press	4	5	5	5
Absence of prior decimation of inter-mediate groups	4	5	5	5
Freedom of party organiza-tion and non-exclusion of parties	3	5	5	4
Absence of prior murder of political party officials and cadres	4	4	5	4
Absence of institutionalized state terrorism, direct and through vigilante groups	4	5 ·	5	4
Freedom *not* to vote	2	5	5	5
Absence of coercion at ballot box	3	4	4	5
Absence of ballot box stuffing and post-elec-tion inflating the vote	x	x	4	5

Source: Based on estimates derived from preceding chapters and sources cited there.

**Rating values:
1. Very good, highly compatible with valid election.
2. Good
3. Fair—borderline compatibility
4. Poor, incompatible with valid free election
5. Very poor.
X. Uncertain

It is illuminating to compare U.S. media treatment of the Polish election with that accorded U.S.-sponsored demonstration elections. As it was sponsored by the Soviet Union, serving to consolidate control of a satellite government, the U.S. government and its allies vehemently protested the electoral abuses so evident in Poland, and the western media followed suit. In terms of dramatic and symbolic structure, there was a reversal of roles as compared with U.S.-sponsored elections: the sponsoring government and its puppet were behaving outrageously, cynically manipulating democratic symbols for undemocratic ends; dissident parties that denounced the election and were abused by the government were noble victims; government terror was heavily featured and passionately denounced; and anti-government terror and obstruction were neither featured nor criticised as unjustifiable disruptions of a democratic event.

The most interesting and revealing discrepancies in formulating the media drama relate to left "disruption" and the meaning and significance of "turnout." In an election of good guys, as in El Salvador, the media give enormous weight and publicity to the alleged disruptive efforts of the bad guys on the security forces' death lists. We saw that this disruption focus was based on a propaganda lie foisted by the government to forward its dramatic scenario, and that the mass media disseminated this lie heavily and uncritically. In Poland immediately after the war there was an active anti-Soviet (and anti-Semitic) underground—a holdover of World War II—with strong Nazi and Ukrainian fascist remnants. This resistance was gradually weakened by warfare and a series of amnesties, but it was still in existence at the time of the January 1947 election. One would have to read the papers very closely to know this. *Newsweek* never mentioned the fact; *Time* mentioned it only once (in a sentence dismissing it as a government excuse to engage in terror). Sidney Gruson, reporting in the *New York Times*, mentions it several times, but toward the end of articles focusing on other matters. At the conclusion of one report, "Election in Poland Rigged by Terror," it turns out that there is "Terror on Both Sides" (a subhead). Gruson writes that

> The Government has made much of the terror used by the underground. It is considerable. More than twenty of the bloc [Communist and allied] parties' election officials have already been murdered and eight Communist workers were recently killed and mutilated on the highway near Warsaw in a particularly revolting crime.[43]

In another article Gruson mentions in a brief end-of-article comment that the underground is still active, but is limited to "small-scale murders [sic] and attacks." Elsewhere Gruson mentions the government's use of this underground terror to smear Mikolyczyk and the Peasant Party and to justify its own use of terror.[44] This is also the opinion of historian Jan Ciechenowski, who notes that "The existence of terrorists was convenient for the communists, because it gave them a good reason to strengthen the security forces and to postpone holding elections until they had tightened their hold on the country."[45]

Nevertheless, it is still enlightening to see how Gruson and company cannot be fooled by dissident "disruptions" in Soviet-sponsored elections, while accommodatingly gullible in their own government's dramatic offerings. If the Polish and Soviet press duplicated the U.S. mass media in El Salvador and Vietnam, they would have taken the underground's violence and pushed it front and center, added a nice dose of government fabrications, and made this violence the dramatic counterplay to the forces of law and order who were trying to allow the Polish people to express their preferences and "control their own destiny."

"Turnout" was also stood on its head. The Polish government used it to show support for themselves. Mikolyczyk urged a boycott of the election by his supporters in areas where Peasant Party candidates had been removed from the ballot, but the turnout was only 10% lighter in those areas. The turnout was claimed to be 90% of the electorate. In U.S.-sponsored demonstration elections a high turnout is interpreted by the U.S. media as a triumphant proof of support for the U.S. offering and a heart-warming step toward democracy. In Poland, the turnout was a simple product of coercion. The media demonstrated this by a concentrated focus on the use of pressure and coercive threats. In perfect symmetry, the equally potent coercive elements present in El Salvador and Vietnam were ignored and readily available information was suppressed.

The U.S. mass media did not hesitate to condemn the Polish election even before it was held as a "foregone conclusion," "rigged," a "fraud and a farce," and "wholly fraudulent." We have pointed out that the media never designate our own staged frauds in such invidious language. On the contrary, there is always a hopefulness or cautious optimism, or more commonly a breezy assurance that we are witnessing steps toward democracy and meaningful tests of local opinion.

Let us look briefly at some of the main criteria of a free election, which are off-the-agenda for the U.S. media in their reporting on U.S. sponsored demonstration elections, and see how the U.S. media addressed these in their reporting on the Polish election.

1. Free speech and freedom of the press. The U.S. mass media stressed unrelentingly that the Peasant Party's press was under constraint, that the radio speeches of Mikolyczk were censored, and that the omnipresent security police were quietly listening. The fact of "government control of all propaganda media" (*Newsweek*) was a central theme of media coverage. The point is very well taken, but the contrast with media treatment of the same subject matter in El Salvador is Orwellian. As we showed earlier, government censorship of the press of El Salvador, the elimination of the independent papers, and the murder of journalists were given only the most muted attention, with no suggestion in the *Washington Post, New York Times, Time, Newsweek,* or the TV networks that these had any bearing whatever on the March 1982 election.

2. Political casualties and state terrorism. The presence of "170,000 Russian-trained security police" (*Newsweek*) was front and center in the U.S. media treatment of Poland. Security police harrassment, the arrests of some candidates and many voters in areas strongly supporting the Peasant Party, and physical attacks on PP cadres, appear near the beginning of every article on the election, often in its title.[46] The U.S. media described this as a "regime of rifle butts," and "Red terror." The number of security police was mentioned daily. *Time* stressed that "the secret police may arrest without warrant anyone in Poland except district secretaries and higher officials of the Communist Party." The same was true in El Salvador in March 1982, but *Time* never mentioned that fact. The number of opposition political officials and ordinary citizens killed by the security forces in El Salvador was many times greater than in Poland for the six months or year prior to the election. The U.S. media's description of the importance of "Russian-trained security forces" in the election outcome of Poland was essentially valid, but its hypocritical selectivity in portraying the "U.S.-trained security forces" of El Salvador as guardians of a valid democratic process is striking.

3. Exclusion of parties and candidates. The U.S. media were closely attentive to the Polish government's exclusion of Peasant Party candidates from the ballot. The government justified this primarily on the basis of alleged ties of Peasant Party members to the underground. *Time* magazine pointed out that "the underground, official label for practically any group that opposes the government, is also the official excuse of [security force] activities." *Time* was right, but its sophistication and ability to look below the facade of propaganda claims is limited to enemy-sponsored elections. In Vietnam, the country's only mass-based political party was off the ballot, and the military junta ruled "neutralists" ineligible and removed from the ballot generals who might have provided serious competition to the self- and U.S.-selected junta. Several hundred local candidates were also arbitrarily shoved off the ballot. *Time* never noticed. In El Salvador, the rebel opposition was on army death lists and was off the ballot *by plan*, but the U.S. media played as the drama required.

CHAPTER 6

The Future of the Demonstration Election

The future of the demonstration election is closely tied in with the evolution of U.S. intervention, to which it is a public relations (PR) complement. The point of planning, publicizing, and holding demonstration elections is to *buy time* for military pacification. By putting forward a prospective "free election," we demonstrate our good intentions, our willingness to rely on an honest test of the internal support of our military junta, and thus the legitimacy of both the client and our own interventionary plans. It is difficult for the domestic opposition to challenge the manipulation of such a formidable symbol as "free elections." The government can manage the drama in such a way that even where there are no opposition candidates, where a system of pervasive terror is openly displayed in the form of 150 mutilated corpses each week, and where the victim population is legally obligated to vote, "turnout" is still interpreted by our media as a triumphant vindication of democratic values. In both Vietnam in 1967 and El Salvador in 1982, furthermore, the consensus of polls and reporters was that the primary interest of the electorate was in "peace," yet peace was not an electoral option in either case![1] One must stand in awe at a government and Free Press that can pull off an election for "democracy and peace" (the PR version) in order to consolidate military rule and clear the decks for intensified warfare (the real purpose and effect).

While a demonstration election buys time for further pacification, as pacification proceeds the escalating violence tends to engulf the victim client state and its nearby neighbors. By 1971, for example, the Vietnam war had escalated to the entire Indochinese peninsula. Given the ends, logic, and unrelentingly militaristic orientation of the Reagan administration, the Indochina pattern seems about to be repeated in Central America. It is now clear that the present administration is bent on not merely winning the Salvadoran war, but also using it as an excuse to destabilize Nicaragua and overthrow its revolutionary government. Just as the Johnson and Nixon administrations were perfectly prepared to destroy Indochina in order to save it, so the Reagan administration shows a positive eagerness to do the same for Central America. It has therefore armed and encouraged the *somocistas* and the Honduran army, and turned Honduras, Costa Rica, and Nicaragua into armed camps. The provocations of Nicaragua are clearly intended to induce retaliation, thus justifying direct U.S. armed action to defend Hondurans against "aggression." U.S. military forces can then be deployed to reestablish "democratic government" in Nicaragua as well as El Salvador.

The escalating violence of pacification also erodes any lingering institutional foundations of democracy. Just as the election for "peace" is followed by intensified warfare, so the "step toward democracy" initiates more ruthless crackdowns on political dissent. We saw that the South Vietnamese elections of 1966 and 1967 prepared the ground for further escalation and for the consolidation of an increasingly repressive police state. Elections were still being held in South Vietnam in the early 1970s, but by then they had served their purpose of facilitating escalation and were seen as an irritant, a source of "turmoil and conflicts" (Kissinger). There was also less stress on the "steps toward democracy" being taken there, given the steady flow of information on junta unpopularity, venality, institutionalized torture, and the rise in the number of political prisoners toward the 200,000 mark.

Similar conditions obtain today in El Salvador. As we have seen, the staged election of March 1982 was carried out in a polarized and terrorized society in which none of the fundamental conditions of a free election were met. What is more, the *trends* were all unfavorable, with pluralistic elements in the society under siege and disappearing by death or enforced retreat underground, and terror and social anomie enlarging steadily. These continued into the postelection period, as described in chapter 4. The fact that electoral conditions in early 1984 promise to be still less favorable to a free election than those of March 1982 will be no bar to holding one and getting a fine turnout.

The groundwork is now being laid for further military intervention and for the demonstration elections to come. The underlying ideological premises—our own natural right to intervene, our hatred of violence and terrorism, our "national security" interests, etc.—are being inculcated on a daily basis. The second Salvadoran demonstration election is already well into the planning and publicity phase, and similar exercises are undoubtedly being prepared for Grenada, Guatemala, Honduras, and perhaps even a "liberated" Nicaragua.

The Clichés of Interventionary PR

There is a standard set of clichés and patriotic symbols that are mobilized to justify U.S. intervention. The media pass them along as self-evident truths and use them as the basis on which to frame the news. They rarely analyse these truths, and almost never suggest that they have been employed with boring regularity as manipulative devices in the past. Some of the main ones, which are in active use today and may be expected to service our next interventions, are as follows:

1. **Our natural right to intervene and set things straight**. It is impressive to see how Washington can express outrage at arms and advisers going to El Salvador's rebels from *foreign countries* (Cuba, Nicaragua, etc.) without any audible voice being heard asking: on what ground may the United States arm and advise the military junta without justifying equal condemnation? The hypocrisy and blatant double standard here are remarkable, as is the mass media's subservience. In terms of the virtue of the people being supported, we have seen that the government of El Salvador is "deserving" only in Reaganspeak—in the same sense in which Guatemala's Rios Montt was given a "bum rap." It is true that the El Salvador government has received the imprimatur of a "free election," but as we have shown in detail in chapters 4 and 5, the El Salvador spectacular of 1982 was a vintage "demonstration election," marginally more fraudulent than even the classics of Poland in 1947 and Vietnam in 1967.

Our right to intervene comes down to this—we are *us*, and therefore good; we are a democracy, an agent of freedom, justice, civilization, and of God, who has given us money and helicopters. Proof may be seen in our success, our GNP, and the refugees flocking to our shores. Examined more closely, these are the premises that have regularly come to the fore in the prior empires of ancient Egypt,

Assyria, Athens, Persia, Rome, Spain of the conquistadores, and Great Britain. As we look at the imperial rationales of these other great systems, in retrospect and with the objectivity of nonpartici-pants, it is quite evident that they were self-serving ideologies covering the use of power to serve particular interests. The ideological cover employed by the United States will appear equally self-serving in the perspective of history.

2. **We oppose foreign intervention**. This is the counterpart to our own right to intervene, resting on the redefinition of *foreign intervention* to exclude ourselves. This redefinition rests on the premise that we are historically unique in being essentially good and above the corrupting din of material interests. As the world's only true neutral, seeking self-determination and free elections above all else, we may deploy our power to assure that no small country is being coerced, intruded upon, or managed from abroad. Some foreign countries have been known to come into small client states and stage phoney elections to justify their sitting astride the client and legitimizing their chosen local instruments. This is the kind of thing the United States is in Central America to prevent!

In short, the United States intervenes massively in the alleged interest of opposing intervention. In reality, its own interventions in Latin America have exceeded the sum of those of all the world's other powers by a large factor. Each U.S. government PR campaign carried out in the midst of its own vast interventions in Vietnam and El Salvador, alleging somebody else's "foreign intervention," has been repeatedly exposed as riddled with lies and deceptions. This has not prevented the mass media from providing full-scale and uncritical deployment of these claims in each succeeding intervention.

Another important feature of U.S. intervention in the Caribbean and Central America, very conspicuous today, has been to use active subversion and the threat of invasion to *drive* a disfavored liberal-left rebel group or regime to seek the support of Communist powers, and then to cite weapons purchases by the intended victim as proof of international Red domination. This tactic of planned self-fulfilling prophecy worked in the case of Guatemala in 1954 and is now in full display in the Reagan policies toward El Salvador and Nicaragua today.

2. **Our "national security" is at stake**. This is solemnly intoned by U.S. leaders as the last and definitive word. It is the ultimate Linus blanket, to which there is no answer, for how could we deny to this pitiful giant the right to defend its national security against the threat arising out of the taking over of their own country by a couple of

million very poor people, traditionally kept in the state of pack animals by our "friends"? This magical phrase clearly has endless possibilities as a justification for intervention by any great power. For example, it might be said that U.S. arms, air bases, and spying stations in Turkey pose a threat to *Soviet* national security. Would they not justify a Soviet destabilization effort, or even an invasion? Does international law still apply where "national security," no matter how remote, can be invoked? Do people in foreign countries lose their right to self-determination if their free choice would have some hypothetical small negative effect on our national security? Do *others* have a right to national security? Is is possible that "national security" is a blind for a desire to maintain control for other reasons? Do left regimes necessarily threaten our national security? Would a Yugoslavian-type regime on our borders threaten our national security?

The media have failed to note that the national security argument is not consistent with the contention of U.S. neutrality and disinterest. It suggests rather a desire to shape other countries' politics to suit *our* interests. If used elastically, as it has been, national security can also provide a cover for much more mundane purposes, such as the desire of multinational corporations to maintain a very hospitable investment climate in which those millions of peasants *stay* in the condition of pack animals.

We believe that "national security" is a PR cliché that obscures the real basis of U.S. intervention in Central America. The United States could have brought Nicaragua, even Cuba, within its orbit of friendly neighbors, but didn't want to. Such an arrangement would have allowed too much autonomy, too little subservience, and too little freedom of U.S. investment. It would have helped strengthen an institutional form contrary to basic U.S. multinational corporate interests. Tiny deviants like Cuba and Nicaragua hardly pose a real threat to the United States, and they have a strong self-interest in accommodation,[2] but an aggressive and expansionist capitalism nevertheless seeks to cripple and destroy them.

4. We support democracy. The Reagan administration has used the word "democracy" and the institutional mechanism of elections as instruments in its struggle *against* democracy. Democracy has to do with the power and rights of the majority of the population. As noted by C. B. Macpherson, democracy was originally a leveling doctrine, feared by men of substance and learning. It meant "rule by the common people, the plebians,...the sway of the lowest and largest class."[3] Democracy can be transformed into its opposite by removing its substantive stress on majority interest and power, identifying it with certain *forms*—notably elections—and using these forms for manipulative purposes. Nicaragua, for example, was vastly more democratic in 1983 than it was under the Somozas, or than Guatemala, Turkey, Chile, or the Philippines were in that year. For the first time in almost a half century the majority of the population was an end, not merely a means. In Somoza's Nicaragua, or in contemporary Chile, Guatemala, Turkey and the Philippines, there was or is elite class rule and a deliberate effort to repress the majority, to keep them in their traditional status of political, economic, and social subservience. In these states this has necessitated the use of force and extreme terror. In none of them are elections used in other than token fashion. The correlation between nonelite orientation in Nicaragua, and the U.S. demand for elections there, and the elite rule and greater terror under Somoza, Rios Montt, Pinochet, Evren, and Marcos, and the U.S. unconcern and lack of urgent and indignant demand for elections, suggests that it is the very *democratic* features of Nicaragua that bother Reagan and Washington. It is surely not its electoral deficiencies. The *form* of democracy is used selectively by the United States as an instrument for encouraging the *substance* of elite rule and state terror.

We note, also, that in contrast with the Reagan administration's insistent concern over the plight of the Miskito Indians of Nicaragua, the structured exclusion from political life and severe repression of the vast black majority of South Africa has not caused the Reagan team any apparent discomfort, let alone proposals for covert operations aiming at destabilization. On the contrary, under the cover of "constructive engagement" the warmth of the U.S. toward South Africa is clearly evident. Elite rule and an open door to foreign investment are the touchstones that cause a radically undemocratic underpinning to be given positive support.

We pointed out in chapter 4 that at the three strategic moments when democracy was at stake in El Salvador—in 1961, 1972, and 1979—the United States threw its weight against democratic outcomes. The United States is now once again supporting the same forces that subverted democracy over the past 40 years. It has helped militarize the country and encouraged a pacification program that has destroyed the basic institutional conditions needed for electoral democracy. The Reagan administration sponsored elections in March 1982 in El Salvador for the same reason that Lyndon Johnson was keen on elections in Vietnam in 1967—namely, because under conditions of military occupation, pacification, and state of siege, an *official* armed minority can easily win a staged demonstration election.

5. We oppose "terror" and "violence." These words are actually used with a straight face by Kirkpatrick, Reagan, and Shultz. They get very emotional about rebel violence in El Salvador and the Sandinista persecutions of the Miskito Indians. Their sympathetic understanding of the problems of Botha and Rios Montt, on the other hand, who are all getting a "bum rap," displays an amazing bifurcation of mind. But it also reflects a spiritual camaraderie, a common set of values, a similar world view, that we believe is essential to explaining the easy relationships between a Vernon Walters and Pinochet, a Richard Stone and Lucas Garcia, a Ronald Reagan and Rios Montt, and a Jeane Kirkpatrick and the Argentine military and South African secret police.

In its *Special Report on Guatemala* of July 1982, Amnesty International listed and provided details about 60 different massacres by the official forces of Rios Montt in the three months between March 24 and June 30, 1982, with an estimated 2,186 civilians slaughtered. While the Reagan administration destabilizes Nicaragua, it does its best to enter into warmer and more supportive relations with Guatemala. Mass murder under rightwing auspices is simply not "terror" or "violence"; it is by definition a response to terror or a reasonable effort to restore stability under regrettable provocations. In El Salvador it is clear that the causality has run from security force-oligarchy violence to induced rebellion; and the evidence is overwhelming that the security force murders, rapes, and mutilations completely dominate the Salvadoran scene. Using the words *terror* and *violence* in their literal senses, the Reagan administration sponsors and warmly supports terrorism and violence. Assailing the Salvadoran rebels for terrorism is like defenders of the Nazis speaking passionately about Jewish violence against the Germans in 1944.

6. We oppose "armed minorities" trying to seize power by force. Again, this cliché stands reality on its head. The military junta in El Salvador is itself an armed minority that refused any democratic and peaceful response to mass demands—any kind of majority rule— prior to the rebel resort to arms. Thus the rebels were literally driven to arms by the system of death squads to which Washington has given unstinting support.

7. We support reform. Although claiming our devotion to reform in both Vietnam and El Salvador, the United States aligned itself with forces of the right that have always been the primary obstacle to reform. This regular attachment to oligarchies and military factions which are antireform points up the fact that reform is hardly a first-order U.S. aim. First in line is "stability,"* which is achieved on the desired terms through an amenable oligarchy and military establishment. As the friends of U.S.-style stability don't like reform, reform is not easy to implement. But without reform, rebellions tend to grow, and they are accelerated by the rapid and large U.S. input of weapons, military advice, and counterinsurgency training that are put in place while "reforms" are still pending. In each case, reform is gradually sloughed off as the United States is obliged to protect "stability" by supporting goons of the extreme right.

In both Vietnam and El Salvador, technocratic land reforms formulated in the United States were imposed from above, with a main objective of defusing discontent. They failed abysmally from any standpoint except that of preserving the PR image of our devotion to reform. In both countries the reform was structured to affect minimally the basic socio-economic structure, and neglected most of the small peasants and virtually all of the already landless. In both cases the administration of the land reform was incompetent and corrupt, and the reforms themselves were too little and too late. In both cases too it was implemented hand-in-hand with antipeasant counterinsurgency warfare, whose negative impact on the rural poor was vastly greater than any positive benefits of the puny reforms. In each case the land reform gradually lapsed, while killing and deliberate refugee generation took complete charge. Because the United States aligns itself with the oligarchies of the status quo, and has its own bias toward military solutions, we may note this ironic fact—the military cost of the Vietnam war would have allowed the United States to buy up and redistribute to peasants all the cultivable land in South Vietnam, leaving over a large taxpayer saving. The same is already true for El Salvador. But the U.S. leadership prefers to kill.

8. We must stand by our allies. Most of our allies who are vulnerable to retribution in the event of a rebel victory would easily escape to Miami, where the Reagan administration would no doubt welcome them as victims of Communism (in contrast with the present large flood of El Salvadoran refugees). While the administration feels attached to these freedom fighters, possibly we should give less weight to preserving their power to kill further than to preserving the lives of their prospective thousands of innocent victims.

9. Marxists-Leninists are worse than the mass murderers we currently support. It is always an adjunct of foreign intervention to make the enemy out to be truly villainous. In the old days of Teddy Roosevelt, Woodrow Wilson et al., we were justified by the fact that rebels in the Caribbean were mere "bandits" and bloodthirsty savages. On that basis, anything that we did to them was acceptable and the rule of ourselves (i.e., civilization and reason) could only be an improvement. In recent decades, "terrorists" have displaced bandits and savages. We have also evolved the selective use of "Marxist" regimes to show the probable end product of rebellion. The logic is as follows: if Marxists-Leninists win, we may expect a Pol Pot in power in due course. Although the regime we are supporting seems murderous, Pol Pot was worse. Furthermore, as the regime we support is under our tutelage, in the long run it will mellow.

The fallacies in this line of argument are numerous. Our tutelage does not always bring mellowness (see cliché 10). Pol Pot was not a representative case of Marxism-Leninism, a category that covers a wide range of possibilities. In comparison with U.S. Third World clients, regimes like Cuba and post-Somoza Nicaragua look very good in both democratic orientation and actual economic-social performance.[4] The ensuing shift in the role of the majority —from pack animals and a "cost" in serving a domestic and foreign elite (Argentina, Brazil, Chile, Indonesia, the Philippines, Somozan Nicaragua) to being the direct object of national policy—has had dramatic effects on malnutrition and literacy rates, health care, and income security.[5] These improvements have been made even when the radical states were under U.S. siege. They do not have elections and their freedoms are limited, but the U.S. satellites have neither elections *nor* other elements of democracy.

Whether popular movements *become* Marxist-Leninist in the first place, and their degree of humanity and inhumanity, is often very much affected by western attitudes and policies. Western intervention, incineration, subversion, and boycott may bring out the worst in radical regimes by intensifying violence and motives of vengeance, and by the adverse effect of impoverishment. It is apparent in the cases of contemporary Nicaragua and post-1971 Indochina that it is and was the intent of U.S. policy makers to produce a poor and vindictive radicalism to show just how awful radical regimes can be. The worse we can make Nicaragua, the easier it will be to support the "goons of convenience" in El Salvador and Guatemala. We strive for a negative demonstration effect for Nicaragua, a positive one for El Salvador and Guatemala.

10. Our intervention will be a plus for human rights. This cliché is based on sheer nationalism, the rewriting of history, and the faulty reasoning that as we have a relatively democratic and humane order at home we will export these abroad. Sometimes the United States is even criticized for excessive devotion to democracy and human rights abroad, at the expense of our "interests." These critics have absolutely no basis for complaint. Study after study shows that U.S. aid in the Third World is correlated with a rise in torture and other measures of deteriorating human rights.[6] The new interventionism of the Kennedy years and later was associated with the rapid proliferation of military dictatorships of the most abusive sort in our sphere of influence. It was only by dint of great media patriotism and self-discipline that the emergence of these National Security States, following so closely upon our greatly expanded aid and training programs to counter "Castro-Communism," was not seen as a clear product of U.S. policy.

The reasons why our intrusions are not helpful to human rights start with the fact that we consistently line up with the forces of the status quo in the Third World. It is these that will protect an open door to investment and collude with our multinationals and military-security establishment to help provide "stability." By giving military aid and training to the local security forces (the "enforcers") to provide a bulwark against popular upheavals, we strengthen the most repressive elements in these societies and encourage them to kill rebels rather than to strive for solutions addressed to underlying social conditions. U.S. training in "human rights" and "democracy" has been a miniscule and self-deceptive cloak over the reality of our own overwhelming stress on the Communist menace.[7] Frederick Nunn has pointed out that "subject to United States military emphasis on anticommunism the professional army officer [trained by us] became hostile to any sort of populism."[8] It is well known that Brazilian officers trained in the United States led the coup that terminated democracy in Brazil in 1964.[9] The Salvadoran military personnel recently returned from the United States have not distinguished themselves for human rights concerns. AI's Report of 1982 describes the work of the U.S.-trained Atlacatl brigade as follows:

> In November reports were received that the new Atlacatl brigade had carried out a sweep of an area in northern El Salvador in which at least 250 would-be refugees were killed. Witnesses states that the would-be refugees had been positioned between the army and the opposition forces at some distance from the opposition. They categorically

rejected the government explanation that the 250 casualties had occurred in clashes between government and opposition forces. In December 1981 the Atlacatl brigade was again named as responsible for the massacre of hundreds of non-combatants, mainly women and children trying to reach Honduras from Morazan.[10]

Scholarship has also helped rearrange the historical record to show our regularly beneficent impact on liberty. Samuel Huntington, Professor of Government at Harvard, for example, concludes that the "cognitive dissonance" which seems to affect U.S. moralists is actually a function of cognitive misperception. In the correct perception, the rise of military regimes in Latin America in the 1960s and 1970s was a consequence of "the decline in the role of the United States" in that area in the "late 1960s and early 1970s."[11] Huntington chooses his years well, although a bit vaguely, carefully omitting the critically important Brazilian coup of 1964. He thus can disregard the very active and positive U.S. role in the Brazilian coup, its importance as a model, and its large number of "follow-ons" extending into the late 1960s. He fails to note that our direct interventionary "role" declined only *after* the Brazilian and numerous other coups, which might be interpreted as reflecting satisfaction with the results and a correspondingly reduced *need* to intervene, given that our agents were already in power. His analysis of the U.S. "role" does not encompass the impact of its investment in military and police aid, counterinsurgency advice, or training—its "insurance policy" against Castro-Communism—which materialized in authoritarian government. Did the United States ever engage in action to *prevent* a military takeover in the period of its reduced "role," comparable to its endeavor to prevent the return of Juan Bosch to the Dominican Republic?

Huntington even explains the Chilean counterrevolution of 1973 as a consequence of the decline in the U.S. role, through "a somewhat more complex process"—namely, by our failure to intervene with sufficient intensity to prevent Allende's victory in 1970! By adequate subversion of the democratic process, using on a larger scale the techniques we had employed in the Chilean election of 1964, "the destruction of Chilean democracy in 1973 might have been avoided."[12] Huntington never points out that the United States contributed both directly and indirectly to the literal overthrow of Allende in 1973, and to the exact qualities of the successor regime, by its encouragement and support of the military in the coup process, its extensive contributions to the polarization and subversion of Chilean democracy from 1970 to 1973,[13] and its strong support of Pinochet during the period of mass murder that followed. The Huntington reasoning is thus somewhat tortured—by analogy, a Soviet Huntington might explain the fall of Czech democracy in 1968 as a result of a failure of the Soviet Union to carry out a prior purging of the Czech leadership, which would have precluded the later necessity of a Soviet invasion and direct placement in power of more responsible officials.

The Tactical Gambits Pending

In the first months of 1983 the Reagan administration had to face the fact that the Salvadoran military was losing the war, and that Congress had become increasingly reluctant to provide the levels of military aid deemed necessary to save the situation. In February UN Ambassador Jeane Kirkpatrick, a member of the National Security Council, was dispatched to El Salvador to survey the situation. In the ensuing weeks an interdepartmental task force chaired by President Reagan reviewed U.S. options and chose to escalate the war. Thomas Enders and Deane Hinton, apparently willing to consider some kind of negotiations with the guerillas, were fired and replaced by policy makers who, under the direction of Kirkpatrick and National Security Adviser William Clark, would pursue military victory.

To provide the necessary PR accompaniment to this strategy, the Reagan administration prepared a number of gambits designed to reassure Congress and the U.S. public, as well as our European and Latin American allies, that the United States remains open and flexible and is employing force only as an accompaniment to its search for a peaceful solution. The first of these gambits is a new "free election." A second gambit is a new version of the Johnson administration's "peace-move-intended-to-fail-and-thereby-show-enemy-intransigence"—the Richard Stone mission. The Kissinger Commission of bipartisan Cold Warriors is a third PR instrument for building public acceptance of escalated "foreign intervention which is not foreign intervention." Beyond the status of a mere gambit is military escalation, which takes advantage of the public's propensity to support our boys (wherever they may be) as the basis for a buildup of short-run political support. This tactic was manifest and temporarily successful in the invasion and occupation of Grenada in October 1983. We will look briefly at the plans and prospects for these PR and other tactics.

1. The Second Salvador Demonstration Election. By the end of 1982 the political and military stalemate in El Salvador had put the Reagan administration's strategy for the region in jeopardy. The March 1982 election had been a great PR success, but the positive PR impact of the election had been slightly weakened by the failure of Duarte and the Christian Democrats, which removed the reformist figleaf. With D'Aubuisson as head of the Constituent Assembly and long-time army front-man Magaña as President, the dominant role of the security forces in the management and rule of El Salvador was also more conspicuous. Furthermore, not only was the Constituent Assembly slow to perform its task of writing a constitution, but it was also reluctant to go along with any gesture attempting to incorporate the FDR "moderates" into discussions leading toward the next presidential election. Thus in October, after a proposal for discussions by the FMLN-FDR, more than a dozen FDR and allied labor leaders were abducted from a meeting by security forces, and at least five of the FDR activists "disappeared." The sustained guerilla offensive which followed culminated in the temporary occupation of the important town of Berlin, and showed that the government forces were far from achieving military superiority.

Thus there were both political and military pressures put on the United States to achieve greater control over events in El Salvador, and the presidential election scheduled for March or April 1984 was perceived as an opportunity to achieve this. New elections would allow a repeat of the tremendous PR benefits reaped in March 1982. They might also provide a greater measure of political stability and a more unified political authority to work through, which would give greater legitimacy to any Salvadoran invitation to the United States to send troops. They might also succeed in detaching some elements of the FDR from the opposition, which would enhance the credibility of the election, as Bishop Muzorewa's candidacy did in the Zimbabwe Rhodesia election of 1979.

The drawback to this strategy was that the elections were so far away, while the situation in El Salvador pressed for a solution. For this reason Reagan chose a "Special Envoy for Public Diplomacy," former Democratic Senator Richard Stone of Florida, to approach Magaña secretly about moving the elections up, perhaps to as early as October. The administration hoped that Magaña could be persuaded to propose earlier elections as though it were his own idea, which would then be welcomed by the Reagan administration as a Good Thing, and would possibly be endorsed by the Pope, whose visit to

Central America was then imminent. This in turn would put increased pressure on the rebels to enter into the election charade or be seen by international opinion as rejecting dialogue and an attempt to peacefully resolve the Salvadoran conflict. Unfortunately, on his return flight from El Salvador Stone was overheard by a Tampa television reporter discussing the plan with some National Security Council aides. Despite entreaties to preserve the secrecy of the mission and thus "national security," the story was broken and the PR impact of another Salvadoran step toward democracy was lost.

The decision to hold an earlier election was nevertheless pursued. Richard Scammon and Howard Penniman, observers in the March 1982 election, were dispatched to El Salvador along with State Department representatives to advise the Central Election Council on such things as the form of the ballot and voting hours, and to make other arrangements for controlling the election. The question of a new voting list proved to be a stumbling block, however. One election council official told a reporter that "there have been many unreported deaths, a lot of people have left the country, and many people seem to have more than one identity card," perhaps not remembering that these facts had proved no obstacle to a free election in March 1982.[14] Fearing delay, the United States hastened to put up $6 to $8 million to provide the Central Election Commission with the necessary computers, and to cover other anticipated expenses. One administration official told the *New York Times* that, at an additional undisclosed cost,

> The Central Intelligence Agency plans to support the election by intensifying its collection of intelligence information about the guerillas' military plans and operations so as to help the Salvadoran military block anticipated efforts to disrupt the voting.... Because the State Department and the Salvadoran Government lack expertise in conducting elections, the officials said, a lot of the work will be turned over to private contractors. They said, for example, that a concern in El Salvador or the United States would likely handle an extensive print and television advertising campaign to promote the major voter registration drive that the Salvadoran Government hopes to conduct.[15]

By the end of the summer, however, the computers had not arrived in El Salvador, nor had the Constituent Assembly completed a new constitution. Because only the Christian Democrats among the parties in the Assembly seemed to have any interest in an earlier election, the United States was reluctantly forced to acquiesce in a postponement to March or April 1984. The decision in the summer of 1983 to greatly enlarge the U.S. military commitment to the region, however, has if anything increased the importance of the election's PR aspects. The significance of the election will be enhanced even further if it occurs in the midst of the U.S. presidential campaign, and could contribute significantly to framing the way in which Central America is discussed in the U.S. presidential race. The energy and resources which will go into trying to control the public perception of the election should thus be great.

We may expect the observers and major media to play their parts once again, focusing on the drama of the leading personalities, the happy and wonderful people eager to record their vote for democracy and peace (i.e., the rule of the security forces and the commitment to fight to the finish), and the possibility that the guerillas might disrupt the election. They will carefully avoid dwelling on whether conditions for a free election prevail in El Salvador—free speech, freedom of the press, the ability of candidates of all factions to run and campaign on basic issues, or freedom from the fear that the state will kill and mutilate dissenters under a state of siege. Instead, they will express wonderment that elections can be held under conditions of "conflict," under threat of disruption and force on the part of those not joining in this exercise in free choice. Any legal obligation to vote and pressures from the forces of law and order will be suppressed, and the historic correlation of high turnout with military occupation and totalitarian conditions will be ignored.

Leading political commentators will anxiously scan the results, hoping that the returns will give Washington a working majority powerful enough to bring the security forces under control, reduce the number of civilian casualties, and put to more effective use the counterinsurgency lessons the United States learned in Vietnam. Once again there will be the hope that the phantom "center" of Salvadoran politics can be revived. Little thought will be given to the meaning of the Salvadoran government's offer to the opposition to allow them to campaign from outside the country by means of radio and TV. Much will be made of the guerillas' refusal to participate in the election, and U.S. congressional opponents of the military build-up in El Salvador will be largely disarmed by their inability to penetrate and expose the hypocrisy of the free election gambit.

2. The Search for Peace. While Washington has been able to score points in the media with its claim to be aiding a freely elected government, its refusal to accept the FMLN-FDR's offer for negotiations did less well in the marketplace of ideas. It was for this reason that the Reagan administration made Richard Stone a Special Envoy to the region, and launched him on a high-visibility tour of Central American capitals. The "search for peace"* gambit had been refined over many years during the Vietnam war. During these years each U.S. "peace offensive" became the prelude to a new escalation of the war, while more genuine peace feelers from within the South Vietnamese political elite were preempted by a quick escalation of the bombing. For more than a decade, successive U.S. administrations used a deliberately manufactured and misleading *appearance* of an intent to negotiate to quiet domestic critics of the war. The *Pentagon Papers* and other documents have confirmed that these "peace moves" were frauds, designed to fail and thus justify continuing the fighting. We may expect a similar pattern in Central America, where the appearance of a diplomatic offensive to find a peaceful resolution to the conflict will be a necessary complement to the continued U.S. commitment to a military solution.

The Stone mission, while not complete as of this writing, is almost certainly only the first of a series of search-for-peace gambits to be staged in Central America. Many Special Persons are doomed to fly from capital to capital in Central America, and then back to Washington to confer with the president and his advisers, before the Central American war is finished. On the basis of early returns, however, we venture to predict the following pattern:

—Neither the media nor Congress will denounce the search-for-peace as a PR device, but will continue to accept at face value each initiative as sincerely intended to avoid further military involvement on the part of the administration.

—The media will studiously avoid any investigation into the biases of the Special Person, lest this hinder the search for peace. Thus the facts about Richard Stone's tenure as a lobbyist for the cutthroat regime of Lucas Garcia in Guatemala were not pursued by the press, even though they would have shown Stone to have been deeply involved in trying to circumvent the arms embargo to Guatemala, receiving at least $10,000 a month for his efforts. Nor did Congress, which had pressed for a Special Envoy as a condition for agreeing to an increase in military aid to El Salvador, raise this issue during his confirmation hearings, even though his close identification with the military and the right in Central America make him hopelessly unqualified to serve as an intermediary. His appointment was an audacious slap in the face to members of Congress who opposed a purely military solution in El Salvador. As with his appointment of Kenneth Adelman as arms control negotiator, Reagan put forward someone hostile to the very mission supposedly advanced by the appointment—saying, in effect, I will get a bit of PR advantage out of this nonsensical effort, but as to substance, I tell you by my selection that I intend this *solely* for PR. And Reagan gets away with this by the strength of imperial office and media subservience.

—The media also will not explain that the announced constraints on the mission for peace set the stage for its failure as a genuine peace mission. The media, particularly the television network news, almost invariably failed to note that Stone's mandate was to bring the guerillas into the election process, which was to be organized once again by us and our military junta. This is a proposal which the rebels have consistently rejected until other conditions were achieved which would allow a genuinely free election. By refusing to negotiate about anything else, Stone's mission is confirmed as designed for PR purposes alone.

For the foreseeable future the point of the Stone mission and similar searches-for-peace will be to obscure the level of intransigence of the Reagan administration and to allow the administration to portray their military buildup as one reluctantly pursued after all attempts at negotiation had failed. The guerillas, meanwhile, will be forced to play along with the game, cooperating in the charade lest they appear unreasonable and intransigent, thus weakening their international position. Their cooperation, of course, helps to legitimate the search-for-peace gambit, and thus contributes to congressional acquiescence in the military buildup. And as in Vietnam, we may expect any "back-channel" negotiations to be revealed by the United States at critical moments in its campaign for continued domestic support for the war, particularly as the presidential election campaign draws to a close.

3. The Kissinger Commission. Faced with issues that have deeply divided the electorate but have not fallen along clear party lines, the Reagan administration has successfully employed the device of a bipartisan panel. This has been the means by which the administration addressed the issues of Social Security and the MX missile. In the latter case, with the Scowcroft Commission, the administration was able to create a bipartisan majority for producing the MX by detaching a number of influential advocates of arms control from the anti-MX forces in Congress in exchange for a promise by President Reagan to follow the recommendations of the Commission to pursue arms control more vigorously. This promise, an ambiguously worded scrap of paper, was the next-to-last step in a prearranged and highly choreographed set of maneuvers by which the panel judged not so much *whether* to produce the MX missile, as how to sell it to Congress and the public.[16]

It was on the heels of the success of the Scowcroft Commission that the Reagan administration decided to try the bipartisan panel gambit in rallying support for its Central American policy. Claiming that their aim was to emulate the commission that had given rise to the Marshall Plan in the late 1940s, the sponsors of the bipartisan panel said that they were concerned that the roots of the Central American conflict—"poverty, misery, illness and human rights"—be addressed by U.S. policy in the region.[17] The PR goals of the use of the bipartisan panel gambit were clearly revealed, however, with the naming of Henry Kissinger as its chairman and the exclusion from the panel of any Latin American experts known to be critical of administration policies. By naming Kissinger to head the panel the administration guaranteed that the Commission's deliberations would be newsworthy and its final report received as a serious document. Notwithstanding the recent work of the Linowitz Commission— which contained several area experts, was admirably bipartisan, and whose conclusion (that negotiations in Central American must be seriously pursued) was studiously ignored by the Administration— the mass media generally hailed the establishment of the Kissinger panel as a step in the right direction.

The Kissinger Commission can be expected to support the administration's strategy for conducting free elections in El Salvador and to restate the need for a long-term strategy for economic development, presumably by maintaining a favorable investment climate and achieving political stability. The panel will call for strengthening the political center in Latin America, promoting respect for human rights, and training the security forces in civic action and other means of gaining the support of the civilian population. While warning against the dangers of an exclusively military approach to the problems of the region, the Kissinger Commission will give its endorsement to covert action and military intervention if employed judiciously and after attempts to resolve tensions through diplomacy have failed.

These and undoubtedly other tactical gambits will be employed by the Reagan administration to diffuse conflict over its policy in Central America and divert the attention of the press from the civilian slaughters which the administration's policy actually sup- ports. As long as the military situation does not require large numbers of U.S. troops, or appear about to involve the United States in conflict with the Soviet Union, the media can be expected to cooperate in treating each of these gambits as a serious gesture of peaceful intent and an indication that the Reagan administration has not locked itself into a strictly military strategy for solving the region's problems. Yet the military "solution" is in fact what these gambits are designed to achieve; and commission, elections, and searches-for-peace will be about as much consolation to the people of Central America as they were to the people of Indochina.

The Invasion of Grenada and the "Thatcher Factor"

The U.S. invasion and occupation of Grenada in October 1983 was a major step toward more direct U.S. involvement in Central American warfare, readying the country psychologically for greater U.S. participation and at least temporarily strengthening the hand of the war party. The invasion followed closely the loss of over 200 U.S. Marines in Lebanon and was, in part, a form of "horizontal escalation" designed to score points against the "enemy" (whoever he may be) and to alleviate public distress by a low-budget victory. It also followed shortly upon the murder of Maurice Bishop and other leaders of the New Jewel Movement and the takeover of Grenada by a military faction of uncertain political aim and in some disarray. This allowed the Reagan team to invade on a number of contradictory and shifting pretexts, including the usual appeal from interested local parties, the need to "protect our citizens," and the airport and assorted other indicators of a Soviet-Cuban presence that threatened U.S. national security. The mass media, especially the TV networks, collaborated with better than average gullibility in helping put over this shifting propaganda stream, barely noting the blatant illegalities, the slight imbalance in size of the contestants, and the fact that it was Maurice Bishop who was friendly with Castro and that Cuba regarded the anti-Bishop coup as a defeat and the end of the Grenadan revolution!

The jump in administration ratings in the polls and the collapse of the Democratic Party opposition to the invasion is ominously suggestive of the potential of military adventurism as a means of political bailout of failing policies. Lyndon Johnson found escalation politically profitable in Vietnam in 1965-67, but only temporarily, with the immediate euphoria and poll effects dissipating and the polls reaching new lows rather quickly. The so-called "Thatcher Factor," however, by which Mrs. Thatcher's successful recapture of the

Falkland Islands from Argentina aroused the   British public to patriotic fervor and helped her win reelection, points to the possibility of more durable political gains from a forward military policy crowned by "success."

The rest of the world has generally not been happy with the Reagan foray into Grenada, and his action has provided new food for thought for people everywhere as well as ammunition for the European (and other) peace movements. Thus far, however, the political benefits to the war party have outweighed any obvious damage, although the circumstances were special, the victory was cheap, and the costs may be somewhat lagged. An invasion of Nicaragua would be more expensive and raise a greater outcry, although the taste of blood and the puniness of the opposition to the Grenada invasion must surely make a Nicaragua replay look more feasible. A more likely scenario may be to rely on proxies from Guatemala, Honduras, and perhaps Panama to invade Nicaragua or provoke it into retaliation, which would quickly call forth Free World aid to repel Nicaraguan "aggression" by U.S. forces conveniently saturating the area. The prospects are frightening given that the level of resistance in the United States and elsewhere in the Free World to steady escalation in Central America has been dangerously modest. There is no reason to doubt that the Reagan administration will use whatever degree of force is needed to maintain or put in place amenable clients in Central America, unless it is checked by vigorous and determined opposition at home.

Concluding Note

Attentive readers will have rightly concluded that we are not optimistic that the tactics described above will be exposed as frauds in the mass media, or that the next use of "free elections" to aid a military pacification campaign in the Third World will be met with the instant ridicule and sustained public opposition that it deserves. Indeed we have written this book precisely because we see the free election-pacification strategy as a powerful one, likely to be successful in disarming or limiting opposition to U.S. intervention or U.S. support for fascist clients in the Third World.

The year 1984 may bring a "free election" to Grenada as well as El Salvador. We have seen that such elections are designed to appeal to the most idealistic strains in the U.S. political culture, including the right of all peoples to self-determination through peaceful political processes. That such freedoms have been transformed into tools of pacification and chains of enslavement by the interventionary strategies of the last two decades needs to become part of the common currency of our opposition political culture. In this book we have tried to contribute to this understanding, in the hope of disarming, if even by only one weapon, the arsenal whereby one great imperial power continues a role foreseen by Simon Bolivar more than a century ago: "to plague Latin America with misery in the name of liberty."

Glossary of Current Orwellian Usage*

Armed Minority. The origin of a civil upheaval which we oppose. Military juntas are invariably armed and a minority, but they are never an Armed Minority.

Authentic Democracy. A client state that is almost democratic, which we are in process of making less so by mobilization for counterrevolutionary warfare.

Authoritarian. Totalitarian but Free (q.v.).

Demonstration Election. A circus held in a client state to assure the population of the home country that their intrusion is well received. The results are guaranteed by an adequate supply of bullets provided in advance. (See Free Election.)

Fair Election. One in which, having stacked the deck conclusively in advance, we do not cheat in counting up our exact winnings. As in, "Within the limitations created by the exclusion from the ballot of certain popular candidates and the abuses that marked the earlier stages of the campaign [South Vietnam, 1967], most observers believe that on the whole the voting was fairly conducted." (NYT editorial, Sept. 4, 1967.) Also, one in which our carefully selected observers see no one beaten up as they are escorted in limousines past carefully selected voting booths.

Force. The principal language of the stronger. By a process of transference said to be "the only language *they* understand."

Free. Non-Communist.

Free Election. A post-pacification election, in which the "hearts and minds" of the survivors are shown to have been won over by the force of pure reason.

Free World. The group of countries that maintain a door open to private foreign investment.

Freedom. See Free.

Freedom House. A small fabricator of credibility; a wholly-owned subsidiary of the White House.

Independence. See Independent.

Independent. Aligned with us. (See Satellite.)

Leverage. That which we seek in aiding amenable tyrants, but which we find unaccountably without effect on their actual behavior.

Loyalist. Siding with the oligarchy, police, and us.

---

*These definitions are taken, sometimes in truncated form and without citations, from a book to be published by South End Press in the latter part of 1984: Edward S. Herman, *Beyond Hypocrisy: U.S. Political Language from the New Frontier to the Last Roundup.*

Military Solution. That which we eschew in favor of Negotiations (q.v.) and a Search for Peace (q.v.).

Negotiations. The process of accepting the surrender of the ill-gotten gains of the enemy. Syn. Victory.

Pacification. Returning a restive population to its traditional state of apathy by killing on the requisite scale; subjugation.

Peaceful Change. Repression punctuated by Free Elections (q.v.); as in "It is true, El Salvador's path has been a hard one. Peaceful change has not always been easy or quick." (Reagan, speech to the Longshoremen, NYT, July 19, 1983).

Quiet Diplomacy. Unconditional support. Syn. Constructive Engagement.

Revolution Without Frontiers. The threat of the mouse to home and tradition, as seen by the cat.

Satellite. Aligned with them. (See Independent.)

Search For Peace. Public relations ploys that will allow us to continue to pursue war.

Security. Control by force or the threat of force; as in "political identification of the people with the Government [Saigon] has not proceeded as fast as the security situation has..." (William Colby, head of the Phoenix Program.) Syn. Insecurity.

Security Forces. Armed agents of the government whose function is to provide the people with security (q.v.).

Stability. A political arrangement free of open warfare and satisfactory to our interests.

Step Toward Democracy. In a friendly client state, any verbal assurance no matter how vague and remote and any formal act no matter how empty of substance.

Terrorism. Killing people retail. (See Pacification.)

Turnout. The statistical proof of the public's devotion to the military junta and security forces in U.S.-sponsored elections; the index of successful coercion and intimidation in those sponsored by the enemy.

Vietcong. A Vietnamese peasant, especially one that we have killed.

Appendix Table 1: Number† of Political Assassinations‡ in El Salvador by Occupation and Month, January Through December 1980

OCCUPATION	Jan	Feb	Mar	Apr	May	Jun	Jul	Aug	Sep	Oct	Nov	Dec	Total
Peasants	129	126	203	198	800*	365	423	297	378	338	279	336	3872
Workers	8	9	31	30	31	24	16	19	44	42	42	96	392
Students	4	22	47	61	34	111	57	54	59	106	77	112	744
Teachers	8	6	3	12	21	15	21	5	16	9	13	7	136
Human Rights Workers	2	—	—	—	—	—	—	—	—	—	2	1	5
Mayors	2	—	—	—	—	—	—	—	—	—	—	—	2
Professionals	—	4	7	—	4	4	3	1	3	5	4	7	42
Shanty Dwellers	5	5	1	—	—	13	—	—	13	—	—	—	37
Public Employees	2	—	1	—	32	30	23	27	37	62	62	88	364
Priests	—	—	1	—	—	1	1	—	—	1	—	2	6
Religious/Seminarians	—	—	—	—	—	—	1	—	—	—	—	4	5
Bus Drivers	—	—	—	—	—	—	—	5	—	2	—	—	7
Small Businessmen	—	—	—	—	13	22	11	10	15	33	25	38	167
Occupation Unknown	110	64	194	179	306	184	145	142	275	164	277	300	2340
Totals	270	236	488	480	1241	769	701	560	840	762	781	991	8119

†Data presented is limited to only that which the Legal Aid Office has compiled. Due to the silencing of news sources and to repression in the conflict zones in the country, information gathering is restricted. The Legal Aid Office emphasizes that this data reflects information processed by objective collection methods and is subject to revision with additional information.

‡Those held responsible are the National Army, the Military Security Corps and the Paramilitary Organizations.

*On May 14 and 15, at least 600 peasants were killed in a massacre at Rio Sumpul, near the Honduran border by the National Army, the National Guard and the Paramilitary group, ORDEN.

Source: Legal Aid Office, Archdiocese of San Salvador, El Salvador, Central America, *Orientacion*, January 11, 1981.

Appendix Table 2: Number of Political Assassinations in El Salvador by Occupation and Month, January Through December 1981

OCCUPATION	Jan	Feb	Mar	Apr	May	Jun	Jul	Aug	Sep	Oct	Nov	Dec	Total
Peasants	176	313	1224	1765	187	203	114	110	159	174	600	98	5123
Workers	36	28	40	50	31	50	45	34	28	15	15	15	387
Students	46	26	39	87	48	25	27	10	19	9	8	2	346
Employees	21	80	84	76	56	51	44	30	38	32	25	17	554
Teachers	10	9	9	6	5	5	6	1	3	6	—	2	62
Small Businessmen	12	12	17	21	16	19	13	17	15	22	19	20	203
Professionals	4	6	3	—	1	6	2	1	1	1	—	1	26
Clergy	—	—	—	—	—	3	1	1	1	—	—	—	6
Journalists	—	—	—	2	—	—	1	—	—	—	—	—	2
Health Workers	3	2	2	1	—	—	1	—	—	—	—	—	9
Unknown Professionals	2336	427	504	303	192	572	293	377	208	179	152	240	5783
Total	2644	903	1922	2311	536	934	546	581	472	438	820	395	12501

Source: *Socorro Juridico*, January 15, 1982.

Appendix 1

Freedom House Observers in
Zimbabwe Rhodesia and El Salvador

The Zimbabwe Rhodesia[1] election of 1979 was held under conditions of intense civil war and martial law. The vote was advertised abroad as a test of internal support for a new constitution, which gave the appearance of moving dramatically toward black majority control but actually preserved most of the substance of white rule.[2] U.S. conservatives supported the new regime and urged that the Carter administration lift economic sanctions against Zimbabwe Rhodesia on the basis that it had held free elections. The election failed to end the sanctions, both in the United States and internationally, and another election was held the following year. Unlike its predecessor, the election of 1980 included the guerilla forces of the Patriotic Front. Because this second election presented the possibility of victory by the guerillas, it was regarded with great caution by conservative forces in the United States.

The two elections in Zimbabwe Rhodesia thus provide a test of observer bias under near-laboratory conditions. Our "sample" will be the reports of the observer delegations sent to monitor each election by Freedom House*, a nongovernmental group long serving as an arm of conservative private and government interests, whose findings were described as "influential" by a congressional study of the evolution of U.S. policy toward Rhodesia.[3] We will look at these reports to see if they raise the same questions for each election and adopt a similarly critical stance toward the claims of the election sponsors and the opposition, the winners and the losers. On the basis of our studies of election observers in the Dominican Republic, Vietnam, and El Salvador, we can advance the following hypothesis: that in the 1979 election the observers will display their bias by an uncritical acceptance of claims of election purpose by the authorities and by a superficial focus on the mechanics of the election and voter turnout, rather than by looking closely at the fundamental conditions under which the election was held; and that by one route or another they will find the election, which produced an outcome favored by U.S. conservative interests, to be relatively "fair" and "free." Conversely, we would expect the observers to approach the 1980 election with greater skepticism; to stress, as did the western media in the case of the Polish election of 1947, the fundamental political conditions under which the election was held; and to investigate more closely the ability of all parties to campaign freely and the effects of coercion on voter turnout. As the outcome of the election was detrimental to U.S. conservative interests, we would not be surprised to find that the observers found the election of 1980 to be fundamentally tainted, less "free" and "fair" than they had found the election of 1979.

At Stake in the Elections

Important strategic, economic, and ideological interests were at stake in the two Zimbabwe Rhodesia elections. Within the United States these interests focused on the issue of continuing or lifting economic sanctions against Rhodesia. By 1979 the Carter administration was under serious attack on the issue of continuing economic sanctions. The administration had lost its majority in the Senate and was losing support for sanctions in the House. Congress appeared determined to end sanctions, over the opposition of the Carter administration, at the conclusion of a "free election."

The immediate cause of economic sanctions against Rhodesia was its Unilateral Declaration of Independence in 1965. For more than a decade Great Britain had been winding down its African empire. In the case of Rhodesia it insisted that the white settler regime, which had ruled the colony for nearly a century, guarantee progress toward majority rule by the 95% of the population who were black. Rather than do this the Rhodesian government declared independence. Britain, reluctant to intervene militarily, took the issue to the United Nations, which finally imposed mandatory economic sanctions against Rhodesia in December 1966. Security Council resolutions supported by the United States completely banned trade with Rhodesia, and executive orders by President Johnson made these UN resolutions binding on U.S. firms.

Sanctions were only half-heartedly supported by the Nixon administration, and in 1971 little executive opposition was made to passage of the so-called Byrd Amendment, which allowed United States companies to import Rhodesian chrome, a necessary mineral in making high-quality steel. The major alternative sources for chrome were South Africa and the Soviet Union; and dependence on the latter for a mineral necessary in many military applications was the cause of much congressional criticism. Perhaps not surprisingly, however, opposition to sanctions against Rhodesia was led by conservative segregationists like Senators Eastland, Stennis, and Helms, whose hearts and minds were closely linked to white settler regimes like Rhodesia. Congressional opposition to the Byrd

Amendment finally prevailed, however, and in 1977 economic sanctions were restored. Although sanctions were supported by the Carter administration, this policy was quickly caught up in the emerging New Cold War. The establishment of leftwing regimes in the former Portuguese colonies of Angola and Mozambique, the defense of Angola by Cuban troops against attacks from South Africa, and Soviet and Cuban support for Ethiopia in its war with Somalia were seized upon by U.S. conservatives as additional reasons why the pro-U.S. and anticommunist regime in Rhodesia should be supported.

This was the background to the promulgation of a new constitution in Rhodesia in March 1978. In an attempt to gain international support for both the Rhodesian economy and the war against the guerillas, white leader Ian Smith engineered a settlement with three black leaders, which provided for a form of majority rule while preserving white control over the civil service, military, and internal security forces. The constitution was denounced as a fraud by the externally based guerillas, who had formed the Patriotic Front, but it was supported by the well-known Methodist Bishop Abel Muzorewa, whose United African National Council (UNAC) was expected to be the main black beneficiary. The constitution was overwhelmingly approved by white voters in a referendum from which blacks were excluded, and on the basis of this constitution elections for a new parliament were scheduled for April 1979.

Although the "internal settlement" received support from no black African country, congressional conservatives in the United States maintained that the elections would establish a black parliamentary majority under a black prime minister, and that sanctions should therefore be lifted. Outright support for the repeal of sanctions in the Senate was averted only by the passage of the so-called Case-Javits Amendment, which declared that sanctions would be lifted when the President determined that "(1) the Government of Rhodesia has demonstrated its willingness to negotiate in good faith at an all-parties conference, held under international auspices, on all relevant issues; and (2) a government has been installed, chosen by free elections in which all political and population groups have been allowed to participate freely, with observation by impartial, internationally recognized observers."[4] After Ian Smith told the Senate Foreign Relations Committee that he was willing to attend such an all-parties conference, a presidential determination that Rhodesia had held free elections would apparently clear the way for the restoration of economic relations with Rhodesia, and the likely continuation in effective power of that country's white minority.

The Freedom House Mission

The issue of election observers divided Congress. A bipartisan effort in the Senate, sponsored by Senators McGovern and Hayakawa, voted to send an official observer team to monitor the April election. The proposal was blocked in the House in committee, however, in part on the grounds that sending an observer team would in itself prejudge the legitimacy of the election, which was contested by both the guerilla forces and many U.S. allies. Indeed, Freedom House stated in its report on the election that the failure of Congress to send an official delegation was "one immediate cause" of its decision to send a mission to monitor an election for the first time in its 30-year history.[5]

In arguing against sending an official observer delegation, one congressman remarked that "it seems to me [that] nobody can be sure what conclusion the observers will come to, and I am not sure that we would want to support a resolution which, in effect, gives franchise for American policy to a group of private citizens, in the sense that, I think you would agree, if such a commission where established, whatever conclusions they reach will become politically binding on the administration."[6] While Freedom House's report did not become politically binding on the Carter administration, which succeeded in maintaining sanctions until after the second (1980) election, the Freedom House observer mission was given quasi-official status by both the media and Congress. In the *New York Times'* reports at the conclusion of the voting, for example, the Freedom House report was singled out as supporting the relative freedom of the election, and some members of the nine-man observer team were quoted to say "they expected the report to increase pressures on the Administration to end efforts to isolate Rhodesia diplomatically and economically."[7] On May 10, 1979 Freedom House released its report, from which the *New York Times* featured the claim that the election was a "relatively free expression of the will of the people," and quoted Freedom House's executive director Leonard Sussman saying that the United States should "change its policy to meet the new situation."[8] Five days later the Senate overwhelmingly passed a resolution stating that the requirements for a free election embodied in the Case-Javits amendment had been met by the Zimbabwe Rhodesia election. Though some Freedom House representatives later denied that they or their report said that the elections were without blemish, or that they recommended the immediate lifting of sanctions against Rhodesia, in fact their report was a superb instrument for the purposes of the pro-Smith faction in the Senate and was frequently invoked as such.

It is instructive to look at the reasons why the Freedom House report was so useful to senators who wanted to lift the sanctions. The election had resulted in a substantial majority for Bishop Muzorewa's UNC, which was pledged to support the 1978 constitution over the opposition of the guerilla forces. Supporters of sanctions argued that the April election was meaningless because (1) the constitution under which it was conducted had been approved only by white voters; (2) the electorate was not informed that the election was being interpreted and propagandized by the Smith government for foreign consumption as a vote for the constitution and the settlement, nor were the facts about these presented or discussed; (3) the electorate was urged to vote on grounds that it was their "duty" and a "step toward peace"; and (4) the relatively large turnout (50% to 65%) was achieved through massive government propaganda, intimidation and coercion. While the Freedom House report did acknowledge the limits of the new constitution and settlement, it asserted that "the transitional government of Zimbabwe Rhodesia asked for international observers to judge the authenticity of the transition to black majority rule" (*Report* , p. 351). This asked a great deal of international observers in a strange land for a few days! In effect, this is a cop-out, which simply accepts both the good faith of the Smith government and the adequacy of the constitution and settlement. An alternative premise might have been that the Smith regime was offering the minimal concessions needed to retain dominant white power, to continue the civil war, and to avoid *major* steps toward black rule. That this alternative view had a great deal of merit was shown by the later settlement, in which a far greater level of black rule was achieved within two years.

While Freedom House concluded that the election was "a relatively free expression of the will of the people," it was vague on what it was that the people were "willing." The government declared openly that the point of the exercise was to get the outside world to see that the Zimbabwean Rhodesian people accepted the new constitution and the internal settlement. Were the constitution and internal settlement addressed in the election? Could or did the media criticize it? Were any alternatives discussed, pointed out, or advocated by anybody? How can a people be said to vote for X if X is never addressed? What exactly was the basis on which people were encouraged to vote? Freedom House never faced these questions. It conceded in passing that the issue of the settlement could not be debated, but it drew no inference from this. In fact, the black populace was encouraged to vote on the ground that it was their "duty" and that the vote would be a "step toward peace." "Duty" in a patriarchal, tribal society with extensive dependency relationships is a manipulative and potentially coercive way to get people to vote. Freedom House never discussed this subject. The appeal to vote for peace by a regime intending to pursue civil war to the bitter end was deceptive and hypocritical. The substance of this ploy also could not be discussed in the election campaign in Zimbabwe Rhodesia, and Freedom House carefully avoided mentioning this issue as well.

Freedom House thus accommodated itself completely to the fact that the public was kept in the dark about the meaning of the election (as it was portrayed by the Smith regime to the outside world) and was subjected to a highly deceptive and manipulative hard sell on "duty" and "peace." Freedom House still contended that "observers" would say that there was a "tacit acceptance" of the settlement if people got to the polls even if they were given no information that *that* was the issue. It is clear that *Freedom House* would draw this conclusion, but whether nonpartisan observers would is doubtful.

The Freedom House report noted that "the government's efforts in the campaign were directed almost entirely toward achieving a maximum poll rather than the success of any particular party" (*Report*, p. 374). This cries out for a discussion of whether the "particular parties" exhibited any meaningful policy variation. It suggests that this lack of interest in party differences might have rested on the fact that the new constitution left so little power with the blacks that exactly who held nominal power was of little import to the white rulers. No such questions were raised by Freedom House. The issue in the election was "the settlement," but only "tacitly."

Concerning the possibility of coercion, Freedom House claimed that white pressure to have a high poll was balanced in part by guerilla opposition to the voting, and that the existence of at least a one-third abstention rate suggested that people were free not to vote. The greatly increased presence of government military force throughout the country at the time of the election, it claimed, was in response to the guerillas' threats to disrupt the election. This accepted without question an assertion of the Smith regime. Arguing that the election was formally free in the sense of being open to all parties which acknowledged the legitimacy of the 1978 constitution, and formally fair in that the ballot boxes were apparently not stuffed or the vote miscounted, the Freedom House Mission judged the election to have been "a relatively free expression of the will of the people of Zimbabwe Rhodesia" (*Report*, p. 351).

The Freedom House findings were sharply at variance with those of two different British observers. A report by Britain's Lord Chitnis on behalf of the British Parliamentary Human Rights Group, for example, concluded that "the recent election in Rhodesia was nothing more than a gigantic confidence trick designed to foist on a cowed and indoctrinated black electorate a settlement and a constitution which were formulated without its consent and which are being implemented without its approval."[9] Professor Claire Palley, in a report prepared for the Catholic Institute for International Relations in London, concluded that "the election was neither fair nor free by any electoral standards applicable in Western democracies or even according to those prevailing in elections preceding the grant of independence to developing African or Asian States."[10]

Let us compare the British and Freedom House observer reports on their treatment of the factors affecting voter turnout. The Freedom House report noted that "channels of nonviolent communication of opposition positions were . . . extremely limited in the country," and that the "government effort to get out the vote was a campaign for [sic] the most important issues—the election and the constitution it represented." Freedom House did not even mention the content of the campaign, the terms on which people were urged to vote, the arguments presented to them, or the framing of the issues. Thus its claim that the effort to get out the vote was a campaign *for* issues (election, constitution) was deceptive ambiguity—not *about* issues but *for* issues! The report provided no detail on the scope and character of government efforts to get out the vote, and the only encouragements to vote provided by white employers mentioned by Freedom House were in giving workers time off and transportation to the polls. The Freedom House assessment of pressures for voter turnout concluded that "the government generally did not bring out the vote by compelling the population to participate," and that such pressures were counterbalanced by real and feared guerilla violence which kept people from the polls.

The British observers saw a quite different election. Unlike Freedom House, they stressed the intensity and cruelty of the war which served as the context of the election. Lord Chitnis estimated that 100 to 200 people were being killed each day as the election approached (a proportional equivalent of 3,000-6,000 a day in the United States). He also pointed to the unleashing of an unprecedented government military offensive in the pre-election period, which included an unsuccessful assassination raid against a guerilla leader in Zambia. Unlike Freedom House, he noted that 90% of the country was under martial law, giving security forces nearly unlimited powers over the black majority. The British observers' reports, unlike that of Freedom House, contain numerous refugee accounts of the terror campaign conducted by the security forces against villagers in areas of the country suspected of being sympathetic to the guerillas. Claire Palley provided extensive evidence that the paramilitary "auxiliaries" of the black candidates Muzorewa and Sithole used coercion on a large scale, and that they and their forces behaved frequently in ways that should have disqualified them according to explicit election rules.[11] "It is the war," concluded Lord Chitnis, "and not the groups of singing and dancing party supporters or the relative calm of the urban polling stations, which is the context in which the elections are being held and should be the focal point for any assessment of whether or not the elections were free and fair" (*Sanctions*, p. 308).

The impressive detail in the reports of the British observers makes it clear that Freedom House seriously understated the scope of the effort and the degree of pressure applied by the "auxiliaries," the government, the security forces, and the white power structure to turn out the vote. Lord Chitnis, for example, reproduced an open letter from the Chairman of the National Election Directorate which included the following passage:

> A high percentage poll is the most effective way of proving to the western world that we have majority support for the internal settlement. In this way we also have the best opportunity of achieving recognition and the lifting of sanctions, which must be the aim of all Rhodesians. We appeal therefore to all white Rhodesians for their utmost co-operation in assisting their black employees to vote in the April election. . . . All white Rhodesians can assist immeasurably by helping their black employees to understand the election procedures, dispelling any fears they may have and, where possible, actually going to the polls with them. (*Sanctions*, p. 338)

Chitnis estimated that some 30% of black voters consisted of employees or their spouses living in urban areas or near mines, or engaged in construction, domestic service, education, or the public service, who would thus be readily subjected to pressure from their employers. A further 17% of the black electorate consisted of employees and their spouses working on white farms; and about one-third of this total were immigrant workers from other black African countries who had no civil rights whatsoever in Rhodesia, but who were made eligible to vote just in this election and escorted to the polls by their employers. Chitnis described several visits to white-owned farms and estates where the several hundred African workers—or in one case 35,000 black residents—were in the process of recording polls of greater than 90%, under the watchful eyes of their employers. As Claire Palley concluded: "There is no doubt that persons in positions of influence and authority and able to confer economic benefits have used their position to ensure that those subject to their influence have voted."[12] In addition to employers, those pressing for a high black turnout included the white civil service, whose pensions and job tenure were guaranteed by the 1978 constitution; the presiding officers at the polling stations, who were all white; and the government security forces, who were empowered to escort people to the polls "when requested," and who distributed a leaflet warning "if you try to stop the people from voting you will be going against the will of the people and the Zimbabwe People's army will kill you" (*Sanctions*, p. 317). Chitnis's report included a sample of case studies of security forces turning out the vote, particularly in the so-called "protected villages"—more nearly concentration camps— near the Mozambique border, and observed that "not surprisingly there was a clear correlation between a high poll and areas where there was a concentration of security forces" (*Sanctions*, p. 319).

In contrast with the Chitnis and Palley analyses of the factors affecting turnout, the Freedom House report is notably lacking in factual detail, expressing its positive conclusions and judgments "on the basis of many contacts with the process throughout the country." The vagueness as to the precise numbers and identity of the "many contacts" is suspect, as is the failure to explore the numerous opportunities for abuse in a militarized and patriarchal-racist society in the midst of a civil war. Inferring a free vote because in "some places" the vote was *not* gotten out is a nonsequitur, the authors ignoring (among other things) the positive relationship Lord Chitnis found between security force presence and voter turnout. Chitnis observed that "many foreign observers took the view that the proper conduct of the polling process was the most important part of assessing the election. This is not surprising since it was at precisely this point of the electoral process that foreign observers were invited in." This accurately describes both the Freedom House report and the activity of their mission, which arrived at the conclusion of the campaign and observed only the five days of the balloting, whereas Palley was in Rhodesia for nearly four weeks of the campaign itself, and the two members of Lord Chitnis's team were in the country for one and two weeks prior to the actual balloting. As a spokeswoman for the United Church of Christ noted in congressional hearings:

> Under these circumstances it is virtually impossible to determine whether the conduct of the Rhodesian elections was free and fair and whether the elections involved all population groups. Observers were regularly transported to the voting areas by South African planes and escorted by Rhodesian Security Forces (those same forces which the Rhodesian Catholic Commission for Justice and Peace reports burning African homes in a "scorched earth" policy). Few election observers spoke Shona or Matabele, most were white, many had their way paid by organizations with a bias toward the elections, none represented international organizations as official observers.[13]

While Freedom House was delivering up its judgment that the Rhodesian election was relatively free and fair, and while its conclusion that the vote represented "a relatively free expression of the will of the people of Zimbabwe Rhodesia" was being used by U.S. conservatives to justify lifting sanctions, Lord Chitnis concluded his report to the British Parliamentary Human Rights Group as follows: "Foreign observers were invited in to watch this brilliantly stage-managed performance so that, deceived by political sleight of hand, they could subsequently impress international opinion through their favorable reports. We cannot play our appointed role in this process and endorse this blatant attempt to perpetuate a fraud and justify a lie" (*Sanctions*, p. 283).

The 1980 Election

The election of 1979 was not followed by a reduction of guerilla violence and international recognition, as the framers of the 1978 constitution had predicted. Instead the war intensified, and Bishop Muzorewa was unable to govern effectively. Nor did the return of a Conservative government in the British general election of 1979 give Zimbabwe Rhodesia the military and economic support that the Ian Smith forces had anticipated. The Thatcher government invited all parties in Zimbabwe Rhodesia, including the two major guerilla organizations, to a conference at Lancaster House. After long negotiations new, all-inclusive elections were scheduled for February 1980.

The Freedom House mission to the second Zimbabwe Rhodesia election faced a far more uncertain outcome than the first mission. Pre-election polls indicated that the parties of the two major guerilla organizations might capture half of the 100 seats in Parliament, with another quarter going to the party of Bishop Muzorewa. As a result of the Lancaster House Agreement, 20 seats were reserved for whites, which were expected to be won by Ian Smith's Rhodesian Front. Thus the election was expected to produce an outcome closely divided between supporters of the incumbent government and supporters of the guerilla forces. The engineers of the settlement hoped that the more moderate of the two guerilla forces could be persuaded to break with the ZANU "extremists" and work out compromises retaining many of the privileges and much of the effective power of the white minority. As it promised to end economic sanctions and the embargo on military aid, therefore, the election represented the last possible means of survival for an increasingly divided white minority, while running the risk of an outright guerilla victory.

The results of the 1980 election surprised most observers, particularly those who had judged the previous year's election "relatively free." Where the first election had resulted in an overwhelming victory for Bishop Muzorewa, the second election saw his share of votes reduced from 65% to 8%. His party gained just three seats in Parliament; 77 were won by the two parties representing the major guerilla forces. If both elections were "relatively free," how could such a change in black opinion occur in less than 12 months? And if the first election represented a vote for peace and an overwhelming rejection of guerilla violence, how were we to read the second election? These were among the problems confronting the Freedom House mission in February 1980.

We earlier advanced the hypothesis that in an election which might result in a leftwing victory, conservative observers would suddenly become conscious of the surrounding political context and potential for "intimidation," while downplaying the importance of fairness in the mechanics of the election in judging its overall validity. This indeed describes the turn taken by the Freedom House delegation. The report on the February 1980 election mentioned almost in passing that, owing in part to the administration of the election itself by British authorities, the mechanics of the election were superior to those of April! But the bulk of Freedom House's two essays on the election—an "Interim Report" completed on March 1, after the balloting was completed but before the results were known, and a later "Supplementary Analysis of the Election"—were concerned with issues of voter intimidation and the likelihood that the ensuing regime would not be a democratic one.[14]

Let us look again at the issue of voter turnout. In the second election the number of votes cast was nearly one million more than the first election, and several areas with a light turnout in the first election increased their polls by more than 100%. In their Interim Report the Freedom House delegation acknowledged that, in spite of the many charges of intimidation against the three black political parties, "the bulk of the population nonetheless was conscious of the messages of two or more competing parties," and that "the majority, perhaps because of the secrecy campaign and the experience of the April election, apparently believed that their votes would be secret. This reduced the effect of intimidators on electoral choices" (p. 21). In the report written after the results were known, however, the Freedom House delegation stressed the issue of intimidation largely to the exclusion of all other factors. They ascribed most of this intimidation to the Patriotic Front, though they noted that in areas controlled by the Patriotic Front the fact of occupation itself had nearly no effect if it conflicted with tribal loyalties. "This suggests," they noted, "that what intimidation did to these voting percentages was accomplished through long-term political-military controls rather than the simple area presence of outside military units" (p. 23). No effort was made by the Freedom House delegation to apply this bit of wisdom in retrospect to the April 1979 election, and to ask what degree of military force must have been used to overcome tribal loyalties in the earlier instance. Although most press reports claimed that even without intimidation the parties of the Patriotic Front would have received sufficient votes to form a majority government, Freedom House could conclude only that the Patriotic Front "had considerable noncoerced support, but its dimensions cannot be estimated."

In its conclusions the Freedom House report remained agnostic about the kind of political outcome the elections would engender. Although it expressed the hope that the new government of Robert Mugabe would be led by the realities of power toward a cautious and pragmatic position, it expressed the fear that "once the reins of power are taken firmly by ZANU (PF), a rapid radicalization will occur that strictly follows hard-line party manifestoes released as late as January." It therefore urged that U.S. economic assistance to the new regime be given cautiously and incrementally, "contingent on the maintenance of those democratic institutions that brought the Mugabe government to power" (p. 24).

No such caution was expressed in a *Wall Street Journal* article by Bayard Rustin and Leonard Sussman, members of both Freedom House missions, on March 7, a week after the conclusion of the voting and before the new regime had taken power. Rustin and Sussman stressed the factor of voter intimidation to the exclusion of all others. Phrases like "pervasive fear" and "climate of fear" appear throughout and are given great importance in assessing the freedom and fairness of the 1980 election. Although in 1979 the Rhodesian army and other security forces had killed and intimidated on a much larger scale than the rebels, and at least as ruthlessly,[15] no such invidious language was ever employed in the Freedom House report on the 1979 election; and the possibility that voters were intimidated by the white racist government was given no serious weight. Another point of emphasis by Rustin and Sussman, which Freedom House did not see fit to include in its official report, was the claim that Mugabe's ZANU-PF party "capitalized on the traditional belief in magic as well as fear. They repeatedly claimed they could foretell the future and discover how individuals voted." Rustin and Sussman passed on the information given them by "one sophisticated African" that as many as 80% of the rural citizens believed in magic. They had characteristically failed to raise this objection in their earlier, more benign review of the 1979 election, even though Claire Palley, in her report on the 1979 election, devoted considerable space to the use of "spirit mediums" by the forces of Bishop Muzorewa, based both on the eyewitness testimony of observers and on stories in the Rhodesian press.[16]

Rustin and Sussman further accused the ZANU party of keeping its real, "Marxist-Leninist" agenda secret from the electorate, concentrating instead on issues such as land reform and black rule. They expressed considerable indignation that "Zimbabweans were not told about" the Marxism-Leninism. Again, in their report on the 1979 election they had failed to concern themselves at all with the programs of the African parties supporting the 1978 constitution, or that neither the constitutional framework nor the substance of "black rule" was presented to the electorate in any form or shape. They had ignored completely the manipulations on "civic duty" and deceptive claims of a "peace" outcome. The government's deceptions in selling the 1979 election were far more comprehensive than those attributed to Mugabe, but for Freedom House the voters casting their ballots in complete ignorance of all substantive issues were benignly regarded as "tacitly accepting" the settlement. Bias could hardly be more dramatic.

Finally, where the first Freedom House report had given no thought to the role of observers in the Rhodesian election process, nor expressed any doubts that appearance was the same as reality, in the 1980 election they learned their lesson: "Our observation of election observers led us to the conclusion that good observation results not so much from the time spent in the field or the number of observers as it does from the extent of institutional limitations under which the observers work. We felt that many observing groups ...were so tied to the political interests of their governments that an independent verdict was literally impossible" (pp. 23-24). This was not, of course, thought to be applicable to the Freedom House missions: in fact, it was unintended self-criticism of exceptional aptness.

Thus, consistent with our hypothesis, the Freedom House mission to the second Rhodesian election reversed the perspective which they had brought to the first one, and found that what determined the freedom and fairness of an election which produced an undesirable outcome was not the mechanics of the election but the fundamental political parameters under which it was conducted.

Freedom House on the El Salvador Election of March 1982

A Freedom House report on the El Salvador election of March 1982 conforms perfectly to the hypotheses just shown to apply so well to the Zimbabwe Rhodesia elections. As the election was sponsored by the United States itself, it would necessarily be an advance of democracy—"a referendum on itself, a test of political party strength, and a mandate for peace."[17]

According to Freedom House, "the sizable turnout demonstrated the determination of the Salvadoran voters to fulfill their civic obligations even in the face of possible danger." Note first the use of the legitimizing and warming phrase "civic obligation." Freedom House would not use this phrase, we believe, to describe the Polish election of 1947 or any other election not favored in advance. If they had taken seriously the thousands of civilian murders and regarded the unelected regime as a "deranged killing machine," or if they had been able to entertain the hypothesis that the election was a staged fraud, they would not have presanctified it with "civic obligation." A second element of immediately observable bias is the implication as

to the source of "danger" in voter "determination" to vote. Determination to vote might have reflected fear of being murdered by those
imposing the civic obligation, but Freedom House clearly implies
that the danger is posed by those who want the citizenry *not* to vote.
This is, of course, the propaganda line of the election sponsors, and
the Freedom House team builds it into their mode of expression even
before they address the issue.

On the question of evidence, Freedom House observers talked to
a number of voters, but they acknowledge that "the security situation
and the fears of our respondents limited responses and explanations." Thus, their direct evidence was worthless. Similarly, their
claim that voters could be observed fulfilling their civic obligation
"pleasantly or even enthusiastically," thus "participating positively"
in the election, is artful manipulation: it is of the same value as
observing smiling faces and jovial people in lines in Poland in 1947
and speaking of positive participation.

How does Freedom House cope with the possibility that there
might be coercion *to* vote? There is brief mention in the report that
"fears of government forces or other nonguerrilla forces if one did not
vote were reported by American media" (p.17). Freedom House
doesn't say whether these reported fears were justified. It does mention that voting was "compulsory" and required by law, but it then
embarks on a discussion of the fact that electoral legal obligations
may not be enforced. This suggests an urgent need to discuss the
substance of *government* intent, pressure, and coercion. Were the
junta and security forces anxious for a large turnout? Did they point
out the legal obligation to vote and make any threats? It hardly
requires explicit mention here that Freedom House did not call
attention to Garcia's published warning that nonvoting was treasonable. Also suppressed was that nonvoting was identifiable by the
security forces.[18]

Was there any basis to be afraid *not* to vote because of prior
security force actions? Freedom House completely suppressed the
details on the behavior of the security forces, the casualty rate, and
the daily deployment and cleanup of mutilated corpses. We noted the
Rustin-Sussman laser-like focus on the "climate of fear" and the
impact of guerilla violence on electoral conditions in Zimbabwe-
Rhodesia *after* Mugabe won the 1980 election! The phrase "climate
of fear" didn't appear as regards the 1979 election, nor can it be found
in the description of El Salvador in 1982, though even a Thomas
Enders and William Doherty speak of a system of justice out of
control, and Juan Corradi describes the regime a bit more accurately

as "a deranged killing machine." This was a U.S.-sponsored demonstration election, and it follows as the night follows the day that Freedom House will find no climate of fear or serious intimidation emanating from the side of the sponsored government. Freedom House focuses, as demanded by the propaganda format, on rebel disruption. For this purpose it relies heavily on the reports of Warren Hoge and Richard Meislin of the *New York Times*, who, as we pointed out in chapter 5, used the "left disruption" theme repeatedly without once citing an independent source for their claims.

Also in accord with our hypothesis on the treatment of "good" demonstration elections by propagandists, Freedom House attends assiduously to election mechanics, the fact that the election "appeared to be" well-managed, and allied questions about numbers and convenience of polling booths. On fundamental parameters, Freedom House mentioned that "grass-roots organization beyond the urban centers seems to have been minimal," but it gave no details, provided no explanation, and drew no conclusions about the impact of this on election viability. Limits on freedom of speech and press were tersely acknowledged, as was the fact that opposition to the election was essentially outlawed (p. 18). No mention was made of the killing of numerous Christian Democrats, the murder of the FDR leadership, or the army death list of 138 center and left political leaders. There was not even a general account of the decimation of journalists and independent media entities. Freedom House says that "this lack of legal opposition was to some extent compensated for by the guerilla radios and word-of-mouth communication and the influence of guerilla violence" (p. 18). An analagous apologetic for the Polish election of 1947 would say: "The harassment of the Peasant Party and the limits placed on the circulation of its newspapers was to some extent compensated for by allowing Mikolyczyk to make two major radio addresses, by word-of-mouth communication, and by the great publicity given to the violence of the Polish underground. Thus it cannot be denied that this step toward democracy was reasonably free and fair."

Appendix 2
Penniman on South Vietnamese Elections:
The Observer-Expert as Promoter-Salesman

Howard Penniman has been the resident specialist on elections at the American Enterprise Institute for many years. He has witnessed and written on elections held in scores of countries including those of South Vietnam (1967), Zimbabwe Rhodesia (1979 and 1980), and El Salvador (1982). His experience gives him the credentials of expertise. His value as an election observer is enhanced by a conservative-nationalistic bias that causes him to view his country's external endeavors in a very positive light. Penniman can thus be counted on not only to find any U.S.-sponsored election highly meritorious, but also to serve as its promoter-salesman.

Neither Penniman's work nor that of election observers in general have ever been subjected to close scrutiny. In light of the important role that observers have played in demonstration elections, we present here a case study of one observer-expert at work. Our analysis focuses on Penniman's assessment of the South Vietnam election of 1967. Not only was Penniman one of the official experts and observers for this election, his text *The American Political Process* was also "translated into Vietnamese and circulated in Vietnam for instruction in electoral campaign procedures," (*New York Times*, August 29, 1967). He also authored two books on the South Vietnamese election, which provide the main basis for our analysis here. These are a 1967 interview in which Penniman discusses the election which he has just witnessed (*Decision in South Vietnam*, published by the Free Society Association [hereafter, Penniman I]); and a "scholarly" 1972 study, *Elections in South Vietnam* (published by the American Enterprise Institute and the Hoover Institution [hereafter, Penniman II]).

The Penniman Method

In promoting and selling, the rules of scientific evidence cease to be a limiting factor in portraying the merits of the commodity being sold. We noted in chapter 4 that Penniman asserted the absence of government coercion to vote in the El Salvador election of 1982, without mention of the legal obligation to vote and on the basis of no possible *observed* evidence that would support such a conclusion. We will see further in this appendix that Penniman's writings on South Vietnamese elections are dominated by three nonscientific criteria:

(1) the patriotic inference (if my government or its friend says so, I will take it as true); (2) what the sociologist Howard Becker called the "preferential method" of research (I like and therefore use *this* fact, not that one); and (3) risk avoidance (don't look under rocks and you will not find any snakes).

As a promoter-salesman, Penniman is always impressed with the quality of the product and its steady improvement. On the apparent weakness of the Saigon army's morale and fighting qualities, for example, Penniman claimed in 1967 that "those in the military" told him that the Saigon soldiery is "improving" and that they are "working out fine" in combined U.S.-Vietnamese units (I-42). The *Pentagon Papers*, in contrast, stated that all recent advances were the result of "unilateral U.S. actions," and that "the GVN at all levels has grown weaker, become more corrupt and, today, displays even less vitality and will than it did one year ago...."[1] The historical record shows that from 1955 to 1975 the Saigon government never made a good showing against enemy soldiers (as opposed to unarmed civilians). As Penniman never recognized this inability of our Saigon agent to mobilize the population on behalf of "freedom," he naturally didn't feel compelled to explain this phenomenon.

According to Penniman, "Americans in the trenches are so eternally optimistic and so completely dedicated" (I-42). This is typical Penniman: generalizing beyond any possible sources, always finding the upbeat truth he is looking for, and being spectacularly wrong on the facts. Fragging, desertions, drug abuse, and serious morale problems in the army were already conspicuous and growing in 1967.[2] As a promoter of the Vietnam war, Penniman was not only upbeat on its progress, but also very down on the negativism of the media, always seeking out fraud and stories about corruption and abuses. Penniman does not look for fraud.

Penniman was most struck by the "complete commitment to the Vietnamese people" of the Americans in Vietnam, particularly the Green Berets (I-41). They were all, of course, devoted to winning the war and achieving U.S. goals in Vietnam, but this was consistent with devotion to the South Vietnamese people. In neither of the works discussed here did Penniman ever consider for as long as a single paragraph the nature of U.S. pacification strategy, the use of B-52s to engage in "area" bombing of the countryside of South Vietnam, or the number and character of civilian casualties or refugees. Even Arnaud de Borchgrave reported in 1967 that military opinion claimed ten civilian casualties for every insurgent.[3] In these works of

Penniman, the following words or phrases never appear: B-52, napalm, defoliation, fragmentation bombs, flechettes, free fire zone, interdiction bombing, Provincial Interrogation Center, Operation Cedar Falls, Operation Speedy Express, Operation Ranch Hand, or the "mere gook rule."[4] It is not at all clear in the writings of Howard Penniman that the United States or its ally in Saigon ever hurt a single noncombatant.

Promotional History

Throughout this book we have noted that observers are of two minds concerning the historical background or fundamental parameters of the election they are observing. In elections staged by an official enemy of the United States, like that in Poland in 1947, or in an election which might well be won by enemies, like that in Zimbabwe Rhodesia in 1980, the patriotic election observer will focus on the political context or immediate historical background of the election. Deck-stacking maneuvers and the role of coercion in turning out a high vote or a vote for a particular party are highlighted in the observers' reports. Conversely, in an election stage-managed by the United States, these factors recede into the background, and are replaced by a focus on the mechanics of the election. In accord with this hypothesis, neither Penniman nor any of the other observers in South Vietnam in 1967 paid much attention to the context of the election.

Nevertheless, in the two works of Penniman under review, a version of Vietnam's recent history is developed. In the following pages we will show that Penniman rewrites or ignores the history of Vietnam according to the requirements of patriotic dramaturgy. We call this historical methodology "promotional history," and we believe that it describes the historical and analytical efforts of the observer-expert profession as a whole.

The legitimacy of Diem. In his 1972 study, *Elections in South Vietnam*, Penniman failed even to mention the Geneva Accords of 1954 or the unheld election of 1956! Diem appears on the scene in 1954 out of the blue; the origin of the "state" of South Vietnam is unexplained. Penniman even notes matter-of-factly that Diem had no indigenous base in 1954, quoting the journalist Robert Shaplen to the effect that "except for his family and a few Vietnamese friends and his American supporters, he literally stood alone" (II-19). This would seem to raise questions concerning the legitimacy of the Diem regime. Penniman simply postulates U.S. imperial rights to carve out a piece of Vietnam, establish a "state," and impose a leader of its choice. On any logic but that of imperial rights, the United States effectively "invaded" Vietnam in 1954-1955, and then and later engaged in massive violations of the principle of self-determination and the rule of law. North Vietnam could never "invade" a South Vietnam that had no legal or moral basis to exist. Penniman bypasses all of this by patriotic assumption.

Diem, the Vietcong, and terrorism. Penniman never uses the word "terror" to describe the actions of Diem or his successors. He says that in 1955-1959 the Vietcong (VC)[5] "resumed" its campaign of terrorism (II-25). Why did the VC do so? Penniman never tells us. But there is a large body of evidence that Diem had initiated terrorism in the form of murderous pacification operations that took place long before VC terror began. Penniman cites Jeffrey Race on assassinations by the VC, but Race states that "the government terrorized far more than did the revolutionary movement. . . . "[6] He quotes Joseph Buttinger, but disregards Buttinger's evidence of Diem's prior and far more massive terror cited in chapter 3. Penniman says: "Attempts to protect villagers from the Viet Cong by transplanting them to strategic hamlets sometimes angered the peasants more than it protected them" (II-25). A book could be written on the distortions in this one sentence, which is a microcosm of Penniman's social science. This is as close as Penniman ever gets to saying that Diem ever killed people. As we indicated in Chapter 3, Diem killed and relocated vast numbers to establish "control," not to "protect" the peasants.

The concept of "protecting" the peasants from the Communists was standard pacification jargon appearing regularly in Pentagon press releases. The evidence of Buttinger, Race, and the *Pentagon Papers* shows that the peasants needed protection from Diem—and later from Ky, Thieu and the U.S. army and air force. Penniman never at any point discusses the policies of the Communists, their basis of support, or any similar substantive question. Nor does he ever assess the *extent* of Communist support. He operates strictly with clichés and myths that can be refuted by the writings of official analysts like Douglas Pike.

Penniman's dichotomy between VC and official terror is maintained into the post-1964 election years. Penniman mentions VC terror and killings frequently and provides details, expressing considerable indignation at this resort to force. With respect to Saigon and U.S. actions, Penniman is silent. He does not disclose that there were very large numbers of police, informers, political prisoners, and torturers, and that extensive political murder was carried out by the official forces of Free Vietnam. This manipulation of evidence on the use of violence provides the background for his explanation of why it was appropriate to exclude the NLF from the elections of 1966 and 1967:

> Contrary to the view apparently held by some critics of the South Vietnamese government, these people are not just a bunch of nonviolent "hippies": they're engaged in open and violent rebellion. And there is, in my view, no reason to encourage voting by those who have committed themselves against Vietnamese society—who have deliberately *removed* themselves from this society and are seeking to destroy it. (I-24)

Penniman mentions "rebellion" and South Vietnamese "society" without feeling obliged to discuss real history (such as Diem's route to power), or real political science (such as the issue of the authenticity of the South Vietnamese state). He never mentions the fact that an election which would have allowed the only mass-based party in South Vietnam—the Vietminh (later, NLF)—to take power by peaceful means was rejected by the United States and its puppet. Under Diem there was never any route to power except force. What is the "society" of South Vietnam from which the rebels removed themselves? Penniman means the political order imposed by the United States in 1954, which never at any time ruled with internal consent. The Vietminh (NLF) leadership did not "remove" itself from a social order—it was excluded and subjected to a policy of extermination from the time the United States entered Vietnam. In short, Penniman's rationale for excluding the NLF falsely portrays both the sequence and relative use of violence, and it completely avoids the fundamental questions of the origin of the Diem regime and what right the United States had to impose its chosen vehicle on South Vietnam.

The U.S. role. As a promoter of the U.S. enterprise in Vietnam, Penniman disregards not only the tremendous damage done to the South Vietnamese land and people by the U.S. military machine, but also the continuous U.S. intervention in South Vietnamese politics. Penniman acknowledges U.S. involvement in the overthrow of Diem, but after that he states:

> The United States has generally kept hands off internal Vietnamese politics. The U.S. government has supported every South Vietnamese government that has been in power. While doubtless pleased with the relative stability of the post-'67 period, it has not intervened in behalf of

President Nguyen Van Thieu. On the contrary, most of the
evidence suggests that Ambassador Ellsworth Bunker, to
the extent that he played any role at all, sought to make the
1971 presidential election something other than the one-
man race it eventually turned out to be. (II-3)

The first thing to note about this statement is its seeming naiveté. The
Saigon government was essentially a creation of the United States
and on the U.S. dole from 1954 onward; and by 1966-1967 South
Vietnam was also subject to a huge direct military as well as advisory
presence. That this would make the United States a very important
factor in South Vietnamese politics would seem inescapable and
obvious. Penniman maintains the contrary by ignoring both logic
and fact. The *Pentagon Papers*, which Penniman cites, are full of
evidence that the United States continuously manipulated the details
of Saigon politics.[7] But for Penniman, if his government *says* it is not
intervening this must be so. It is intriguing and even touching to see
his faith in the word of U.S. officials. In his 1972 book, Penniman
devotes three entire pages to quotations from U.S. Presidents on our
objectives in Vietnam, which by implication Penniman takes at face
value. In a case where the candidates opposing the Thieu-Ky ticket in
1967 claimed abuse, Penniman notes that Ambassador Bunker
himself accepted the Thieu-Ky explanation (I-17). For Penniman this
is authoritative evidence.

But Penniman is not even consistent within the brief statement
just quoted. He claims that the United States was neutral and kept
hands off, but at the same time "supported every South Vietnamese
government." How do you support a government without helping it
contain and defeat its internal opponents? If Thieu is the head of state
and you support the "government," how can you fail to intervene on
behalf of Thieu? If you give the military regime advice and logistical
support in crushing the organized Buddhists, and help it build
prisons and run interrogation centers, this would seem not merely
intervention but highly political intervention. What the United States
did in South Vietnam was to use its enormous power to put into place
a military faction, and then allow a certain amount of shuffling in the
composition of the military leadership. For Howard Penniman,
Professor of Government at Georgetown University, this is non-
intervention.

Penniman's remark on Bunker's role in the 1971 election is of
special interest given the strong evidence subsequently provided by
Frank Snepp and Seymour Hersh that the CIA played a major role in

the 1971 election and colluded with Thieu in pushing through legislation to get Ky removed from the ballot. This was done to avoid splitting the power of the military faction and to allow the U.S. choice to defeat General Minh.[8] It involved substantial bribery and the manipulation of the legislature and courts. Nowhere in Penniman's discussion of any South Vietnamese election does he ever mention the CIA, or suggest that the United States ever used bribery. His treatment of the legislation that made Ky ineligible in 1971 never suggests that this was a political maneuver sponsored by Thieu and the CIA. In Penniman's version the origins of the law excluding Ky are shrouded in mystery. Penniman says that Bunker only intervened to keep Minh in the race, ignoring the fact that Minh had quit because of the Ky gambit. Penniman never mentions the CIA bribe attempt to keep Minh in the race. In short, Penniman's account of the 1971 election misses or suppresses every element of substance.

Military Occupation, State Terror and Free Elections

We noted that Penniman never mentions the police, or prisons, or interrogation methods and practice. As the Saigon government was fighting against Communists who had "removed themselves" from "society" and had actually used force against the non-violent hippies in Saigon and Washington, it was appropriate to outlaw them and their ideas and to try to exterminate them. Penniman never gives details. The constitution and election laws of 1966-1967 also forbade "neutralism" and acts that might aid Communism "indirectly." Penniman does not discuss the meaning of these words and their application in practice. Many observers contended that the military regime used anticommunism as a basis and cover for suppressing all serious dissent. Penniman does not address this subject.

Nor does he discuss the murder of Tran Van Van, an important opponent of Marshal Ky, or the assassination attempt against Dr. Dan, another non-Communist dissident, which we mention in Chapter 3. On the day before the vote that removed Thanh from eligibility as a candidate in the 1967 election, the private secretary of the president of the Saigon Bar Association was murdered. Wurfel claims that this bar leader was the only independent-minded member of the officially dominated Central Election Council, established to evaluate the qualifications of candidates. Wurfel argues that this was part of a coercive pattern, and that "in this context, implied threats were sufficiently effective against Constituent Assembly members." Penniman relegates the secretary's murder to a footnote in which he suggests that critics have no "proof" of the relation between the murder and the decision on Thanh (II-60).

In his 1967 interview Penniman never discusses freedom of speech and press. In the 1972 volume, while he says nothing about this subject in his chapter on the 1967 election, he devotes an entire but separate chapter to freedom of the press. Organizing his book in this way, he never has to address the issue in evaluating the quality of each specific election treated in separate chapters. The chapter on the press itself deals mainly and superficially with the evolution of laws and rules on the subject. It contains a minimum of substance on the structure and control of the media, the forms and process of state censorship and other forms of discipline, and the impact of actual and threatened intervention on the scope and intensity of debate.

Penniman says nothing about the impact of the military regime on intermediate organizations. Although he records the general fact of attacks on the Buddhists, Penniman at no point suggests the possibility that there might be legitimate grievances underlying the Buddhist unrest. His version is that the Buddhists "started up again" creating "disorder," "stirring up trouble" and upsetting "stability." This makes the government's "reestablishing control" by force OK (II-33). These are the kinds of clichés that a repressive government uses: opponents are unruly and power hungry; only the government represents legitimate interests. A Soviet or Polish Penniman would say the same about the power-hungry officials of Solidarity and their periodic stirring up of trouble.

Pacification and Coercion in the Countryside

Penniman mentions "pacification" a number of times, but without any details. He implies that it was just a matter of killing terrorists and then bringing the saved civilians back into the democratic society. He points out that in the Diem period rural voters always went heavily for Diem, in contrast with voters in Saigon. The evidence from the Diem era is so clear in suggesting coercion of the hostile rural populace, that Penniman at least quotes Robert Scigliano to that effect and doesn't deny the possibility (II-22). But he carefully avoids discussing the matter in any detail. Showing how the "forms" of democracy failed to correspond to the substance in the early years of Free Vietnam would have opened a Pandora's box which Penniman keeps tightly shut.

A close examination of pacification in the Diem years and later would reveal that it was an extremely brutal activity. Air attacks, artillery shellings, and search and destroy ground operations all involved extensive killing, destruction of homes and crops, torture, imprisonment, and the imposition of direct military-police rule with omnipresent maltreatment and threat of damage. With the emergence of the Phoenix program in the late 1960s, literally thousands of mainly rural civilians were murdered in an attempt to root out NLF political influence. Even the Phoenix program's director, William Colby, admitted that these murders were sometimes based on less than adequate "intelligence,"[9] and others claimed that it was a system of uncontrolled and arbitrary violence. Penniman never mentions the content of pacification as it would destroy his pretense that the forms of electoral processes had any bearing whatever on voting in pacified areas. Voting still took place in these locations, turnout was excellent, and Thieu and Ky did very well.

Thus the Penniman method of dealing with the rural vote, the tradition of coercion, and the likelihood of enhanced coercion under pacification is first and foremost massive suppression of evidence. No details are provided on the Diem terror, and the facts on the incredible violence applied to the rural population by the U.S. military machine in 1966-1967 are blacked out.

Penniman on the 1967 Election

Penniman's non-treatment of pacification prepares us for his analysis of the 1967 election. An understanding of the content of pacification is essential to making any sense out of the important rural vote, where contradictions abound and the issue of coercion is so important. It constitutes a background fact, a basic parameter, that ruled out the possibility of a free election and an uncoerced vote long before election day.

In his explicit discussions of coercion and fraud in the 1967 election, Penniman relies heavily on the fact that data are necessarily hard to come by. He says that "there is no evidence that anyone saw a soldier or civilian vote or attempt to vote twice on election day" (II-79). Who would provide such evidence in a police state? What fraction of rural voting was seen by observers? Wurfel says that "what is really meant is that no foreign observer, or no Vietnamese willing to risk torture and imprisonment by testifying in a judicial or quasi-judicial proceeding, saw such an attempt."[10] Penniman says that the charge that extra voter cards were passed out to soldiers "is equally hard to substantiate" (II-78). This is partly a function of how hard one tries to substantiate negatives. But in this case, Thieu himself actually admitted the practice and "substantiated" the fact for Penniman, which suggests non-trivial numbers.

Wurfel also contends that in many rural villages the local chiefs voted "on behalf" of the villagers. Such a process would help explain the large progovernment turnouts in rural areas from Diem to Thieu. Penniman does not refer to this important contention. We noted in chapter 3 some very credible claims of instructions to get out the vote sent by the military regime to its rural agents. Penniman doesn't discuss these or take such leads and pursue them. The famous incident in 1971 when General Minh released a document on Thieu's plans for fraud,[11] Penniman relegates to a skeptical footnote. He clearly didn't look hard at the document or check out its validity; its content being antagonistic to the official line, Penniman quietly sets it aside.

Besides averting his eyes and depending on the absence of evidence under authoritarian research conditions, Penniman puts great weight on the *forms*—multiple observers were stipulated in the rules, and admirable procedures were spelled out in handbooks 40-50 pages long which were given to the head of each polling place. The naiveté and political bias in putting any substantial weight on these forms in South Vietnam are remarkable. Even more so is the jump from the forms to alleged empirical fact: "In every important detail, the prescribed procedures were followed scrupulously" (I-13). Penniman's assertion could not be based on observation, as he and the other observers had only visited a small fraction of the polling stations. We cited in chapter 3 the statement of the Chairman of the Central Electoral Commission that 28% of the reports from the polling places showed irregularities, so serious in the aggregate as to cause the Commission to vote to invalidate the election. Penniman's claim of universal scrupulousness in the following of prescribed election procedures is thus patriotic promotion and salesmanship lacking in minimal self-restraint.

Penniman also says that "there were very few reports of problems at the polls" (II-67). Characteristically, he does not say reports by whom, to whom, or the number that constitutes "few." If he means reports of official observers, the conclusion is a meaningless truism. He claims that short supplies of ballots in particular polling places did not penalize voters or provide the basis for potential ballot-stuffing because voters could vote anywhere in a district. Once again he implies without evidence that a legal form corresponds to a substantive reality. Wurfel states that "the behavior of voters on election day made it very clear that they did *not* know that they could vote at another place within their district."[12]

Penniman makes an attempt to prove "scientifically" that there was a fair vote in South Vietnam. His argument proceeds along these lines: as the Buddhist candidates did well in Buddhist areas, and Dzu did well in VC areas, the general character of the vote was just as we would predict. Ergo, the vote was fair and uncoerced. This is a non-sequitur. Under conditions of complete and/or unscientific fraud perhaps the Buddhist candidates wouldn't do any better in Buddhist areas than elsewhere, but if the fraud is well done, or only partial and just sufficient to attain the desired end, Penniman's test is without value. Penniman never explains why there was a lower turnout in Saigon than in the "pacified" areas, and why the military ticket lost there but won regularly in the countryside.

Thieu and Ky did very well in the contested rural areas. In a table showing the distribution of winners and losers by degree of Saigon control it turns out that in the most hotly contested regions Thieu-Ky won a plurality in eight of nine cases (Dzu only won one). Now why would peasants in the countryside, long hostile to Saigon governments, and now being subjected to an inferno of state terror, vote for the military ticket? Saigon had a relatively high proportion of military personnel, civil servants and middle class people—a relatively conservative constituency. Why would the peasant vote be relatively large and more favorable to the military ticket than that of middle class Saigon? An obvious hypothesis is that, as in the Diem period, coercion was relatively low in Saigon and high in the countryside. Penniman does not consider this possibility.

The only place where Penniman acknowledges the presence of coercion is in the territory where Dzu got a fair number of votes. He suggests that this was a result of VC coercion, and "in marginal regions, the pressures on voters must have been intense from both sides" (II-75). Having evaded all suggestions of terror on the part of the cops, Penniman can't restrain himself in blaming votes for Dzu on VC terrorism. The robbers are really bad guys and use force. The bias here attains the pathetic. Penniman even slips momentarily. Because he is eager to tie the Dzu vote to terror and pressure, he actually suggests pressure from both sides. This is the only place where Penniman allows the possibility of pressure from the non-violent democrats in Saigon and the Godfather in Washington.

The constitution and the stacking of the electoral deck. In addressing these issues Penniman's prime method of apologetics is to merely report "objectively" the elements of the constitution, the retention of de facto governmental power by the military junta throughout the constitution-making and election period, and the assertion of the power to amend the constitution by military fiat with one-third support of the General Assembly.[13] As noted, he never questions the right of the military junta to rule, and he never suggests that it had self-serving or ulterior motives. He plays dumb on the power of incumbency, strives hard to make the Constituent Assembly an independent body, and understates the ability of the junta to get its way with the Assembly. If some blatant action is approved by the Assembly or an Electoral Commission, he uses this to convey the impression that the military junta had nothing to do with it—it was done by others. The constitution, in fact, had loopholes big enough to allow the maintenance of a state of siege. In addition, because real power was retained by the junta, this was a paper constitution anyway.

We described in chapter 3 a series of deck-stacking characteristics of the pre-election maneuvering that led to a foreordained conclusion. First, both voting and candidacy were restricted by vague language that ruled out "pro-Communist neutralists" (can't vote) and "persons who work directly or indirectly for Communism or neutralism" (excluded as candidates). There were no definitions of these words, and anybody opposing government policy could have been said to be indirectly helping Communism or neutralism. Penniman quotes this language, but he fails to discuss or defend it (except for its exclusion of Communists) or to analyse how it worked out in narrowing the range of options.

Penniman then pretends that the election proved that the public wanted war because it voted predominantly for candidates who supported war—never once mentioning that *by law* and effective exclusion peace candidates could not run. Penniman relies on the Dzu candidacy to show a peace option, describing Dzu as an "extremist" advocate of peace, without ever describing his specific campaign claims. As Dzu received only 17% of the vote, the pro-war candidates "won." But Dzu was only allowed to run by an unexplained failure to enforce the prohibition of neutralists. Penniman never discusses this point; nor does he ever raise the question of the meaning of a vote on war and peace where it would be criminal to openly advocate the peace option. Penniman notes that Dzu was an unknown of dubious background, without organization or any obvious source of financing, but the bearing of this on the size of his vote is unmentioned. He never calls attention to the irony of ruling off the ballot Thanh and Minh, *strong* peace candidates, while allowing a weak one to run—or the implications of this nice discrimination on the size of the "peace" vote. Penniman sneers at the suggestion that Dzu represented a CIA ploy, but his research methods precluded any serious investigation of the matter. The idea is plausible. It may help explain Dzu's ability to remain in the campaign as a neutralist. Furthermore, some very well informed former insiders testify to Dzu's earlier relationship with the CIA.[14]

A second deck-stacking device was to allow and encourage a proliferation of civilian candidates, while consolidating the military ticket. Penniman mentions the subsidization of candidates, but pretends that this was a wonderfully generous and democratic idea. He never suggests that this might have been part of a strategic design to encourage proliferation, including the unknown Dzu and his peace symbol, to diffuse the vote in the interest of the military ticket. He says that "it was relatively easy to become approved candidates for the highest offices in the country" (II-61), disregarding the convenience of this to the military ticket and (in the words of Wurfel) "ignoring that 'ease' was in direct proportion to the political insignificance of the candidate and the identity of his views with that of the government."[15] That the United States contributed to this diffusion process—and to Ky's willingness to run second to Thieu on a military ticket—by advice, pressure, and bribery, Penniman denies a priori: the United States is by definition a neutral, although supporting the government in power!

A third deck-stacking device was the arrangement to have no vote run-off, but instead to allow a plurality on the first vote to win all. This was again perfect for the military ticket, but for Penniman this was not a reflection of the manipulative power of Thieu, Ky and the United States, it was based on a ruling by the independent Constituent Assembly. Once again, the contribution of the democratic Assembly to the welfare of the military ticket was fortuitous. For Penniman, the Constituent Assembly was sometimes guilty of "politics"—when it challenged the military ticket—but when it accommodated to the ticket this was democracy at work.

The exclusion of General Minh and Thanh. Nowhere are Penniman's biases so clearly evident as in his apologetics for the exclusion of Minh and Thanh from candidacy in the 1967 election. He explains that "in the case of Au Truong Thanh, the former finance minister in the Thieu-Ky government, the Assembly excluded him on the perfectly understandable ground that, in its judgment, he was pro-VC or neutralist—both terms were used" (I-34). Note first the unquestioning acceptance of the stated reason for exclusion as constituting the real reason. Once again, the surface of events and the nominal suffice when Penniman examines acts by those whom he supports. Is it possible that Thanh represented a serious challenge to Thieu and Ky and that a plausible reason had to be found to justify his exclusion? The question doesn't arise for Penniman. Thanh had been a member of the Ky government shortly before being declared ineligible for candidacy in 1967, which suggests the phoneyness of the charge. There is also the problem that, if it was perfectly understandable to exclude Thanh as a neutralist, why wasn't Dzu also excluded? Penniman does not mention this strange dichotomy. In his 1967 report, Wurfel pointed out that the civilian candidates and their supporters in the Assembly also had a strong political or self-interest in excluding a powerful competitor like Thanh—an obvious point, but Penniman merely quotes Wurfel in a footnote and then blithely ignores its significance.

In discussing the National Assembly's vote on the validity of the 1967 election itself, Penniman is very alert to the "political considerations that influenced the votes of some of the deputies [that] could have included their own public situations" (II-83). The same is obvious in the case of the exclusion of Thanh, but in the latter instance the action was "perfectly understandable" based on "principle" and the integrity and independence of the various bodies. Penniman's asymmetry in argument—time and again resorting to "politics" in criticizing actions hostile to the military government, and sticking to the nominal and playing dumb in defense of the junta—is as regular as the tides.

Penniman nowhere discusses either the justification for excluding "neutralists" or the criteria employed in identifying them. These encompass the substantive issues and premises of the whole Saigon enterprise, and Penniman steers clear of substance. He was willing to stick his neck out to explain why Communists should be excluded, as we described earlier—but neutralists are a little more touchy, so Penniman just asserts baldly that it was perfectly understandable to exclude them. In his "scientific" effort published by the AEI and Hoover, Penniman is less brash, just recording the "facts" that *both* the Central Electoral Committee and a Special Committee agreed that Thanh was pro-Communist. Penniman pretends that these political entities are independent of one another and not subordinate to the military regime, although he never discusses this issue in any depth. Thus if they come separately to an identical conclusion this is presumably compelling. Did they have any overlapping membership? What fraction of the various committees was made up of government officials and employees? Were bribery or threats ever employed by the military regime to accomplish their ends in dealing with these bodies? Penniman doesn't raise such questions. In chapter 3 we summarized a 1971 interview with the Chairman of the Central Electoral Committee, who claimed that extensive bribery and a variety of coercive threats were employed to affect Committee and Assembly votes. South Vietnam was a remarkably corrupt police state in 1967. But Howard Penniman was not looking for fraud.

In accepting the perfectly understandable rejection of Thanh's candidacy, Penniman never took an independent look at the evidence on which that conclusion was based. He also tells us that the police "linked" Thanh to a Communist group, but he made no independent investigation of the "link," but instead relied completely on the integrity of the Saigon police. Then Penniman quotes Charles Joiner to the effect that the Communists planned to support one non-Communist peace candidate. The implication is that Thanh may have been this candidate, although Joiner himself says there was never any proof linking this plan to Thanh.[16]

General Minh's exclusion from the ballot in 1967 leads Penniman into some real drolleries. Minh was kept off the ballot on the ground that the new constitution of South Vietnam excluded former French citizens as candidates, and Minh's running mate was a former French citizen. Now this might appear a technicality, but as Penniman explains, such a proviso "may be crucial to a developing country searching for self-identity. Particularly abhorrent under these circumstances is allegiance to the former colonial power" (II-59). On the matter of technicalities, the Assembly had, of course, passed a law earlier that no active officers could run for high office while on duty. This was changed by the Assembly to allow Thieu and Ky to run. Here was a technicality that could be overcome. Could it be that the exclusion of Minh on a technicality was an excuse covering over the real reason—his threat to the military ticket—and that the firmness on this technicality and the removal of a real challenge to Thieu and Ky reflected *power*? Penniman never raises these questions.

Finally, Penniman's remarks on the pride of developing countries and their sensitivity to allegiance to the former colonial power run into the problem that Thieu and Ky were both trained by and worked for the former colonial power, France, before they switched to the service of the United States. Penniman also failed to note that

Article 11 of the 1967 election law prohibited the candidacy of "those who have been sentenced for criminal or light offenses of political character or for political reasons before April 1, 1967. . ." This ruled out anyone arrested by the French or Japanese for political reasons. Thus the only group not discriminated against in the election law was those who *collaborated* with the French! This "developing country seeking self-identity" was thoroughly occupied in 1967 by another distant foreign power that was in process of returning it to the Stone Age, and utilizing for this purpose the former French hirelings. It takes a truly true-believing and foolish promoter to play the "anti-colonialist" game with Thieu and Ky as the heroes.

Appendix 3
Fraud in the 1967 Vietnam Election: An Extract from a Report by Election Observer David Wurfel*

1. *Fraud on election day was extensive, perhaps producing 300-500,000 votes and inflating the total number of voters by the same number; in addition hundreds of thousands of votes were produced by pressure exerted by the government through the military and the civil service.*

The manufacture of votes without voters was relatively easy because there was no effective check on whether the voter ever appeared personally at the polling place. The only record which officials could present was a string of voting card corners ostensibly clipped as voters entered the polls. But this proved nothing. Officials themselves could have brought dozens of voting cards to the polling place, clipped them, and then deposited an equivalent number of ballots in the box after the polling place closed. I personally witnessed two policemen who presented voting cards to be clipped just before the polls in a Cholon precinct—*without* themselves receiving *any ballot.* Though a list of registered voters was compiled before election day by district, in most provinces it was *not* compiled by polling place, so that voters could easily cast their ballots anyplace in the district; the voting card itself was the only proof of registration.

My estimate is based on my own observations and discussions with dozens of Vietnamese election observers in the week following the election. I talked also with American journalists and with Vietnamese school teachers who had been members of polling place committees. I also analyzed the returns in several provinces rather carefully. For example, in Can Tho, where I had access to returns by polling place four days after the elections, officials readily admitted discrepancies amounting to several hundred votes. At least several thousands in Saigon and Gia Dinh were not allowed to vote either because the voter was not given his voting card before election day, with a variety of excuses, or because ballots "ran out" at the polling place early in the day, even though two million extra ballots were

---

*"Dr. David Wurfel Reports on Vietnam," was published by the Methodist Division of Peace and World Order, September 21, 1967. This report was based on a four-week visit to Vietnam at the time of the 1967 election. This was his sixth visit to that country, in which he had a great many friends and other contacts.

printed by the government's own admission. *No* record has been kept of what happened to those ballots, which were supposedly insurance against "VC theft of ballots."

In Gia Dinh, Thieu and Ky received over 100,000 votes more than their nearest rival, by far their largest margin in any province. Yet this is a dominantly urban province, most of whose inhabitants are of the same occupational, religious and educational make-up as citizens of Saigon, where Thieu and Ky came second. Gia Dinh is also the province in which there was the most spectacular rise of registered voters from June to August, an increase of over 80,000.

In a province where Dr. Phan Quang Dan, Mr. Suu's running mate, was a popular and well-known public figure, elected to the provincial council and to the Constituent Assembly, the Suu-Dan ticket came in a poor fourth with less than 10% of the votes in the province. The province chief of Gia Dinh is a relative of Gen. Loan, head of national police. Dr. Dan himself, in an interview the day after the elections, estimated that fraudulent votes probably amounted to about 10% of the total, i.e. 480,000. But he was unwilling to associate himself with any public charge of fraud. He is running for the premiership.

It has sometimes been said that the fact that Thieu and Ky received only 35% of the vote is proof of an honest ballot. For such an unpopular regime, however, this is a nonsequitur. While Ky had predicted that his ticket would get as much as 50% of the vote, Thieu had been more modest with 40%. There were two kinds of pressures operating on them. On the one hand, they might gain legitimacy before the world by winning a majority. But, given their unpopularity, this could only be achieved by massive fraud. Fraud on such a scale would have produced stronger domestic repercussions and might even have been noticed by foreign observers. It is probable that the US Embassy advised against a push to get a majority.

Reports of government pressure on the military and the civil service to support the Thieu-Ky ticket were innumerable. A military reorganization was announced before the election to be implemented after the election. This served to keep corps commanders, as well as province and district chiefs, on their toes. Even before the election there were some arrests, removals, and transfers of military officers for failure to support the government ticket; for example, the assistant province chief of Long An province was removed to Saigon ten days before the election. The major was a member of the Tan Dai Viet party which supported Dzu.

The distribution of undesignated slush funds to Hoa Hao

leaders by Gen. Ky was an important means for gaining support in the delta.

2. *Rigging of the Senate race was generally believed by knowledgeable Vietnamese to be much more blatant than in the presidential election, i.e. the final outcome of the Senate race was the result not simply of vote counting but of bargaining between Thieu and Ky during the week's delay in publishing the results.*

Voting for the Senate was so complex that most Vietnamese selected at random. My observation at polling places on election day was that the average voter did not spend more than 1 to 2 minutes in the voting booth to select 6 out of 48 ballots. Some reported a formula of "the three top and three bottom." In some polling places the preferred six were on top when distributed. Other places the ballots of important opposition slates were not distributed at all.

The belief that the outcome was finally determined by a joint decision of Thieu and Ky was universal among defeated candidates. One powerful bit of circumstantial evidence is that, during the week before the reporting of final returns, the votes of some tickets went down, while others went up. The Tran Van Lam ticket, for instance, dropped out of the top six because of a *loss* of more than 40,000 votes! (*Two* weeks after the election he was restored to the select six.)

The Senate which resulted is dominated by Northern Catholics, many of whom were prominent during the Diem regime. Though this is probably in part due to rather effective Northern Catholic bloc voting, the unrepresentativeness of the Senate's composition confirms in the minds of Southerners the presence of fraud. The Constituent Assembly is showing great reluctance to proclaim officially the results of the Senate election.

Somewhat surprisingly the U.S. Embassy in Saigon claimed that the Senate election was again proof of the honesty of the process. It was pointed out that the six tickets which, according to press reports, were receiving government backing did not all win. However, according to my Vietnamese informants, this merely means that "deals" with some Senate tickets were not lasting and/or that Thieu and Ky intentionally gave the impression to some candidates that they were backing slates which they, in fact, had abandoned. The intense competition between Thieu and Ky certainly increased the fluidity of these arrangements.

3. *Major techniques of fraud were issuance and use of multiple voting cards, ballot box stuffing, and alteration of returns; some documentary evidence can be presented, but proof of the extent of these techniques is impossible because of fear.*

I have photostatic copies of voting cards issued to two women in Gia Dinh. Both received two cards on the same day at the same office, reporting the same address. The serial numbers make it clear that the two women were together when they received their second, as well as when they received their first, voting card. This double issuance was hardly accidental. If such multiple issuance was possible for civilians, how much more so for military men?

Every family that I talked to in Viet Nam who had a relative in the military reported that he had more than one voting card. Until two days before the election both the U.S. and Vietnamese governments denied knowledge of this situation. Then on Friday night before the election a radio broadcast by the Vietnamese Joint Chiefs of Staff reported "regretfully" that there had been a "mistake" and that some soldiers had received more than one voting card; they were asked to turn them in to their commanding officers. Whether they were turned in or not, these extra voting cards, perhaps amounting to hundreds of thousands, could have been used on election day. The returns in Gia Dinh, where there is a concentration of military camps, strongly suggests that many were.

Ballot box stuffing, in the sense of officials, not voters, placing ballots in the box, is of two types. In one the voting card to match the ballot was surrendered voluntarily to the official; in the other, officials refused to distribute voting cards to voters. I have already mentioned that the latter was widespread in urban areas. I found no one, however, who was willing to risk retaliation by signing an affidavit to this effect. Those I asked were persons I had every reason to trust. The former type was widespead, I learned, in the September 1966 elections, particularly in the villages. Obliging village or hamlet chiefs would advise peasants to hand over their voting cards "so the VC would not try to take them away," as occasionally did happen. They were also warned about the dangers of going out on election day and thus were only too happy when village and hamlet chiefs offered to fulfill their voting obligation for them. (Mr. Patterson of the official observer team discovered in the delta how natural the idea of proxy voting seemed to a village elder.) It will probably take months, as it did in 1966, for news of such proxy voting to get to the cities. This is, of course, an effective means for increasing the percentage of voters voting, as well as for rigging the results. In Phong Dinh province my inspection of precinct-level returns gave a hint that this technique may have been used in outlying villages. The percentage of invalid ballots reported was *much* lower than that in urban areas. Yet illiterates would naturally have more difficulty with the complex voting system than literates.

I am in possession of a signed statement by a chief of a polling station in Gia Dinh that there were 20 more ballots in the box at the beginning of counting than there were clipped corners of voting cards. At the polling station which I observed in Cholon there were 40 more voting card corners than there were ballots. They seemed quite embarrassed. Perhaps they were not expecting the presence of a foreign observer even after the polls closed.

The counting of ballots was generally so secret that the suspicion of fraud was created even if there was none. Police removed voters from the schoolyards where polls were usually located as soon as the polling places closed. Probably less than 10% of polling places throughout the country had opposition candidates' observers; there were none in the villages. This was a result both of poor organization and of the fear of local people to be openly identified with an opposition leader. Under these circumstances it is understandable that a chief polling clerk could be told—as he reported to me—to produce an 80% turnout and a 50% vote for Ky and Thieu at his station.

It is hard to know how honest the counting process itself was. The printing of illegal ballots certainly made honesty more difficult. I am in possession of a photostat of a ballot (I saw the original) which has the symbol and picture of Mr. Dzu, which would be noticed by the illiterate, but the name of Mr. Suu and his running mate. It is the latter which would probably be counted, though properly the ballot should have been invalidated. In one polling place in Gia Dinh a Vietnamese friend reported to me that the district chief came into the polling place during counting, asked the total number of voters who voted, was told 553, and then said, "Give Thieu 200."

Most Vietnamese believed, however, that manipulation of the returns was more common between the district and the province. My own experience was that province chiefs were reluctant to reveal district-level returns. Mr. Dzu's complaint to the Constituent Assembly charged that his provincial representatives were frequently refused the right to see district returns. From two sources it was reported to me that in one district of Vinh Long province the number of votes first reported was greater than the number of registered voters. Later the higher number was adjusted to fit the lower, all the votes being taken away from one civilian candidate.

Further documentation of fraud would strengthen my charges. I had very little time to gather or analyze district-level returns, however. And to expect to get signed statements by ordinary Vietnamese regarding instances of fraud in the present context there is totally unrealistic.

Footnotes

Preface

1. "Cauldron in Central America: What Keeps the Fire Burning?," *New York Times*, December 7, 1980, p. E3.
2. See Hannah Arendt, *The Origins of Totalitarianism*, Meridian, 1958, Part 3; William Kornhauser, *The Politics of Mass Society*, Free Press, 1959, Part 1; Franz Neumann, *Behemoth*, Oxford, 1944, *passim*.
3. *Presidential Certification on El Salvador*, House Committee on Foreign Affairs, 97th Congress, 2nd Session, 1982, vol. I, p. 330.
4. "El Salvador; A Culture of Fear," (Review of *Salvador*, by Joan Didion) *Dissent*, Summer 1983, pp. 287-8.
5. Reagan speech of March 10, 1983 before the National Association of Manufacturers, in *New York Times*, March 11, 1983.
6. See Richard DuBoff and Edward S. Herman, *America's Vietnam Policy, The Strategy of Deception*, Public Affairs Press, 1966; David Kraslow and Stuart Loory, *The Secret Search for Peace in Vietnam*, Random House, 1968; Franz Schurmann et al., *The Politics of Escalation*, Fawcett, 1966.
7. Ben Bagdikian, *The Media Monopoly*, Beacon, 1983, Chapters 1-2, 8-9.
8. See especially, *ibid.*, Chapters 10-11 and Eric Barnouw, *The Sponsor*, Oxford, 1978; also, Edward S. Herman, *The Real Terror Network*, South End Press, 1982, Chapter 4.
9. For summaries of these developments, see "Salvadoran Rights Worker: 'Justice Will Be a Living Reality'," an interview with Jacinto Morales, a member of the Human Rights Commission of El Salvador, *Latinamerica Press*, May 12, 1983; and "We who touch the wounds...," *Index on Censorship*, August 1983.
10. "We who touch the wounds...," *op. cit.*
11. John Newhagen, "Report says $25 million in U.S.-backed loans to El Salvador missing," *Washington Post*, March 16, 1983.
12. "Capture of M-16s Reported," *Washington Post*, March 16, 1983.
13. "El Salvador Weighing Plan to Offer Limited Amnesty to Guerrillas," *New York Times*, March 20, 1983.
14. "We who touch the wounds...," *op. cit.*
15. For other human rights workers murdered by the security forces in El Salvador, see Table 4-2 below.
16. Five weeks after the plane incident, and based on unreleased material probably available within 24 hours, U.S. intelligence experts concluded that the Soviet pilots very probably did not know they were shooting down a commercial rather than military plane. (David Shribman, "U.S. Experts Say Soviet Didn't See Jet Was Civilian," *New York Times*, October 7, 1983.) There had also been information disclosed before then that a U.S. spy plane had been in the vicinity at the time of the shooting; and that the U.S. frequently used bait planes to cause Soviet

radar reactions that could then be monitored, among other matters. By October 7, however, the incident had been milked for all its propaganda value. In the weeks following this new admission there were no second thoughts, apologies, or reassessments.

17. John Dinges, "New Evidence on Missionaries' Deaths in El Salvador Suggests Official Plot." General Garcia himself, the top military officer in El Salvador, was quoted by a local official saying that "We've got to take steps against these missionaries." (Lawyer's Committee for International Human Rights, *Justice in El Salvador: A Case Study*, July 20, 1982, p. 21.) Within a month the murders took place.

18. See *Foreign Assistance Legislation for Fiscal Year 1982*, Part 1, Hearings before the House Committee on Foreign Affairs, 97th Congress, 1st Session, March 18, 1981, p. 163. When families of the victims complained to Haig and the State Department about the Haig allegation, they were told that no State Department evidence from El Salvador had suggested the possibility that the nuns were killed while running through a roadblock, and the FBI also denied this as a likely theory. (Letter of William Ford to Haig, March 25, 1981, discussing his interchanges with James Cheek of the State Department and Harry Brandon of the FBI.) Haig's fabrication seems to have been constructed out of the whole cloth. On Haig's reference to "pistol packing nuns," which elicited laughter in the Committee room, see *Foreign Assistance Authorization for Fiscal 1982*, Senate Foreign Relations Committee, 97th Congress, 1st Session, March 19, 1981, p. 40.

19. In an interview on December 16, 1980, Kirkpatrick stated that "The nuns were not just nuns. The nuns were also political activists." She also suggested that the killers were "death squad" personnel not under government control. (*Tampa Tribune*, December 25, 1980.) They were, in fact, members of the National Guard.

20. Speaking of the assassinations of the rebel leaders, Kirkpatrick's reaction was: "I found myself thinking that it's a reminder that people who choose to live by the sword can expect to die by it." "Cauldron in Central America: What Keeps the Fire Burning?," *New York Times*, December 7, 1980, p. E3.

21. More than four months before the Salvadoran military authorities had completed their alleged investigations, U.S. Ambassador Deane Hinton stated that the investigation should be limited to the six detained guardsmen "who were acting on their own." (Mary McGrory, "Pressure Over Missionairies' Deaths is Only Card Duarte Holds," *Washington Post*, October 1, 1981.) The sergeant commanding the guardsmen alleged to have done the killing "retired" shortly after the incident, and emigrated to the United States. As this sergeant admitted that the killers had confessed to the murders and that he had not done anything about it, he had violated Salvadoran law and was a criminal (aside from the probability of deeper involvement in the case). This was no bar to his entry and residence in this country. He was not very closely questioned

by U.S. authorities. For details on this and scores of other pieces of evidence of U.S. collaboration in the cover-up, see the series of documents put out by the Lawyers Committee for International Human Rights: *A Report on the Investigation Into the Killing of Four American Churchwomen*, September 1981; *Justice In El Salvador; A Case Study*, July 20, 1982; and *Update, Justice in El Salvador; A Case Study*, February 1, 1983.

22. See Miles Wolpin, *Military Aid and Counterrevolution in the Third World*, Lexington, 1972, *passim.*; Noam Chomsky and Edward S. Herman, *The Washington Connection and Third World Fascism*, South End Press, 1979, Chapters 2-4; Herman, *The Real Terror Network*, Chapter 3.

23. Quote from Metin Demirsar, "Turkey's Rejection of 12 Political Parties Raises Doubts About Plan for Democracy," *Wall Street Journal*, August 25, 1983.

Chapter 1:
The Rise of the Demonstration Election

1. See Walter LaFeber, *Inevitable Revolution: The United States in Central America*, Norton, 1983, chapters 1 and 2; see also Charles Wright, *American Support of Free Elections Abroad*, Public Affairs Press, 1962.

2. See John Gallagher and Ronald Robinson, "The Imperialism of Free Trade," *Economic History Review*, vol. 6, no. 1, 1953, pp. 1-15.

3. Jules Benjamin, *The United States and the Cuban Revolution of 1933: The Role of United States Hegemony in the Cuban Political Economy 1880-1934*, Ph.D. dissertation, University of Pennsylvania, 1974, vol. I, p. 50.

4. See Edward S. Herman, *The Real Terror Network*, South End Press, 1982, pp. 33-36. A classic discussion of the use of Communism (an international movement) as an instrument to justify attacks on threatening social change (Kommunism) is in Juan José Arévalo, *Anti-Kommunism in Latin American*, Lyle Stuart, 1963. Arévalo was a liberal-left President of Guatemala in the late 1940s. John F. Kennedy approved a military coup in Guatemala in 1963 because of the "Kommunist" threat posed by an imminent return of Arévalo to run in a free election. See Stephen Schlesinger and Stephen Kinzer, *Bitter Fruit*, Doubleday, 1982, pp. 243-44.

5. See the next chapter.

6. An editorial in the Dominican Republic newspaper *Listin Diario*, dated August 9, 1915, entitled "The Godfather," called attention to the recent U.S. invasion and occupation of Haiti in July 1915, and expressed concern that "the fire is getting close, and any spark may set off our powder." The Dominican Republic was subject to a U.S. occupation beginning in May 1916 and lasting until 1924. (Quoted in M.M. Knight, *The Americans in Santo Domingo*, Vanguard, 1928, p. 68.)

7. See Jean Kirkpatrick, "Dictatorships and Double Standards," *Com-

mentary, November 1979, p. 35.
8. University of Illinois Press, 1964, p. 172.
9. See Table 5-1 and associated text.
10. See especially, *Free and Fair? The 1979 Rhodesian Election, A Report by Observers on Behalf of the British Parlimentary Human Rights Group*, May 1979.
11. See the discussion of the observers in the Dominican Republic in Chapter 2.
12. One of the leading Saigon generals, speaking to George Kahin, in George Kahin and John Lewis, *The United States in Vietnam*, rev. ed., Delta, 1969, p. 346.
13. See below, Chapter 4, under "The Election of 1972."
14. These procedures are discussed in greater detail in Chapters 4 and 5.
15. William Kornhauser, *The Politics of Mass Society*, The Free Press, 1959, p. 82.
16. *Washington Post*, April 9, 1981.
17. These are discussed in Chapter 4 below.
18. Austin Ranney and Willmoore Kendall, *Democracy and the American Party System*, quoted in M. Rejai, ed., *Democracy: The Contemporary Theories*, Atherton Press, 1967, p. 86.

Chapter 2:
The Dominican Republic

1. The OAS Charter unequivocally prohibits intervention among the signatory American states, which include the United States and the Dominican Republic. According to Article 15: "No State or group of States has a right to intervene, directly or indirectly, for any reasons whatever, in the internal and external affairs of any other State..." Article 17 states: "The territory of a State is inviolable; it may not be the object, even temporarily, of military occupation or of other measures of force taken by another State, directly or indirectly, on any grounds whatever."
2. See especially Simon G. Hanson, *Five Years of the Alliance for Progress: An Appraisal*, Inter-American Affairs Press, 1967.
3. *Ibid.*, Chapter 5; Richard Walton, *John F. Kennedy and the Cold War*, Penguin, 1975, *passim*.
4. Letter to the *New York Times*, May 12, 1965.
5. Quoted in Melvin M. Knight, *The Americans in Santo Domingo*, Vanguard, 1928, p. 4.
6. *Ibid.*, Chapter 10; Marvin Goldwert, *The Constabulary in the Dominican Republic and Nicaragua: Progeny and Legacy of United States Intervention*, University of Florida Press, 1962, p. 7; Piero Gleijeses, *The Dominican Crisis: The 1965 Constitutionalist Revolt and American Intervention*, Johns Hopkins, 1978, p. 19 (hereafter GL-19).
7. GL-20.
8. GL-18.
9. Goldwert, *op. cit.*, p. 8; GL-18-21.

10. GL-21.
11. Jerome Slater, *Intervention and Negotiation: The United States and the Dominican Revolution*, Harper, 1967, p. 4.
12. Howard J. Wiarda, *Dictatorship, Development and Disintegration: Politics and Social Change in the Dominican Republic*, Xerox University Microfilms, 1975, vol. 3, pp. 1433-4 (hereafter Wiarda-1433-4).
13. GL-187-8.
14. *The Era of Trujillo, Dominican Dictator*, University of Arizona Press, 1973, pp. 187-8.
15. *Ibid.*, p. 187; Wiarda-1438.
16. Dan Kurzman, *Santo Domingo: Revolt of the Damned*, Putnam, 1965, pp. 45-46.
17. Wiarda-1439.
18. Robert D. Crassweller, *Trujillo: The Life and Times of a Caribbean Dictator*, Macmillan, 1966, pp. 70-71.
19. *Ibid.*, p. 274.
20. Kurzman, *op. cit.*, p. 46.
21. The quotations are from Crassweller, *op. cit.*, pp. 324-6, and Kurzman, *op. cit.*, p. 46.
22. That is: an active anticommunism, subservience to U.S. foreign policy, and respect for private property and the rights and interests of foreign investors.
23. Gerald Murphy had piloted the plane on which the abducted Galindez had been taken from New York to the Dominican Republic to be murdered. Murphy's disappearance (in contrast with that of Galindez) produced a major outcry and affected relations between Trujillo and the Eisenhower administration. See GL-340-1; Crassweller, *op. cit.*, pp. 311-23.
24. GL-303-7.
25. GL-47-48.
26. See Walton, *op. cit.*; Edward S. Herman, *The Real Terror Network*, South End Press, 1982, pp. 119-37; Thomas Lobe, *United States National Security Policy and Aid to the Thailand Police*, University of Denver, 1977, *passim*.
27. GL-75.
28. Quoted in GL-76.
29. Quoted in *ibid.*
30. GL-77.
31. *Ibid.*
32. GL-82; Wiarda-1537.
33. GL-83.
34. GL-84ff.
35. GL-87.
36. Quoted in GL-89.
37. Slater, *op. cit.*, p. 38.
38. GL-98.
39. *Ibid.*

40. Quoted in GL-116-7.
41. Norman Gall, "The Goons Again," *New Republic*, February 17, 1964, p. 160.
42. GL-117.
43. GL-118.
44. *Ibid.*
45. *Ibid.*
46. GL-119.
47. GL-125.
48. *Ibid.*
49. GL-161.
50. *Ibid.*
51. GL-217.
52. Quoted in GL-218.
53. *Ibid.*
54. *Ibid.*
55. See especially José Moreno, *Barrios in Arms: Revolution in Santo Domingo*, University of Pittsburgh Press, 1970; Marcel Niedergang, *La Révolution de Saint-Domingue*, Plon, 1966; Tad Szulc, *Dominican Diary*, Dell, 1966; GL-219-81.
56. GL-402-3, n. 87.
57. GL-264 and n. 51, p. 406.
58. GL-207-12.
59. GL-285.
60. GL-406, n. 51.
61. GL-260.
62. GL-264.
63. GL-272-7.
64. Interview, *New York Times*, May 9, 1965, p. E-3.
65. Jerome Slater takes this position as an act of faith, without providing any evidence, in his book *Intervention and Negotiation*, pp. 70, 163ff. See below, footnote 67.
66. "The Dominican Struggle," in Eugenio Chang-Rodriquez, ed., *The Lingering Crisis: A Case Study of the Dominican Republic*, Las Americas Publishing Company, 1969, p. 47. Grant allocates the responsibility for the 1966 election outcome to Bosch's personal defects and strategic mistakes plus his administrative incapacity. The latter reason is offered as the sole explanation of the fact that "the PRD ranks had become greatly disintegrated in the country-side," p. 57.
67. Slater notes this differential treatment (*op. cit.*, p. 132), but its implications escape him. By premise, the United States was neutral, and therefore the arms of the Old Regime would be used neutrally—but if factions are easily controlled, why disarm the Constitutionalists? He also points out that there were "thousands" of cases of harassment and violence brought by rebel victims to the Inter-American Human Rights Commission, but he stresses U.S. encouragement of investigation of these thousands of abuses—he never asks why the United States could not *stop* them, as it had so successfully neutralized the Constitution-

alists, nor does he ask whether this terror might not have political consequences. The breakdown of U.S. neutrality during the truce of early May, helping Imbert subdue the *barrios altos*, apparently never raised the possibility in Slater's mind that the subsequent terror might have been similarly functional and planned.

68. Wiarda-1798.
69. *The Organization of American States and Human Rights 1960-1967*, OAS, 1972, p. 461. The Commission's Reports are contained in this volume, pp. 359-475. The one cited is the Report of the Inter-American Commission on Human Rights in the Dominican Republic June 1- August 31, 1965.
70. Wiarda-1797.
71. Carlos Maria Gutierrez, *The Dominican Republic: Rebellion and Repression*, Monthly Review Press, 1972, p. 11.
72. GL-280.
73. GL-206.
74. Howard Wiarda, "From Fragmentation to Disintergration: The Social Political Effects of the Dominican Revolution," in Eugenio Chang-Rodriguez, ed., *The Lingering Crisis*, pp. 30, 40.
75. Donald Keys, "Observing the Elections," in Chang-Rodriguez, ed., *The Lingering Crisis*, pp. 75, 78.
76. Wiarda-1799.
77. "The Strange Dominican Election," *New Leader*, June 20, 1966, p. 3.
78. *Ibid.*, p. 4.
79. *Ibid.*, p. 5.
80. *Ibid.*, p. 6.
81. *Ibid.*, p. 5.
82. The two leaders of the unofficial U.S. observer contingent, Norman Thomas and Allard Lowenstein, were long-standing conduits of CIA funding in domestic and Third World operations. Thomas' very sympathetic biographer, W.A. Swanberg, noted that in 1967, "As the revelations [of CIA subsidization] continued, the Thomas score in unknown subsidizations was seen to be impressive." This included substantial transfers to Thomas from the Kaplan Fund, which was an important conduit for CIA efforts in the Dominican Republic. (Swanberg, *Norman Thomas: The Last Idealist*, Scribner's, 1976, p. 479.) Thomas claimed that he had been totally unaware of any CIA money behind any of his efforts. Lowenstein had been heavily involved in the CIA penetration and manipulation of the National Student Association prior to his leadership role in the organization of the observer team in the Dominican Republic in 1966. Subsequently, Lowenstein was associated with Freedom House, and served as a member of their mission to Rhodesia in 1979 and 1980. Frances Grant, one of the observers in (and apologists for) the Dominican Republic election showed up as a Freedom House observer in El Salvador in March 1982 (see Appendix 1).
83. This is the estimate given the authors by one of the top coordinators of the U.S. observer team.

84. U.S. military and police aid before 1966 had provided substantial radio communications equipment to Dominican forces; see Fred Goff and Michael Klare, "How U.S. Aid Shapes the Dominican Police," *NACLA Newsletter*, April 1971, pp. 19-28.

'85. Charlotte Roe, "The Committee on Free Elections," in Chang-Rodriguez, ed., *The Lingering Crisis*, p. 61.

86. "An Intervention of Friendship," in Chang-Rodriguez, ed., *The Lingering Crisis*, p. 69.

87. "U.S. Asks Pullout in Santo Domingo," *New York Times*, May 31, 1966.

88. Thomas Powers, *The Man Who Kept the Secrets*, Knopf, 1981, p. 171; quoted from a book by former CIA officer Ray Cline.

89. See especially, Fred Goff and Michael Klare, "How U.S. Aid Shapes the Dominican Police," *NACLA Newsletter*, April 1971, pp. 19-28. The authors show that while the dollar sums expended by the United States were small, they were concentrated in strategic areas such as communications, intelligence, and training in riot control, and were large enough so that (in the words of an AID report) "for U.S. objectives it provides the necessary leverage." Quoted on p. 20.

90. Amnesty International, *Report on Torture*, Farrar, Straus and Giroux, 1975, pp. 211-2.

91. "Santo Domingo: The Politics of Terror," *New York Review of Books*, July 22, 1971, p. 15.

92. Michael J. Kryzanek, "Diversion, Subversion and Repression: The Strategies of Anti-Opposition Politics in Balaguer's Dominican Republic," *Caribbean Studies*, vol. 17, nos. 1 & 2, 1977, p. 98.

93. *Ibid.*

94. See "U.S. A.I.D. in the Dominican Republic—An Inside View," *NACLA Newsletter*, November 1970, pp. 2-7.

95. Goff and Klare, *op. cit.*, p. 21.

96. "A Reporter's Notebook: For the Dominicans the Election is a Test of a Shaky Democracy," *New York Times*, May 27, 1978.

97. A. Kent McDougall, "Caribbean Terror: In Dominican Republic, Political Murders Rise, and so Does Poverty," *Wall Street Journal*, September 9, 1971.

98. L. Erik Calonius, "Caribbean Crisis: Dominican Republic, Mired in Deep Slump, Turns to U.S. for Help," *Wall Street Journal*, January 7, 1983.

99. *Ibid.* Also Gutierrez, *op. cit.*, p. 92.

Chapter 3:
Vietnam

1. Quoted in Richard B. DuBoff, "Business Ideology and Foreign Policy: The National Security Council and Vietnam," in Noam Chomsky and Howard Zinn, eds., *The Pentagon Papers, Critical Essays*, Gravel Edition, vol. 5, Beacon Press, 1972, p. 25.

2. *Ibid.*

3. See B.S.N. Murti, *Vietnam Divided: The Unfinished Struggle*, Asia Publishing House, 1964; Franklin B. Weinstein, *Vietnam's Unheld Elections: The Failure to Carry Out the 1965 Reunification Elections and the Effect on Hanoi's Present Outlook*, Cornell Southeast Asia Program, 1966.

4. John Adams estimated that only one-third of the colonial population supported the George Washington-led insurgency. See John Shy, *A People Numerous and Armed*, Oxford, 1976, pp. 166, 215-7. For estimates of Vietnam and NLF support, see text and associated footnotes below.

5. *New York Herald Tribune*, August 31, 1954.

6. Dwight D. Eisenhower, *Mandate for Chance*, Signet, 1963, p. 372.

7. *Look*, January 25, 1955.

8. George M. Kahin and John W. Lewis, *The United States in Vietnam*, rev. ed., Delta, 1969, p. 106.

9. David Hotham, in R. Lindholm, ed., *Vietnam: The First Five Years*, Michigan State University Press, 1959, p. 346.

10. Kahin and Lewis, *op. cit.*, p. 106.

11. *Pentagon Papers*, Gravel ed., vol. I, p. 254.

12. "Lösung für Vietnam," *Neues Forum*, August/September 1969, p. 459.

13. *Pentagon Papers*, vol. I, p. 255.

14. For a discussion of the use of terror as a semantic tool of propaganda, see Noam Chomsky and Edward S. Herman, *The Washington Connection and Third World Fascism*, South End Press, 1979, *passim.*; Edward S. Herman, *The Real Terror Network*, South End Press, 1982, Chapters 1 & 4.

15. Jeffrey Race, *War Comes to Long An*, University of California, 1971, pp. 110-11.

16. *Ibid.*, p. 197.

17. U.S. officials in Saigon estimated in late 1962 that "about one-half of the South Vietnamese support the National Liberation Front for different reasons, of which 300,000 are active in their support." Robert Scigliano, *South Vietnam: Nation Under Stress*, Hougham Mifflin, 1963, p. 145.

18. Douglas Pike, *Vietcong*, MIT Press, 1966, p. 110.

19. *Ibid.*, p. 362.

20. Untitled paper on pacificiation requirements and problems, circulated within the military in 1965, reprinted in 1967. A copy was given by Vann to professor Alex Carey of the University of New South Wales, Australia.

21. The Paris Agreements, furthermore, were also only a scrap of paper as far as the U.S. leadership was concerned. All of its major provisions on non-intervention, neutrality, equivalent status of the PRG (the successor to the NLF) and Saigon, reconcilation, and unification were immediately interpreted out of existence by U.S. officials, who strove till the final day of exit from Saigon to preserve their anticommunist instruments in power. See Noam Chomsky, "Indochina and the Fourth Estate," in *Towards a New Cold War*, Pantheon, 1982.

22. Kahin and Lewis, *op. cit.*, pp. 240-41.
23. *Ibid.*, p. 242.
24. "Premier Ky Indicates Delay in Elections Until October," *Philadelphia Evening Bulletin*, May 3, 1966.
25. Kahin and Lewis, *op. cit.*, pp. 242-3.
26. *Ibid.*, pp. 238-9.
27. *Pentagon Papers*, II, p. 371.
28. "Lodge Asks Army Role in New Regime," *New York Times*, April 26, 1967.
29. Kahin and Lewis, *op. cit.*, pp. 258-9.
30. Kahin and Lewis, *op. cit.*, p. 260.
31. *Ibid.*, p. 262.
32. On ordnance, casualties, and refugee generation by bombings and scorched earth policies, see Edward S. Herman, *Atrocities in Vietnam: Myths and Realities*, Pilgrim Press, 1970, pp. 42-47, 57, 83-87.
33. Kahin and Lewis, *op. cit.*, p. 189.
34. Paul Joseph, *Cracks in the Empire: State Policies in the Vietnam War*, South End Press, 1981, p. 166.
35. Howard R. Penniman, *Decision in South Vietnam* (Transcript of an Interview), The Free Society Association, 1967, p. 16.
36. "Dr. David Wurfel Reports on Vietnam," Methodist Division of Peace and World Order, September 21, 1967, pp. 2-3.
37. Statement of Alfred Hassler, "Peace and the Vietnam Elections," placed in *Congressional Record* by Senator Ernest Gruening, September 26, 1967.
38. Chomsky and Herman, *Washington Connection*, pp. 254-6; Penny Lernoux, *The Cry of the People*, Doubleday, 1980, Part III.
39. "'If he is a Communist or if he is a neutralist, I am going to fight him militarily,' Marshal Ky said. 'In any democratic country you have the right to disagree with the views of others,' he added." "Ky Warns of Fight if 'Red' Wins Vote," *New York Times*, May 14, 1967.
40. For some details and citations, Chomsky and Herman, *Washington Connection*, pp. 328ff.
41. *U.S. Assistance Programs in Vietnam*, Hearings before Subcommittee of the House Committee on Government Operations, 92nd Congress, 1st Session, 1971, p. 314.
42. Kahin and Lewis, *op. cit.*, p. 348.
43. "Dr. David Wurfel Reports on Vietnam," p. 3.
44. Tran Van Dinh, "The Ky Question," *New Republic*, January 21, 1967.
45. See Appendix 2.
46. Karl H. Purnell, "Marching Out the Horses," *The Nation*, September 25, 1967.
47. William Corson, *The Betrayal*, Norton, 1968, p. 110.
48. *Ibid.*
49. Vann, *op. cit.*, p. 20.
50. See *Pentagon Papers*, II, p. 402.
51. Seymour M. Hersh, *The Price of Power*, Summit, 1983, pp. 435ff; Frank Snepp, *Decent Interval*, Random House, 1972, Chapter 2.

52. These statements in the text are based on the notes taken by George Kahin in an interview with Nguyen Thanh Vinh, Chairman of the Election Commit tee of the Constituent Assembly of South Vietnam, in Saigon, July 27, 1971.
53. Penniman, *Decision in South Vietnam*, p. 13.
54. Notable here were several articles by R.W. Apple, Jr.; see e.g., his "Thieu's Power at Polls," *New York Times*, September 6, 1967.
55. Drew Pearson and Jack Anderson, "How Johnson Feels About Vietnam," *Gazette and Daily*, York, Pa., March 17. 1967.
56. Corson, *The Betrayal*, p. 111.
57. "South Vietnamese Above All Want Peace, CBS Poll Finds," *Gazette & Daily*, York, PA, March 22, 1967 (summarizing an AP report).
58. "Report on Trip to Vietnam, U.S. Study Team," May 25-June 10, 1969, put into the *Congressional Record* by Congressman Ogden Reid, June 17, 1969.
59. Seymour Hersh, *op. cit.*, pp. 432-3.
60. *Ibid.*, p. 437.
61. There were no crematoria in South Vietnam, but methods of torture there were more refined and very broadly employed; even Hitler did not engage in large-scale crop defoliation, wholesale bombing or forced transfer of a large part of his own rural population. See Holmes Brown and Don Luce, *Hostages of War: Saigon's Political Prisoners*, Indochina Mobile Resource Project, 1973; Pham Tam, *Imprisonment and Torture in South Vietnam*, Fellowship of Reconcilation (n.d.). Herman, *Atrocities in Vietnam*, pp. 30-33, 66-70; James Simon Kunen, *Standard Operating Procedure*, Avon, 1971.
62. "As for officers [of the South Vietnamese army]...only one officer above the rank of lieutenant colonel did not serve in the French Army against the Viet Minh in the French Indochina War." (Jonathan Randal, *New York Times*, June 11, 1967.)
63. *Civilian Casualty and Refugee Problems in South Vietnam*, Findings and Recommendations, Subcommittee on Refugees, Senate Judiciary Committee, 90th Congress, 2nd Session, May 9, 1969, p. 36.
64. See Noam Chomsky and Edward S. Herman, "Saigon's Corruption Crisis: The Search for an Honest Quisling," *Ramparts*, December 1974-January 1975, pp. 21ff.
65. *Ibid.*
66. *Pentagon Papers*, II, pp. 402-4.
67. Hersh, *op. cit.*, pp. 427ff.

Chapter 4:
El Salvador
1. Michael T. Klare, *Beyond the "Vietnam Syndrome": U.S. Intervention in the 1980s*, Institute for Policy Studies, 1981, Chapter 1.
2. Phillip Berryman, *What's Wrong in Central America*, American Friends Service Committee, 1983, p. 7.

3. Cynthia Arnson, *El Salvador: A Revolution Confronts the United States*, Institute for Policy Studies, 1982, pp. 22, 33; Tommie Sue Montgomery, *Revolution in El Salvador*, Westview, 1982, p. 31; and *Human Rights Conditions in Selected Countries and the U.S. Response*, Hearings before the Committee on International Relations, House of Representatives, 95th Congress, 2nd Session, 1978, pp. 88-89.

4. Cited in Thomas Anderson, *Matanza: El Salvador's Communist Revolt of 1932*, University of Nebraska, 1971, pp. 83-84.

5. Robert Armstrong and Janet Shenk, *El Salvador: The Face of Revolution*, South End Press, 1982, p. 32.

6. Montgomery, *op. cit.*, p. 103.

7. Armstrong and Shenk, *op. cit.*, p. 78.

8. E.g. Philip Agee, *Inside the Company: CIA Diary*, Penguin, 1975, p. 600.

9. *Human Rights in Nicaragua, Guatemala, and El Salvador: Implications for U.S. Policy*, Hearings before the Committee on International Relations, House of Representatives, 94th Congress, 2nd Session, 1976, pp. 47-48.

10. Stephen Webre, *José Napoleón Duarte and the Christian Democratic Party in Salvadoran Politics, 1960-1972*, Louisiana State University Press, 1979, *passim*.

11. Castillo testimony, *Human Rights in Nicaragua, Guatemala, and El Salvador...*, p. 48.

12. *Ibid.*, p. 49.

13. Armstrong and Shenk, *op. cit.*, pp. 62-63.

14. *Ibid.*, p. 75.

15. Inter-American Commission on Human Rights, *Report on the Situation of Human Rights in El Salvador*, Organization of American States, 1979, pp. 153-56; and *The Recent Presidential Elections in El Salvador: Implications for U.S. Foreign Policy*, Hearings before the Subcommittees on International Organizations and on Inter-American Affairs, House of Representatives, 95th Congress, 1st Session, 1977.

16. *Human Rights Conditions in Selected Countries and the U.S. Response...*, pp. 93-94.

17. *Ibid.*, p. 93; Amnesty International, *El Salvador: General Background*, cited in *Human Rights Conditions in Selected Countries and the U.S. Response...*, pp. 82, 85; and *Religious Persecution in El Salvador*, Hearings before the Committee on International Relations, House of Representatives, 95th Congress, 1st Session, 1977, pp. 82-84.

18. Cynthia Arnson, "The Frente's Opposition: The Security Forces of El Salvador," in Marvin E. Gettleman, et.al., *El Salvador: Central America in the New Cold War*, Grove Press, 1981, p. 137.

19. Testimony before the Subcommittee on Foreign Operations of the House Appropriations Committee, April 19, 1981; reprinted in Gettleman, *op. cit.*, pp. 146-8.

20. CAMINO, *El Salvador: Background to the Crisis*, CAMINO, 1982, pp. 87-90; and Arnon Hadar, *The United States and El Salvador: Political and Military Involvement*, U.S.-El Salvador Research and Information Center, Berkeley, 1981, p. 26.

21. Armstrong and Shenk, *op. cit.*, p. 118.
22. Carolyn Forché, "The Road to Reaction in El Salvador," *The Nation*, June 14, 1980; Jenny Pearce, *Under the Eagle: U.S. Intervention in Central America and the Caribbean*, South End Press, 1982, pp. 220-21; and Montgomery, *op. cit.*, Chapter 1.
23. *Amnesty International Report 1980*, cited in Armstrong and Shenk, *op. cit.*, pp. 120-21.
24. Amnesty International to Warren Christopher, U.S. Deputy Secretary of State, in *U.S. Policy Toward El Salvador*, Hearings before the Subcommittee on Inter-American Affairs of the Committee on Foreign Affairs, House of Representatives, 97th Congress, 1st Session, 1981, pp. 103-4.
25. "Submission by Amnesty International to the Inter-American Commission on Human Rights of the Organization of American States, March 21, 1980," in *ibid.*, pp. 105-31.
26. L. Simon and J. Stephens, *El Salvador Land Reform Impact Audit*, Oxfam America, 1981, cited in Pearce, *op. cit.*, p. 232; and the statement by Martin Diskin on behalf of Oxfam-America, *Presidential Certification on El Salvador* II, Committee on Foreign Affairs, House of Representatives, 97th Congress, 2nd Session, 1982, pp. 124-44 (hereafter *Certification Hearings*, II, pp. 124-44.)
27. Pearce, *op. cit.*, p. 232.
28. "Submission by Amnesty International...." *loc. cit.*, pp. 108-9.
29. Cited in Pearce, *op. cit.*, p. 236.
30. Armstrong and Shenk, *op. cit.*, p. 145; and the testimony of William Doherty, in *U.S. Policy Toward El Salvador...*, p. 290. Of the 134 murders for which the groups responsible are known, 56 were "combined military operations," 23 were at the hands of ORDEN, and the rest were committed by rural police, the army, the cavalry, the treasury police, etc.
31. Memorandum from the Salvadoran Communal Union to President José Napoleón Duarte, December 10, 1981, summarized in Arnson, *El Salvador: A Revolution Confronts the United States...*, p. 77.
32. Pearce, *op. cit.*, p. 228.
33. "Statement by Amnesty International on the Occasion of the Tenth Regular Session of the General Assembly of the Organization of American States November 19-26, 1980," in *The Situation in El Salvador*, Hearings before the Committee on Foreign Relations, Senate, 97th Congress, 1st Session, 1981, pp. 255-56; "Statement by Amnesty International USA," in *U.S. Policy Toward El Salvador*, p. 101; and Arnson, *El Salvador: A Revolution Confronts the United States...*, pp. 84-85.
34. Testimony of former ambassador Robert White, *The Situation in El Salvador...*, pp. 100-159.
35. Pearce, *op. cit.*, p. 230; and Armstrong and Shenk, *op. cit.*, p. 127.
36. Testimony by Hector Dada Hirezi at the Permanent People's Tribunal, Mexico City, February 10, 1981; cited in Hadar, *op. cit.*, p. 6.

37. Hadar, *op. cit.*, pp. 7, 26.
38. Advisers Fontaine, Di Giovanni, and Kruger, *The Washington Quarterly*, Autumn 1980, cited in Pearce, *op. cit.*, p. 239.
39. *New York Times*, February 21, 1981, cited in Arnson, *El Salvador: A Revolution Confronts the United States*, p. 70.
40. *Wall Street Journal*, April 23, 1982.
41. Letter of May 11, 1981, cited in Americas Watch Committee and the American Civil Liberties Union, *Report on Human Rights in El Salvador* (hereafter *Report*), Vintage, 1982, p. 155.
42. FMLN-FDR, "Peace Proposal of the FMLN-FDR," presented to the U.N. General Assembly October 7, 1981; quotations from Americas Watch Committee and American Civil Liberties Union, *July 20, 1982 Supplement to the Report on Human Rights in El Salvador* (hereafter *July 20, 1982 Supplement*), Center for National Security Studies, Washington, D.C., 1982, pp. 155-56.
43. *Ibid.*, p. 154.
44. *July 20, 1982 Supplement*, p. 121; and *Report*, pp. xxx-xxxii.
45. Cited in *July 20, 1982 Supplement*, p. 51.
46. Committee to Protect Journalists, *Chronology of Repression: El Salvador and Guatemala, July 1978-February 1982*, The Committee, New York, 1982.
47. *July 20, 1982 Supplement*, pp. 51-52, 91-92; and *Report*, p. 129.
48. *July 20, 1982 Supplement*, pp. 55-56; and *Report*, pp. 136-39.
49. *Report*, p. 141; and Council on Hemispheric Affairs, "The Perilous State of the Academic Community in El Salvador," cited in *July 20, 1982 Supplement*, pp. 53-54.
50. *Report*, p. 114; and *July 20, 1982 Supplement*, p. 90.
51. *Certification Hearings*, II, p. 430.
52. *July 20, 1982 Supplement*, pp. 60, 123.
53. *Ibid.*, p. 58; and *Report*, pp. 143-46.
54. James Petras, "The Salvadoran Elections," unpublished mss.
55. Robert Armstrong, "The Salvadoran Election," *NACLA Report*, March/April 1982, p. 9; and *New York Times*, April 1, 1982.
56. Howard Friel, "That Famous Election was Hardly Free or Fair," *Boston Globe*, May 21, 1982; CAMINO, *El Salvador 1982: Elections Without Choice*, CAMINO, 1982, p. 24; and *July 20, 1982 Supplement*, pp. 159-60.
57. *Certification Hearings*, II, p. 104; *El Salvador Bulletin*, May 1982, p. 5; and CASA (Boston), "Elections in El Salvador: What Do They Mean?"
58. Information on procedures used in the March 1982 election and not otherwise attributed is taken from *July 20, 1982 Supplement*, pp. 150-79; and Armstrong, "The Salvadoran Election," *loc. cit.*
59. Armstrong, "The Salvadoran Election," *loc. cit.*
60. Cited in CAMINO, *El Salvador 1982: Elections Without Choice*, p. 25.
61. Friel, *op. cit.*.
62. *New York Times*, June 4, 1982.
63. *New York Times*, June 14, 1982.

64. *U.S. Policy in the Western Hemisphere*, Foreign Relations Committee, Senate, 97th Congress, 2nd Session, 1982, p. 33.
65. Statement by Dr. Jorge Bustamente, Chairman of the Central Election Commission, in *Certification Hearings*, II, p. 509.
66. For example, Colonels Garcia, Carranza, and Casanova were all assigned to ANTEL between 1974 and 1977. Tommie Sue Montgomery, *op. cit.*, p. 195. At the time of the election, ANTEL was under the administration of Carranza, who was removed from his post as Under Minister of Defense in December 1980 at the insistence of the United States, following the murder of the four U.S. religious women. Washington Office on Latin America, "Inside El Salvador: January to June, 1983."
67. Thomas Sheehan, "Salvador Vote Inflated, Study is Said to Find," *New York Times*, June 3, 1982; and Christopher Dickey, "Salvadoran Researchers Question Voter Turnout," *Washington Post*, June 19, 1982.
68. *New York Times*, July 30, 1982; and Raymond Bonner, "Secret Pentagon Intelligence Unit is Disclosed," *New York Times*, May 11, 1983.
69. United States General Accounting Office, *Funding of International Election Observers for El Salvador Election*, GAO/ID-82-44, June 25, 1982 (hereafter *GAO Report*); and *New York Times*, September 9, 1981.
70. *GAO Report*, Enclosure 1: "Chronology of Events Relating to International Election Observers for El Salvador, March 28 Elections," p. 1.
71. *Ibid.* This was apparently money well spent. For the lavish entertainment and PR activity for the observers by the Salvadoran government, see *New York Times*, March 28, 1982, p. 17.
72. *New York Times*, February 23, 1982, and March 21, 1982.
73. See Theodore Hesburgh, "The Elections in El Salvador," *America*, May 1, 1982, p. 336. Representative John Murtha (D-Penna.) was a late addition to the observer delegation.
74. Hesburgh, *op. cit.*, pp. 336-37.
75. *Boston Globe*, March 29, 1982.
76. *Philadelphia Inquirer*, March 29, 1982 (Kerr); *Boston Globe*, March 29, 1982 (Livingston); *Certification Hearings*, II, p. 501; and *Newsweek*, April 12, 1982, p. 49 (Penniman); and *New York Times*, March 21, 1982 (Scammon).
77. *New York Times*, July 24, 1982. Their entire report is printed in "The Election in El Salvador," *Freedom at Issue*, May/June, 1982, pp. 15-22.
78. *New York Times*, April 3, 1982.
79. *New York Times*, March 1, 1982.
80. *Washington Post*, March 31 and April 1, 1982.
81. *Washington Post*, April 2, 1982; and *Boston Globe*, April 1, 1982.
82. *New York Times*, April 9, 1982; *Philadelphia Inquirer*, April 24, 1982; and *New York Times*, April 25, 1982.
83. Christopher Dickey, "Changes Slow Land Reform in El Salvador,"

Washington Post, May 31, 1982.

84. Raymond Bonner, "Salvador Evicts Peasants from Land," *New York Times*, May 30, 1982; and Barry Bearak, "Salvadoran Peasants Reap Little from Land Reform," *Philadelphia Inquirer*, May 28, 1982.

85. Roy Prosterman, "The Unmaking of a Land Reform," *The New Republic*, August, 1982, pp. 22-25.

86. Raymond Bonner, "Despite Salvadoran Vote, the Killings are Continuing," *New York Times*, April 25, 1982.

87. *Certification Hearings*, II, p. 522.

88. "Executions in Salvador Denounced," *Philadelphia Inquirer*, July 21, 1982; "Increase Reported in Political Killings in Salvador," *New York Times*, August 29, 1982; and "Groups Deny Abuse Easing in Salvador," *Philadelphia Inquirer*, September 20, 1982.

89. *Certification Hearings*, II, pp. 386-87.

90. *Ibid.*, p. 430.

91. "El Salvador Police Hold Health Chief," *Philadelphia Inquirer*, May 30, 1982.

92. Don Oberdorfer, "Torture Reported in Salvador," *Washington Post*, July 26, 1982; and Christopher Dickey, "Torture Case Poses Problems for U.S. Officials," *Washington Post*, August 2, 1982. Lopez Nuila was later appointed to the government's Human Rights Commission.

93. *Certification Hearings*, II, p. 390.

94. This telegram was made available in photostat on June 24, 1982 by CAMINO (The Central American Information Office), 1151 Massachusetts Avenue, Cambridge, MA 02138. Portions of it were quoted, and the whole was the subject of articles in the *Washington Post* on July 3 and July 8, 1982. According to the latter article, "Embassy officials [in El Salvador] said that the cable was authentic and described it as one of the single documents that best expressed U.S. policy in El Salvador. One of the officials, however, called the recommendations a 'wish list'."

95. John Dinges, "Red Cross Said Ready to Quit El Salvador," *Washington Post*, July 3, 1982.

96. Christopher Dickey, "Wave of Killings Unsettles Salvadoran Party," *Washington Post*, June 1, 1982.

97. Christopher Dickey, "Salvadoran Colonel Turning Rebels' Tactics Against Them," *Washington Post*, June 21, 1982.

98. *Presidential Cerification on El Salvador*, I, Foreign Affairs Committee, House of Representatives, 97th Congress, 2nd Session, 1982, p. 107 (here after *Certification Hearings*, I, p. 107).

99. Christopher Dickey, "U.S. Tactics Fail to Prevent Salvadoran Civilian Deaths," *Washington Post*, June 10, 1982.

100. "Interviews with Refugees from El Salvador," June 21, 1982, Mss., translated by Sharlee Merner Bradley. A report by Janice Hill based on these interviews is in *Certification Hearings*, II, pp. 541-43.

101. Christopher Dickey, "U.S. Tactics Fail to Prevent Salvadoran Civilian Deaths," *loc. cit.*

102. *Certification Hearings*, II, p. 474.

Chapter 5:
Role of the Mass Media in a Demonstration Election

1. A study of the El Salvador coverage of the *New York Times* in 1980 showed that although peasants are more than 50% of the population, in only two of 75 articles (about 2 %) were peasants used as informants. Ivna Gusmao and Alan Benjamin, "The *New York Times'* Coverage of El Salvador," (January 1981, mimeo).
2. Edouard Bailby, "Terror in El Salvador's Countryside," *Le Monde Diplomatique*, January 1981 (authors' translation).
3. See Chomsky and Herman, *Washington Connection*, pp. 72, 184-185; Chomsky and Herman, *After the Cataclysm, Postwar Indochina and the Reconstruction of Imperial Ideology*, South End Press, 1979, Chapters 4 and 6.
4. Congressman Robert Dornan asserted before a congressional committee that Raymond Bonner was worth a division to the Communist terrorists in the hills, *Certification Hearings*, II, p. 348.
5. University of Illinois Press, 1964, p. 174.
6. For a review of the volume and quality of the outpouring, see Chomsky and Herman, *After the Cataclysm*, Chapter 6.
7. According to Reagan administrative representative John Holdridge, "the coalition government of Democratic Kampuchea is a continuation of a political entity which was there as a government when the North Vietnamese, the Vietnamese, attacked." *Recent Developments in East Timor*, Hearings before the Subcommittee and Asian and Pacific Affairs, House Committee on Foreign Affairs, 97th Congress, 2nd Session, September 14, 1982, p. 71.
8. Amnesty International (AI), Concerns in El Salvador, Release of February 2, 1981.
9. *Certification Hearings*, II, pp. 223-4.
10. Warren Hoge, "El Salvador's Election: Issues and Consequences," *New York Times*, March 27, 1982.
11. Joseph B. Smith, *Portrait of a Cold Warrior*, G.P. Putnam, 1976, chapter 7 ("We Make a President")
12. Jan Black, *United States Penetration of Brazil*, University of Pennsylvania Press, 1977, pp. 72-77.
13. Interview with the German magazine *Stern*, reprinted in Los Angeles *New Advocate*, April 1-15, 1972.
14. *Pentagon Papers*, III, p. 669.
15. W.W. Norton, 1972, pp. 248, 294, 322.
16. Philip Taubman, "U.S. Sets Aside $6 Million for Salvador Voting," *New York Times*, May 26, 1983.
17. Philip Taubman, "C.I.A. Chief Tells of Attempt to Aid Salvador Vote," *New York Times*, July 30, 1982.
18. *Ibid.*
19. Wayne Biddle, "The Selling of D'Aubuisson," *The Nation*, July 24-31, 1982.

20. Joanne Omang, "$3.4 Million Asked for Salvador Vote," *Philadelphia Inquirer*, July 12, 1983.
21. Apart from the fact that turnout in the 1982 election was meaningless in the 1982 Salvadoran electoral context, the literature disseminated in the process of getting out the vote was loaded with propaganda bias, regularly claiming that the government in office—an unelected military junta—was "democratic" and asserting that a vote was an important step toward reducing violence. A comic book produced for the 1982 election under State Department inspiration with AID money asserted quite definitively that your vote would bring "peace." Another propaganda piece funded by AID had as its slogan "Ballots, Not Bullets." John Dinges, "El Salvador's Comic Election," *In These Times*, April 6-12, 1983, p. 5.
22. Omang, *op. cit.*
23. *Certification Hearings*, I, pp. 425-6.
24. According to Robert White, "It is in Honduras, the poorest country in the region, that the worst effects of the Reagan policy may be seen. In the face of widespread misery and despair, many Hondurans oppose their government's militaristic policies, demanding deep political, economic and social changes. These dissidents are now treated as subversive and, for the first time in its history, the Honduran military has begun to abduct and kill labor union leaders, intellectuals and others who dissent from official policy. This is the way revolution took hold in El Salvador—with popular outrage against offically-sponsored disappearances." "Perilous Latin Policy," *New York Times*, May 2, 1983 (Op. Ed.).
25. In explaining Bonner's reassignment, *Times* foreign editor Craig Whitney claimed that it had no political significance; that Bonner had been a temporary stringer who had done good work but had no training as a journalist and was reassigned to New York to get that training. (Dan Hallin, "White Paper, Red Scare," *NACLA Report*, July/August 1983, p. 19.) This is completely unconvincing. Bonner's reporting was of higher quality than those left on the job, by the standards of enterprise in seeking out unofficial sources and simple truthfulness (as we note in the text below). Furthermore, the reassignment of Bonner, given the fact that he was under attack by official and unofficial government propagandists, was inherently a policy decision of importance, symbolizing the giving way to the attackers and vindicating their criticisms of Bonner's alleged failings.
26. Jack Spence, "Media Coverage of El Salvador's Election," *Socialist Review*, March/April 1983, p. 29.
27. "Promoting Free Elections," Department of State, Bureau of Public Affairs, Current Policy No. 433, November 4, 1982, p. 3.
28. Spence, *op. cit.*, p. 31.
29. *Certification Hearings*, I, p. 41.
30. *Ibid.*, pp. 375-6.
31. Spence, *op. cit.*, p. 36.
32. *Certification Hearings*, I, p. 230.

33. Teresa Chopoorian and Eli Messinger, "U.S. Medical Aid to El Salvador Must be Condemned," *New York Times*, July 9, 1983 (Op. Ed.).

34. *Certification Hearings*, I, p. 228.

35. *New York Times*, March 30, 1982 (editorial).

36. *U.S. Policy in El Salvador*, Hearings Before the Subcommittee on Human Rights and International Organization and Western Hemispheric Affairs, U.S. House, 98th Congress, 1st Session, March 17, 1983. p. 620.

37. There was a peace candidate in the 1967 election in Vietnam, but he had no chance of winning and may have been an official plant; see Chapter 3 and Appendix 2 for further details.

38. See Joyce and Gabriel Kolko, *The Limits of Power*, Harper & Row, 1972, pp. 204-15.

39. Quoted in *ibid.*, p. 207.

40. Ygael Gluckstein, *Stalin's Satellites in Europe*, Beacon Press, 1952, p. 168.

41. *New York Times*, January 20, 1947.

42. This table clearly rests on judgment rather than on quantitative estimates, and was done with an eye toward reasonableness as to relative values between the four cases.

43. "Election in Poland Rigged by Terror," *New York Times*, January 3, 1947.

44. *New York Times*, January 19, 1947.

45. R.F. Leslie, ed., *The History of Poland Since 1863*, Cambridge University Press, 1980, p. 291.

46. Sidney Gruson, "Beatings Disprove Warsaw's Denials," *New York Times*, January 12, 1947; "Election in Poland Rigged by Terror," *New York Times*, January 3, 1947.

Chapter 6:
The Future of the Demonstration Election

1. As we discuss in Chapter 3, two potentially strong peace candidates were excluded from the ballot. A weak and compromised candidate was allowed to run on a quasi-peace platform, along with nine other civilian candidates, by a sufferance of the authorities that could have been terminated at their discretion as "neutralism" was an explicit basis for exclusion.

2. Their main basis of self-interest is the omnipresent threat of U.S. intervention, assassination attempts against the leadership, subversion, and direct or sponsored invasion. On the massive U.S. efforts to overthrow the Cuban government, see Warren Hinckle and William Turner, *The Fish is Red, The Story of the Secret War Against Castro*, Harper and Row, 1981.

3. *The Real World of Democracy*, Oxford University Press, 1966, p. 5.

4. On Cuba, see, e.g., Sergio Diaz-Briquets and Lisandro Perez, "Cuba: The Demography of Revolution," *Population Bulletin*, April 1981. On

Nicaragua, see Roger Burbach and Tim Draimin, "Nicaragua's Revolution," *NACLA Report on the Americas*, May/June 1980.

5. See Edward S. Herman, *The Real Terror Network*, South End Press, 1962, Table 3-2 and associated text.

6. Lars Schoultz, "U.S. Foreign Policy and Human Rights Violations in Latin America: A Comparative Analysis of Foreign Aid Distributions," *Comparative Politics*, January 1981, p. 162; Noam Chomsky and Edward S. Herman, *The Washington Connection and Third World Fascism*, South End Press, 1982, pp. 42-26.

7. See especially, Miles Wolpin, *Military Aid and Counterrevolution in the Third World*, Lexington, 1972.

8. "Military Professionalism and Professional Militarism," quoted in Jan Black, *United States Penetration of Brazil*, University of Pennsylvania Press, 1977, p. 194.

9. Black, *op. cit.*, pp. 176-8.

10. *Amnesty International Report 1982*, p. 134.

11. "American Ideals Versus American Institutions," *Political Science Quarterly*, Spring 1982, p. 29.

12. *Ibid.*

13. See especially, Fred Landis, "Psychological Warfare and Media Operations in Chile, 1970-1973," Ph.D. dissertation, University of Illinois at Urbana-Champaign, 1975; Fred Landis, "How 20 Chileans Overthrew Allende for the CIA," *Inquiry*, February 19, 1979; *Covert Action in Chile*, 1963-1973, Staff Report of Select Committee to Study Intelligence Activities, U.S. Senate, 1975.

14. Stephen Kinzer, "Lack of Money Imperils Salvadoran Elections," *New York Times*, May 4, 1983.

15. Philip Taubman, "U.S. Sets Aside $6 Million for Salvador Voting," *New York Times*, May 26, 1983.

16. For details on the staging and choreography of the Scowcroft Commission, see Elizabeth Drew, "A Political Journal," *The New Yorker*, June 20, 1983.

17. Martin Tolchin, "Senators Call for Bipartisan Latin Panel," *New York Times*, June 16, 1983.

Appendix 1:
Freedom House Observers in
Zimbabwe Rhodesia and El Salvador

1. According to the constitution agreed to on March 3, 1978 between the white Rhodesian government and several black leaders, the state of Rhodesia would change its name to Zimbabwe Rhodesia following elections and the installation of a new government. This took place on May 31, 1979. Although the first election took place while the country was still called Rhodesia, we have followed common usage in referring to both elections as held in Zimbabwe Rhodesia.

2. Under the constitution, whites (constituting 4 percent of the population) retained a guaranteed 28 percent of Assembly seats and 33 percent of the

seats in the Senate. The President was to be selected by the legislature rather than by direct vote. The black representatives in the legislature were to be voted upon by whites as well as blacks. Property rights were firmly protected by the constitution, and numerous devices were incorporated there to assure white minority domination of the courts, bureaucracy, and executive. Truman Dunn concluded his detailed analysis of this constitution as follows: "There is not a single chapter in the entire constitution which demonstrates even the potential for transition to true majority rule in Zimbabwe." ("The 'New' Rhodesian Constitution," *Southern African Perspectives*, April 1979.)

3. *Executive-Legislative Consultation on Foreign Policy; Sanctions Against Rhodesia*, House Committee on Foreign Affairs, 97th Congress, 2nd Session, 1982, p. 50.

4. *Ibid.*, p. 40.

5. "Report on the Freedom House Mission to Observe the Common Roll Election in Zimbabwe-Rhodesia — April 1979," (hereafter *Report*), reprinted in *Economic Sanctions Against Rhodesia* (hereafter *Sanctions*), Hearings before the Subcommittees on Africa and on International Organizations, House Committee on Foreign Affairs, 96th Congress, 1st Session, 1979, p. 361.

6. Cited in *Sanctions*, p. 49.

7. *New York Times*, April 22, 1979.

8. *New York Times*, May 11, 1979.

9. "'Free and Fair? The 1979 Rhodesian Election,' A Report by Observers on Behalf of the British Parliamentary Human Rights Group — May 1979," reprinted in *Sanctions*, pp. 280-347.

10. Claire Palley, *The Rhodesian Election*, Catholic Institute for International Relations, London, 1979, p. 35.

11. *Ibid.*, p. 12.

12. *Ibid.*, p. 15.

13. Testimony of Gretchen Cassel Eick, *Sanctions*, p. 238.

14. The Freedom House Report is published in *Freedom at Issue*, May/June 1980, pp. 19-24.

15. The Minister of Defense of Rhodesia, Mr. Van der Byl, stated: "If villagers harbour terrorists and terrorists are found about in villages, naturally they will be bombed and destroyed in any manner which the commander on the spot considers to be desireable in the suitable prosecution of a successful campaign...and one can have little sympathy for those who are mixed up with terrorists when finally they receive the wrath of the security forces." Quoted in Catholic Institute of International Relations, *Rhodesia, The Propaganda War*, London, 1970, p. 20. See further the data on pp. 12-21.

16. Palley, *op. cit.*, pp. 14-15.

17. The Freedom House Report on El Salvador is published in *Freedom at Issue*, May/June 1982, pp. 15-22.

18. For details, see Chapter 4 above under "The Mechanics of the Election."

Appendix 2:
Penniman on South Vietnamese Elections:
The Observer-Expert as Promoter-Salesman

1. *Pentagon Papers*, Gravel edition, II, p. 406.
2. See Richard Boyle, *The Flower of the Dragon: The Breakdown of the U.S. Army in Vietnam*, Ramparts Press, 1972.
3. *Newsweek*, March 16, 1966.
4. An expression used facetiously by some U.S. Army legal officers who believed that military courts were lenient on U.S. personnel who killed Vietnamese civilians, who were "mere gooks." See Philip Shabecoff, "Murder Verdict Eased in Vietnam," *New York Times*, March 31, 1970.
5. Vietcong ("Vietnamese Communist") and its abridgement VC were used as expressions of derogation by Diem, his successors, and U.S. officials, frequently encompassing enemies who were not Communists. The NLF and its successors included many non-Communists, but were always designated VC. Penniman naturally uses this language, and we follow him to avoid confusion.
6. Jeffrey Race, *War Comes to Long An*, University of California, 1971, pp. 196-7.
7. See *Pentagon Papers*, II, pp. 277-415; see also Chapter 3 above.
8. Seymour Hersh, *The Price of Power*, Summit, 1983, pp. 433ff; Frank Snepp, *Decent Interval*, Random House, 1972, Chapter 2.
9. *U.S. Assistance Program in Vietnam*, Hearings before the Subcommittee of the House Committee on Government Operations, 92nd Congress, 1st Session, 1971, p. 207.
10. Quoted from letter by Wurfel to Edward S. Herman, dated August 17, 1983.
11. See Seymour Hersh, *op. cit.*, p. 437.
12. Letter to Edward S. Herman, *op. cit.*
13. These points are discussed in more detail in Chapter 3.
14. Two former officials of the Saigon government have asserted this in interviews with the authors of this book.
15. Letter to Edward S. Herman, *op. cit.*
16. Charles A. Joiner, *The Politics of Massacre*, Temple University Press, 1974, pp. 115-17.

Index